SCOTLAND FOR EVERYMAN

SCOTLAND
FOR EVERYMAN

BY

H. A. PIEHLER

WITH AN ATLAS OF 24 COLOURED MAPS
EDITED BY JOHN BARTHOLOMEW, F.R.G.S.

'All I ask, the heaven above
And the road below me.'

R. L. S.

LONDON
J. M. DENT & SONS LTD

FOREWORD

This little volume, a companion volume to the author's Everyman Guides to England, Wales, and Ireland, is a description of the principal scenic beauties and antiquities of Scotland, divided into twelve tours, and adapted equally for the needs of the motorist, the traveller by motor-coach, motor-bus, or railway, the cyclist, and the walker. Each tour, starting where the last left off, covers about 100 to 500 miles, and can be comfortably accomplished in a week or so by the motorist, and, in some cases, almost as speedily by those who make use of public conveyances. A tourist who conscientiously followed out the whole series would, in the course of about 3,000 miles' travelling, see a large proportion of the most charming scenery of Scotland, the cathedrals and ruined abbeys, the castles, the picturesque old towns and quaint villages, and the historic sites.

It would, of course, be impossible to attempt a description of all the touristic attractions of Scotland in such a brief compass without adopting a concise style of writing and abandoning any idea of comprehensiveness. Purely industrial towns and districts are avoided as far as possible. Throughout the volume nothing is mentioned unless it is considered to be well worth seeing, and as a rule the description follows the main routes of tourist traffic.

Introductory sections—some of them directed in particular towards the needs of visitors from overseas—deal with the questions of How to Travel and Where to Stay, Scottish Place-Names, etc., a Scottish Calendar, and Bibliography. The index of places and persons is as full as space allows. At the beginning of the volume will be found Bartholomew's layered and attractively coloured Map of Scotland, on a scale of twelve miles to an inch, and in the form of a twenty-four-page atlas. On it the various classes of roads are clearly distinguished, and road mileages from point to point are given.

The more important properties of the National Trust

for Scotland for Places of Historic Interest or Natural Beauty (offices, 5 Charlotte Square, Edinburgh, 2) are mentioned in the text. Members (10s. per annum) have free access to all National Trust properties in the British Isles.

There are no abbreviations of any kind in the book except self-explanatory ones.

Sir James Barrie, Mr J. J. Bell, Mr George Blake, Miss D. K. Broster, Miss Anna Buchan, Lord Tweedsmuir (John Buchan), Mrs Catherine Carswell, Mr J. Storer Clouston, Dr A. J. Cronin, Mr Lewis Grassic Gibbon, Mr Neil M. Gunn, Mr Eric Linklater, Miss Agnes Mure Mackenzie, Miss Dorothy L. Sayers, Mr L. A. G. Strong, Mr Maurice Walsh, and Mrs Virginia Woolf kindly supplied notes on the settings of their Scottish novels.

Corrections, criticisms, and suggestions of any kind will be received by the author with gratitude. This new edition incorporates many emendations kindly contributed by readers, and has in other respects been brought up to date in readiness for the summer season of 1954.

Finally, it should be noted that full information on any point connected with travel in Scotland may be obtained from the Scottish Tourist Board, 20 York Place, Edinburgh, 21A George Street, Edinburgh (for personal callers), and 20 Academy Street, Inverness. Or from the British Travel and Holidays Association, 64–65 St James's Street, London, S.W.1.

1954.   H. A. P.

CONTENTS

		PAGE
FOREWORD	. . . .	vii
LIST OF MAPS	. . . .	xi
ATLAS	. . . .	I
HOW TO TRAVEL	. . . . . .	25
WHERE TO STAY	. . . . . .	29
A SCOTTISH CALENDAR	. . . . .	31
GLOSSARY OF SCOTTISH PLACE-NAMES, ETC.	.	33
BIBLIOGRAPHY	. . . . . .	36

TOURS:

I. BERWICK TO EDINBURGH	. . .	39
II. EDINBURGH TO MELROSE AND CARLISLE	. .	57
III. CARLISLE TO STRANRAER, AYR, AND GLASGOW		67
IV. GLASGOW AND THE CLYDE	. . . .	80
V. GLASGOW TO ST ANDREWS, AND BACK TO STIRLING		93
VI. STIRLING TO PERTH AND ABERDEEN	.	105
VII. ABERDEEN TO BRAEMAR, PITLOCHRY, BANFF, AND INVERNESS		118
VIII. INVERNESS TO FORT WILLIAM AND OBAN	.	135
IX. OBAN TO FORT WILLIAM VIA LOCH TAY	.	149
X. FORT WILLIAM TO SKYE AND THE HEBRIDES, AND BACK TO INVERNESS	. .	156
XI. INVERNESS TO INVERNESS VIA CAPE WRATH AND JOHN O' GROATS	. . .	179
XII. ORKNEY AND SHETLAND	. . . .	195

| INDEX | . . . . | 205 |

LIST OF MAPS

	PAGE
INDEX TO MAP SECTIONS	1
THE LOTHIANS, BERWICKSHIRE, PEEBLES-SHIRE, SELKIRKSHIRE, AND ROXBURGHSHIRE . .	2–3
AYRSHIRE, LANARKSHIRE, WIGTOWNSHIRE, KIRK-CUDBRIGHTSHIRE, AND DUMFRIESSHIRE . .	4–5
DUNBARTONSHIRE, STIRLINGSHIRE, RENFREWSHIRE, KINTYRE, BUTE, AND ARRAN . . .	6–7
PERTHSHIRE, ANGUS, CLACKMANNANSHIRE, KINROSS-SHIRE, AND FIFE	8–9
PARTS OF ARGYLLSHIRE, INVERNESS-SHIRE, AND PERTHSHIRE	10–11
MULL, JURA, ISLAY, AND UIST	12–13
MORAY, BANFFSHIRE, ABERDEENSHIRE, AND KIN-CARDINESHIRE	14–15
ROSS-SHIRE, INVERNESS-SHIRE, AND NAIRNSHIRE .	16–17
SUTHERLAND AND CAITHNESS	18–19
LEWIS, HARRIS, AND PART OF ROSS-SHIRE . .	20–21
SKYE	22
ORKNEY	23
SHETLAND	24

xi

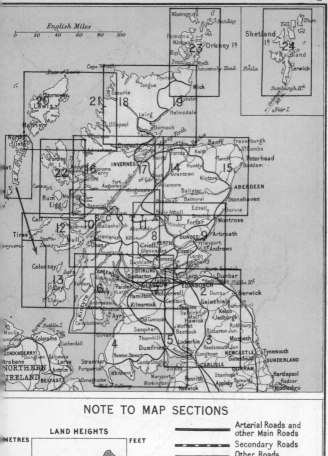

English Miles
0   20   40   60   80   100

Shetland

SCOTLAND

NOTE TO MAP SECTIONS

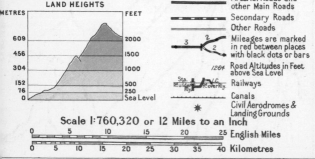

LAND HEIGHTS

METRES		FEET
609		2000
456		1500
304		1000
152		500
76		250
0		Sea Level

Arterial Roads and other Main Roads

Secondary Roads

Other Roads

Mileages are marked in red between places with black dots or bars

1264 Road Altitudes in Feet above Sea Level

Railways

Canals

Civil Aerodromes & Landing Grounds

Scale 1:760,320 or 12 Miles to an Inch

0   5   10   15   20   25   English Miles

0   5   10   15   20   25   30   35   40   Kilometres

John Bartholomew & Son, Ltd. Edinburgh.

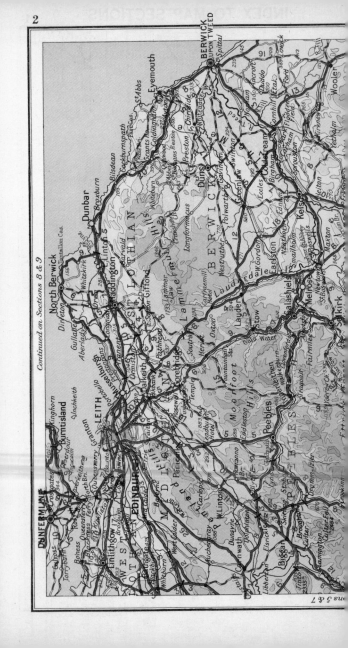

Continued on Sections 8 & 9

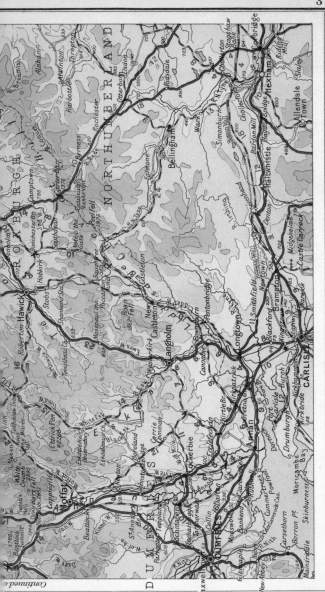

Continued c

For explanation of road marking and
contour colouring see page 1

0 2 4 6 8 10 12 Miles
0 2 4 6 8 10 12 14 Kilometres

John Bartholomew & Son, Ltd. Edinburgh

Copyright.

Continued o

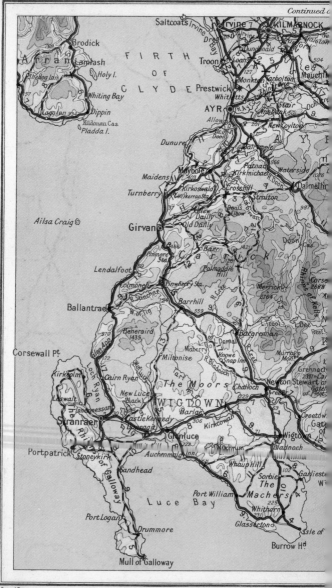

0 2 4 6 8 10 12 Miles
0 2 4 6 8 10 12 14 Kilometres

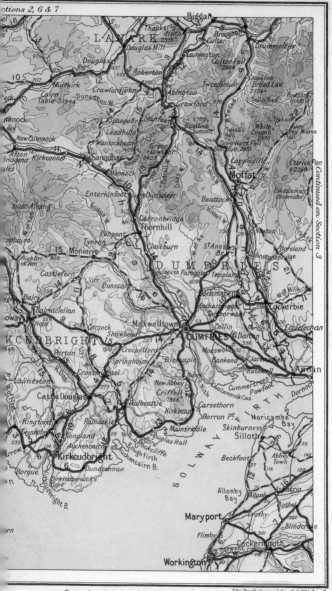

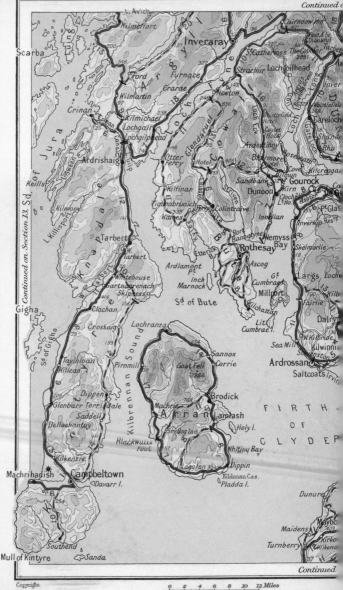

L. Avich
Kilmelfort
Scarba
Inveraray
S.Catherines The Cobbler
Cairndow Inn
2891
Strachur
Lochgoilhead
Ford
Furnace
Crarae
Newton
Whistlefield Hotel
Barelone
Kilmartin
Crinan
Kilmichael
Lochgair
Lochgilphead
Coylet Hotel
Whistlefield Sta.
Ardentinny
Rosencath
Kilcregga
Ardrishaig
Otter Ferry
Hotel
Sandbank
Cove
Gourock
Kirn
Coll L.Ho.
Kilfinan
Dunoon
Pt.Glas
Tighnabruaich
Colintraive
Kames
Innellan
Inverkip Res.
Tarbert
Port Bannatyne
Wemyss Bay
W.Tarbert
Etterick B.
Rothesay
Skelmorlie
Ardlamont Pt.
Inch Marnock
Ascog
Largs Loch
Whitehouse
Gartnagrenach
Skipness
Sd. of Bute
Gt. Cumbrae I.
Millport
Kilchattan
Lit. Cumbrae I.
Fairlie
Clachan
Dalry
Crossaig
Lochranza
Sea Mill
W.Kilbride
Kilwinning
Stevenston
Tayinloan
Killean
Pirnmill
Goat Fell 2866
Sannox
Corrie
Ardrossan
Saltcoats Irvin
Dippen
Glenbarr Torrisdale
Saddell
Bellochantuy
Machrie
Brodick
Lamlash
ARRAN
Holy I.
FIRTH
Shedog Inn
OF
Kilkenzie
Blackwater Foot
Whiting Bay
CLYDE
Machrihanish
Campbeltown
Davarr I.
Lagg Inn
Dippin
Kildonan Cas.
Pladda I.
Dunure
Southend
Sanda
Maidens
Maybo
Mull of Kintyre
Turnberry
Kirko
Kilkerra

0 2 4 6 8 10 12 Miles
0 2 4 6 8 10 12 14 Kilometres

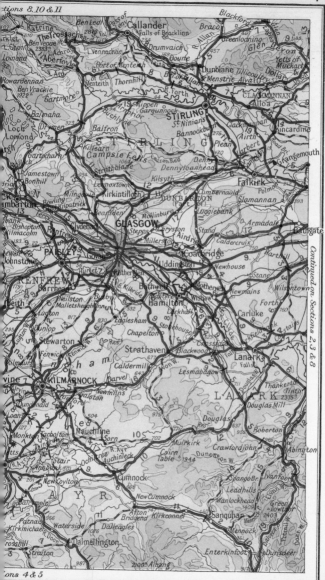

Continued

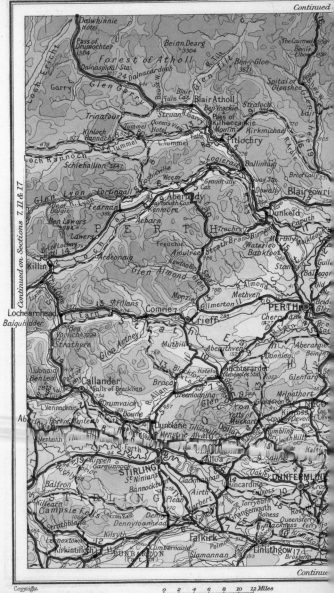

Continued on Sections 7, 11 & 17

Continued

Copyright

0 2 4 6 8 10 12 Miles
0 2 4 6 8 10 12 14 Kilometres

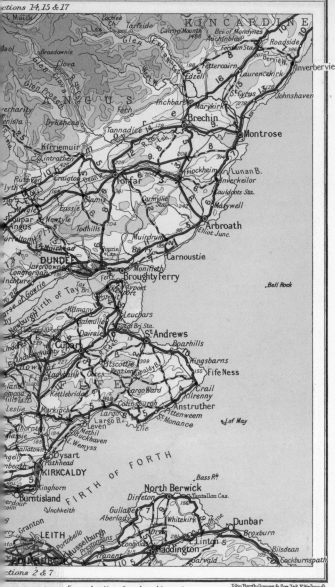

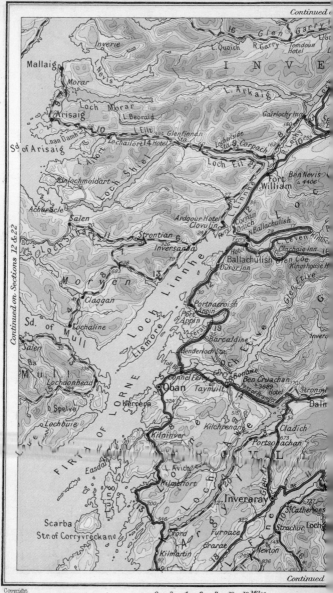

Copyright.

0 2 4 6 8 10 12 Miles
0 2 4 6 8 10 12 14 Kilometres

Continued

Continued on Sections 16 & 22

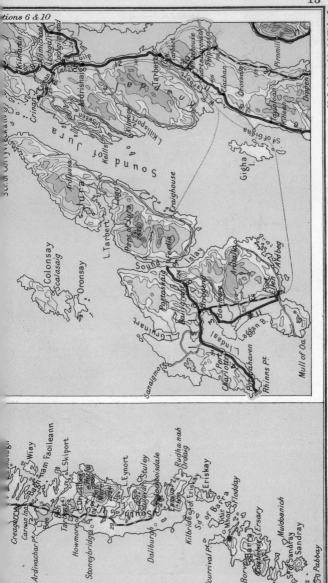

13

tions 6 & 10

Krihtnen
Kilmichael
Lochgilphead
Gilp
Ardrishaig
Crinan
Crinan L.
Keills
Kilberry
Killisport L.
L. Sween

Sound of Jura

Lussa
Jura
Paps of Jura
Feolin
Lagg
Craighouse
Keills
L. Tarbert

Sound of Islay
Portaskaig
Ballygrant or Islay

W. Tarbett
Tarbett
Whitehouse
Clachan
Crossaig
Sd of Gigha
Gigha

Skipness
Pirnmill
Dippen

John Bartholomew & Son, Ltd, Edinburgh

For explanation of road marking and
contour colouring see page i

Colonsay
Scalasaig
Oronsay

Sanaigmore
Gruinart

Ardnahoe
Bridgend
Bowmore
Port
Charlotte
Port
Wemyss
Rhinns Pt.

L. Indaal
Laggan B.
Mull of Oa

Ardalla
Port
Ellen
Ardbeg
Lagavulin

Creagorry
Carnan Inn
Ardivachar Pt.

Howmore
Stoneybridge
Daliburgh

Wiay
Bagh nam Faoileann
L. Skiport
Drimsdale
Bornish
Dalibrog
L. Eynort
Stulay
Eriskay
Boisdale
Rugha nah
Ordaig
Ushinish

Kilbride
Scurrival Pt.
Borve
Barra
Eoligarry
Sd. of Barra
Ottir
Vore
Whot
Sandray
Sea Sandray
Pabbay

S. of Eriskay
Flodday
Ersary
Muldoanich
Sandray

Copyright

0 2 4 6 8 10 12 Miles
0 2 4 6 8 10 12 14 16 Kilometres

14

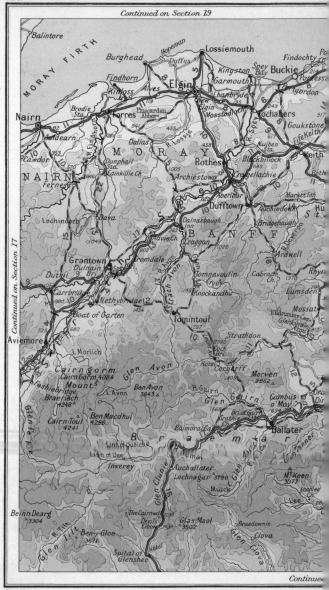

Continued on Section 17

Copyright

0 2 4 6 8 10 12 Miles
0 2 4 6 8 10 12 14 Kilometres

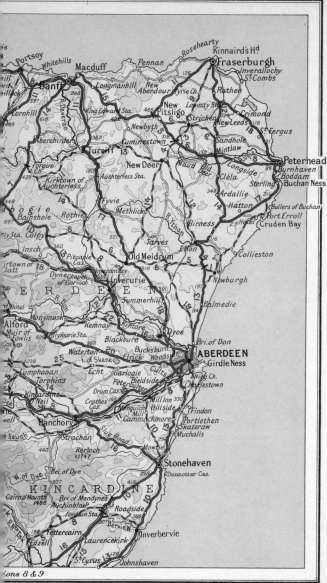

For explanation of road marking and
contour colouring see page I

John Bartholomew & Son Ltd, Edinburgh

Continued

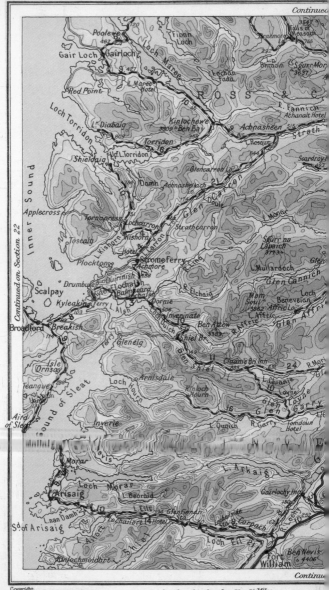

Continued on Section 22

Continued

0   2   4   6   8   10   12 Miles
0   2 4 6 8 10 12 14 Kilometres

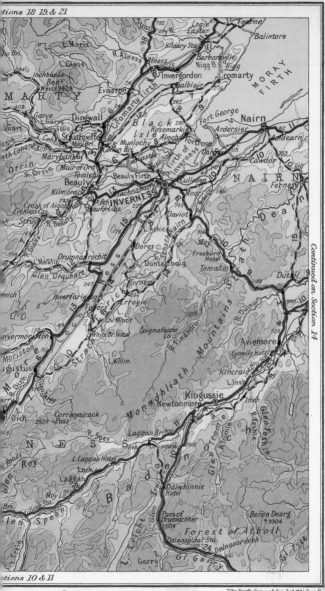

Sections 18 19 & 21

Continued on Section 14

Sections 10 & 11

For explanation of road marking and
contour colouring see page 1

John Bartholomew & Son, Ltd, Edinburgh.

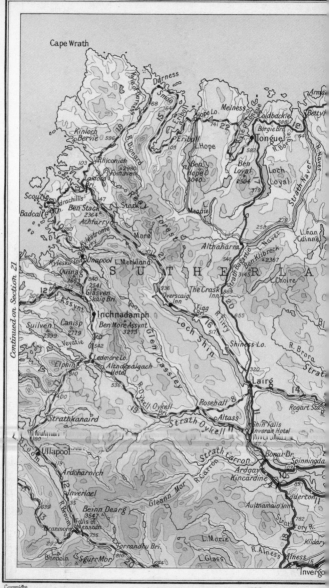

Cape Wrath

Kyle of Durness

Durness

Smoo
68 64

R Dionard

Kinlocho Bervie 596

Hope Lo. Melness

Eriboll
03 L. Hope

Coldbackie
388
Borgie Bri
54

Kyle of Tongue

Tongue
582

R Borgie

Strath Naver

R. Naver

103

Rhiconich
2980
Foinaven

Laxford
Bri.
147

Scourie
Badcall
Ch.
Badcall

Ben Stack
2364

Achfarry

Ben
Hope
3040

Ben
Loyal
2504

Loch
Loyal
379

Meadie

Reay Forest

Stack
More

Westrome
Ferry

Kylesku Inn
Unapool
L. Merkland

Quinag
2651

840
2541

Glasven

Skaig Bri.

S U T H E R L A

Althaharra

Strath Naver

Ben Klibreck
2367

258

278

L. nan
Clainne

R. Brora

Strath

545

3145

936

Overscaig
Inn

The Crask
Inn

869

Choire

Assynt

Inchnadamph

Canisp
2779

Suilven
399

Ben More Assynt
3273

Flag
Inn

R Tirry

16

517

855

Shiness Lo.

Loch Shin

Veyatie

1542

Elphin
810

Ledmore Lo.

Altnacealgach
Hotel

536

R. Oykell

Glen Cassley

320

Lairg

14

Strathkanaird

400

Oykell
Bri.

Oykell

19

Rosehall

8

Altass

Rogart Sta.

Continued on Section 21

Continued on Section 21

Strath Oykell

11

Shin Falls
Invaran Hotel

River Shin

L. Broom

Ullapool

Ardcharnich

Strath Carron

R Carron

Strath

Bonar Br.

Spinningda

103

Inverlael

639

Beinn Dearg
3547

135

Falls of
Measach

Braemore

29

755

Sgurr Mor

Torrandhu Bri.

810

Bhraoin

L. Morie

L. Glass
694

R. Alness

Ardgay
Kincardine

10

Aultnamain Inn

Edderton

842

Strath Rory R.

782

Kildary

Alness

Invergo

Gleann Mor

13

20

Betty

Arna

Copyright

0 2 4 6 8 10 12 Miles
0 2 4 6 8 10 12 14 Kilometres

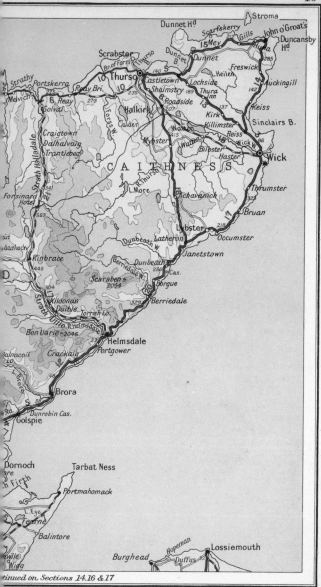

Stroma

Dunnet Hd.
Scarfskerry
15 Mey
Gills
John o'Groat's
Duncansby Hd.
Huna
285
Scrabster
Br. of Forss
Dunnet B.
Dunnet
Freswick
Thurso
5
L. Heilen
Strathy
Portskerra
Reay Bri.
140
Castletown
Lochside
Muckingill
Melvich
6 Reay
273
Shalmstry
189
Thura Inn
142
Golval
Roadside
207
Kirk
137
Keiss
Halkirk
Watten
Killimster
Sinclairs B.
Craigtown
Calder
345
Myster
Watten
Reiss
Dalhalvaig
Trantlebeg
Forss W.
415
Bilbster
Wick W.
86
CAITHNESS
Haster
Wick
R. Thurso
Forsinard Hotel
341
L. More
Achavanich
Thrumster
323
563
Lybster
Bruan
17
Kinbrace
445
Dunbeath W.
Latheron
Occumster
anloch
Dunbeath
Janetstown
304
Berriedale W.
256 Cas.
Scaraben
2054
Borgue
Kildonan
529
Duible
Berriedale
Torrish Lo.
Ben Uarie 2046
R. Helmsdale
33
Balnacoil Lo.
Crackaig
Helmsdale
Portgower
48
Brora
Sta.
98
Strath Ulle
5
Dunrobin Cas.
Golspie
Dornoch
Tarbat Ness
h Firth
Portmahomack
L. Eye
Fearn
Balintore
ville
Wigg
Burghead
Hopeman
Duffus
Lossiemouth

ntinued on Sections 14,16 & 17

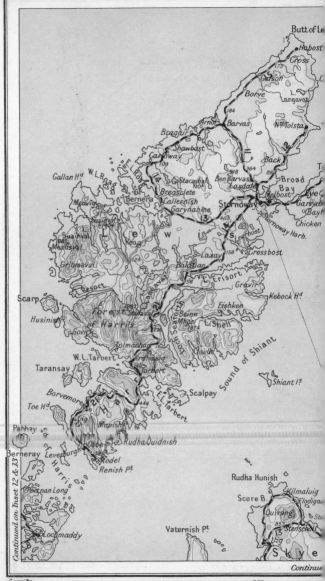

Butt of Le

Habost
Cross
Galson
Borve
L. Langavat
N.th Tolsta
184
Barvas
Arnol
Bragair
Shawbost
Back
Carloway
109
918
Ben Barvas
364
88
Broad
Bay
Stacashal
110?
Laxdale
Breasclete
Melbost
Eye
W.L.Roag
Garrab
Callernish
Stornoway
Bayl
Chicken
Garynahine
Gallan Hd
Bernera
402
Meavig
13
Newbost
Roag
S
Suainval
Crossbost
559
Laxay
Mealisval
Balistan
574
Grimaval
558
Erisort
Gravir
24
Scarp
H. Resort
Kebock Hd
Husinish
Eishken
Forest Sliuaval
Beinn
Mhor
L. Shell
Govig
of Harris
1874
Govig
522
Tolmachan
Sound of Shiant
W.L.Tarbert
Ardhasig
544
Shiant Is.
Taransay
Tarbert
Borvemore
H
Scalpay
Toe Hd
449
E.T.Tarbert
444
Pabhay
Grupish
Rudha Quidnish
Berneray Leverburgh
Obbe
558
Continued on Inset 12 & 13
Rodel
Harris
Renish Pt
Rudha Hunish
Kilmaluig
Shillean Long
Score B.
Flodiga
Lochmaddy
Quirang
Sta
853
Stenschol
Vaternish Pt
13
Uig
Skye
Continue

0 2 4 6 8 10 12 Miles
0 2 4 6 8 10 12 14 Kilometres

Kinloch
Bervie

103

Scourie
Badcall
Eddrachillis
Bay

Pt of Stoer

Handa
Eddrachillis
280

Drumbeg
Clashnessie
Stoer

Kyleskur Inn
Quinag
2653
275

12

Assynt

Lochinver
Inverkirkaig
Suilven
2779

Canisp
399

Veyatie

Ledmore Lol.
Elphin
310

Rhu Coigach

Enard
Bay

Fionascaig

ORTH

Achiltibuie
L. Lurgain
Coigach
400

INCH

Tanera More

Strathkanaird

Greenstone Pt.

Loch Broom
Ardmair
180

Ullapool
13

Gruinard
B.

Laide
225
8

Lit. L Broom
585
Gruinard

10

Dundonnell
Hotel

12

Melvaig

Aultbea
Lit.
Gruinard

220

L. na
Sheallag
3483

An Teallach 1639

R. Broom
135

13

Poolewe
462

Fionn
Loch

Braemore
292

Gair Loch
Gairloch
9

Loch Maree

Lochan
Fada

La
Bhaoin

Red Point
L. Maree
Hotel

10
46

Loch Torridon
L.t. Diabaig
809

Kinlochewe
3309 Ben Lay
358

Achnasheen
515

815

s 16 & 22

For explanation of road marking and
contour colouring see page l

John Bartholomew & Son, Ltd, Edinburgh.

Continued on Sections 16 & 18

Rudha Hunish
Kilmaluig
Score B.
Flodigarry
Quirang
Staffin
853
Stenscholl
Vaternish Pt
Uig
Culnaknock
Rona
Loch
Snizort
Red Point
Loch Torridon
Dunvegan Hd
Stein
285
Hinnisdal Bri
The Storr
2360
Kensaleyre
Applecross
Milovaig
Fairy
Brr.
342
363
Edinbain
152
Bernisdale
Carbost
Roskhill
Dunvegan
Portree
53
Toscaig
Sound of Raasay
Inner Sound
Bracadale
Drumbuie
Toilore
Skye
106
Kyleakin
358
Drynoch
Scalpay
103
L. Bracadale
L. Harport
457
362
Sligachan Hotel
Fuib.
174
Breakish
Broadford
Cuillin
Hills
3309
Blaven
3042
Coruisk
Isle
Ornsay
Surr
Alasdair
L. Brittle
Soay
L. Scavaig
Elgol
L. Slapin
L. Eishort
Teangue
286
Cuillin Sound
Andvasar
Aird of Sleat
147
Sound of Sleat
Sd of Arisaig
Canna
Pt of Sleat
Mallaig
Morar
Kinloch Cas.
Rum
Arisaig
L. nan Uamh

0   2   4   6   8   10   12 Miles
0 2 4 6 8 10 12 14 Kilometres
Eigg
For explanation of road marking and
contour colouring see page I
Muck

Kinlochm
Ardnamurchan
Pt
Achuracle
Ardnamurchan
Sale

John Bartholomew & Son, Ltd. E.

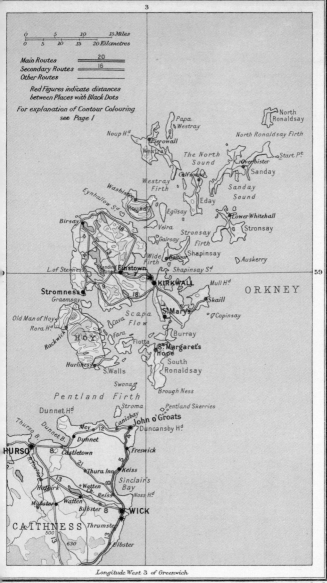

0   5   10   15 Miles
0   5   10   15   20 Kilometres

Main Routes   20
Secondary Routes   16
Other Routes

Red Figures indicate distances
between Places with Black Dots

For explanation of Contour Colouring
see Page 1

North
Ronaldsay

Papa
Westray

Noup Hd   Pierowall   North Ronaldsay Firth

Westray   Start Pt

The North
Sound   Overbister
Calfsound   Sanday

Westray
Firth   Sanday
Sound

Wasbister   Eday

Eynhallow Sd   Rousay   Egilsay

Birsay   Veira   Lower Whitehall

Gairsay   Stronsay   Stronsay
Firth

Wide   Balfour
Firth   Shapinsay   Auskerry

L. of Stenness   Standing   Finstown
Stones   Shapinsay Sd

Stromness   18   KIRKWALL   Mull Hd   ORKNEY

Graemsay   Skaill

Old Man of Hoy   St Marys   Copinsay

Rora Hd   Cava   Scapa
Rackwick   Fara   Flow   Burray

HOY   Flotta   St Margaret's
Hope
Hurliness   South
S. Walls   Ronaldsay

Swona   Brough Ness

Pentland   Firth   Stroma   Pentland Skerries

Dunnet Hd   Canisbay
Thurso B.   Dunnet B.   Mey 12 John o'Groats
THURSO   Dunnet   Duncansby Hd

8 Castletown   Freswick

21 Thura Inn   Keiss

Halkirk 13 Watten   Reiss   Sinclair's
Ch.   Bay
Mybster   Watten   Noss Hd

Bilbster 8   WICK

CAITHNESS   Thrumster

500   Ulbster
630

Longitude West 3 of Greenwich

59

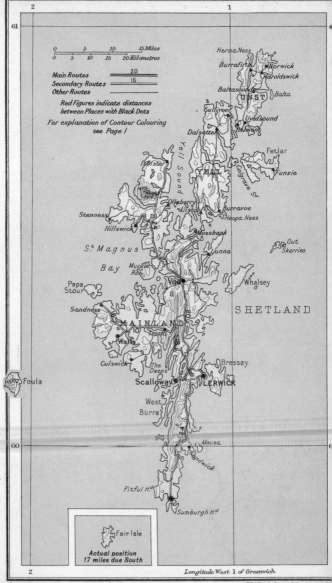

61

2   1

0   5   10   15 Miles
0   5   10   15   20 Kilometres

Main Routes   20
Secondary Routes   16
Other Routes

*Red Figures indicate distances
between Places with Black Dots*

*For explanation of Contour Colouring
see Page 1*

Herma Ness
Burrafirth   Norwick
                    Haroldswick
Baltasound   Balta
                UNST
Saxavord
Uyeasound
Belmont

Fetlar

Dalsetter   Colgrave Sd.   Funzie

YELL

Isbister

1477 Rooa Hill

Ollaberry   Burravoe
Ulsta   Heoga Ness

Stenness
Hillswick   Mossbank
                                 Lunna   Out
St. Magnus   Skerries

Bay   Muckle
             Roe
                         Voe
Papa   Whalsey
Stour
Sandness   SHETLAND

             MAINLAND
             10
             Tresta
Walls

Culswick   The
             Deeps   Bressay

             Scalloway   LERWICK
West
Burra

Foula   Mousa

60

Sandwick

Fitful Hd.

Sumburgh Hd.

Fair Isle

*Actual position
17 miles due South*

John Bartholomew & Son, Ltd., Edinbr.

HOW TO TRAVEL

MOTORING. Motorists—especially those unacquainted with the country—who intend to drive their own cars are strongly recommended to join the Royal Automobile Club (R.A.C.) or the Automobile Association (A.A.), which will acquaint them with the motoring regulations peculiar to Great Britain. The former has offices in Glasgow and Edinburgh, the latter in Edinburgh, Glasgow, Dundee, and Aberdeen. These associations obviate, as far as is humanly possible, every difficulty that the motorist may encounter. They issue maps and handbooks containing lists of recommended hotels and other information useful to the motorist, employ patrols who render assistance to members on the road, plan itineraries, and even provide free legal defence when their members come into conflict with the police. The latest information regarding road conditions, ferries, etc., is obtainable at their offices or from the road patrols.

The laziest and most care-free way of getting about the country is to hire a car and the services of a chauffeur. There are several firms of good repute ready to accommodate the tourist in this way, but naturally this method of travelling demands a purse bursting with gold.

One of the jolliest ways of touring in Scotland is by motor-car and trailer-caravan. Special care is necessary in negotiating the narrow and tortuous by-roads in the Highlands. The Caravan Club (32 Gordon Square, London, W.C.1) and the British Caravanners' Club (a section of the Camping Club; 38 Grosvenor Gardens, London, S.W.1) provide their members with lists of camping sites, exemption from restrictive legislation, technical advice, social activities, etc. Farmers generally charge 1s. a night or more for the use of a site.

In spite of the hilly and even mountainous nature of its surface, Scotland's main roads are well adapted for motoring and, as they mostly follow the valleys, are surprisingly free from severe gradients. Many of the arterial roads have been widened or completely reconstructed in recent years. The road surface varies from county to county, but on the whole is hardly up to the English standard. In the remoter districts of the Highlands the roads are narrow, tortuous, and seldom tarred, with many short and sharp gradients and tricky bridges. Owing to the indented nature of the coastline long detours are frequently necessary between places only a few miles apart as the crow flies. Ferries play a considerable part in the road system of north-west Scotland. They are often expensive, and ply only during restricted hours (sometimes not at all on Sundays). Nervous drivers are warned that loading and unloading a car at some of the ferries is a process of some difficulty, owing to the slope of the jetties and the danger of skidding on the seaweed. The roads over the high passes are often snow-bound for weeks at a time. Garages and filling stations, which are often closed on Sundays, are few and far between in some districts, and ample supplies of petrol and oil, besides a spare inner tube, should be carried. The price of petrol rises slightly as one proceeds north.

Bartholomew's road map of Scotland, on a scale of twelve miles to an inch, is supplied with this volume, and will be found adequate for most motoring purposes. The *'Contour' Road Book of Scotland* (5s.), published by Gall & Inglis, Edinburgh and London, is a series of elevation plans of the roads, with measurements and descriptive letterpress, and invaluable to road-users.

The tourist who does not own a motor-car and cannot afford to hire one can get from anywhere to practically anywhere else either by railway or by MOTOR-COACH or MOTOR-BUS. Motor coaches perform longer journeys and are more comfortably fitted up than the motor-buses. Stops are made at roadside inns for lunch and tea. Smoking is permitted. The motor-coaches have the advantage of being somewhat cheaper than the railway, they pick up and land their passengers at more convenient points, and, as a general rule, they offer less restricted views of the scenery on either side. They are usually heated in winter, and rugs are provided. On the other hand, they are slower than trains, less well organized, and more liable to change of programme, and they do not carry heavy luggage. One suit-case is allowed to each passenger, and there is a luggage rack for light articles. Another drawback is that in summer, when the coaches are often full, a passenger cannot be sure of obtaining a seat unless he has booked it beforehand, and he thus runs the risk of being stranded in some remote spot. Apart from the regular services from point to point, a large variety of whole-day and half-day trips by motor-coach is available at every tourist resort.

There is no complete time-table for motor-buses and motor-coaches with regular services, corresponding to *Bradshaw* for railways; but the time-tables of W. Alexander & Sons (Falkirk), Scottish Omnibuses (Edinburgh), Central Scottish Motor Traction Co. (Motherwell), Western Scottish Motor Traction Co. (Kilmarnock), Highland Omnibuses (Inverness), and the Sutherland Transport and Trading Co. (Lairg) cover the principal bus services throughout Scotland. Details of many services will be found in Murray's Railway and Steamer Time Tables. For the numerous other purely local services (mail-cars, carriers' cars, etc.) inquiry must be made on the spot.

CYCLING. Scotland is a splendid touring country for the cyclist who does not object to a good deal of hill-climbing. As elsewhere, the main roads are apt to be congested with motor traffic. Bicycles are conveyed on the steamers and can be taken over many mountain routes and loch-ferries that are inaccessible to motors. Membership (15s. per annum) of the Cyclists' Touring Club (C.T.C.), 3 Craven Hill, Paddington, London, W.2, offers many advantages. The club *Handbook and Guide* contains a list of recommended hotels and lodgings, besides much other valuable information. The most useful scale for cycling maps is two miles to an inch (Bartholomew's, coloured and contoured).

WALKING. As Alexander Smith wrote in *A Summer in Skye*: 'No one knows a country till he has walked through it; he then tastes the sweets and the bitters of it. He beholds its grand and important points, and all the subtler and concealed beauties that lie out of the beaten track.' Scotland is a glorious country for a walking tour, but there are certain disadvantages. Accommodation is hard to find in the remoter districts of the Highlands, and days' marches of excessive length are sometimes necessary. After 12th August the deer forests and grouse moors are closed to the public, and those who stray from the not very numerous rights of way are liable to be warned off. The climate is uncertain, and rain and Scotch mists are very prevalent, especially on the west coast. Midges are a great nuisance, and citronella or paraffin may be used as a preventive, ammonia as a cure. The necessary outfit for hill-walking includes nailed boots, a rucksack with webbing straps, an ordnance map (one inch to the mile), and a compass. The presence of bog is often indicated by light-green patches or by cotton-grass.

RAILWAYS. The Scottish railways, together with the English, were nationalized in 1948 under the name of 'British Railways.' Return tickets from London to Scotland are available by several routes, and break of journey is allowed on line of route. There are two classes, first and third. The ordinary rate for first-class fares is 2·625d. per mile, for third-class 1¾d. per mile, but day return and excursion tickets are issued at reduced rates. Return tickets, available for three months, are issued at double the cost of a single fare. On Sundays the train services are curtailed or (on branch lines) suspended altogether. A generous allowance of luggage is carried free, but special tickets must be obtained for cycles. Murray's Time Tables cover all the railways and include details of many steamer and bus services run in conjunction.

Comparative times and fares from London to Edinburgh: By railway, in 7¾–8¼ hours, third class, 57s. 4d.; return ticket, available three months, 114s. 8d.—By air, in 2½ hours, £8; return ticket, available one month, £12; in winter, available one week, £8.—By motor-coach of the Scottish Motor Traction Co., in 15¾ hours, 30s.; return ticket, available any period, 60s., going by road and returning by rail, 80s.

STEAMERS, besides being, of course, the usual means of access to the Hebrides and other islands, are often the principal means of communication between the outer world and many of the isolated villages on the west coast of the mainland. Much of the finest scenery, too, is only visible from the sea, and an essential ingredient in a Scottish tour is a steamer trip down the Clyde. Most of the west coast services are managed by David Mac-Brayne Ltd, 44 Robertson Street, Glasgow, the others by British Railways. Small steamers ply also on some of the larger freshwater lochs.

AIR SERVICES connect London with Glasgow (Renfrew) and Edinburgh (Turnhouse), and Glasgow and Edinburgh with Aberdeen, Inverness, Wick, Orkney, and Shetland. There are also regular services from Glasgow and Edinburgh to Manchester, and from Glasgow to Belfast, to Tiree, Barra, Benbecula, and Stornoway, and to Campbeltown and Islay. A direct service connects Inverness with Stornoway. Prestwick Airport is on the international network, with regular services to London, Brussels, Amsterdam, Copenhagen, Oslo, Stockholm, Ireland, Montreal, New York, etc.

WHERE TO STAY

HOTELS. Scottish hotels have the reputation of being expensive, but allowance must be made for the shortness of their season. Good smaller, second-class hotels are somewhat rare, but when found (e.g. the anglers' inns) are hard to beat, with their home-grown fare of beef and mutton, ham, salmon and trout, and oatmeal in all its forms. Many hotels provide fishing and shooting (free or at a nominal rate) for their guests. Hydros, which abound in Scotland, are often licensed and differ little from other hotels except that they usually have extensive grounds, fixed hours for meals, and a more sociable atmosphere. Alcohol is obviously taboo at temperance hotels—which, by the way, rank higher in Scotland than in England—but at private hotels and boarding-houses (often identical in character) the guest may order in a supply from the wine merchant. In many commercial and other second-class hotels the evening meal is 'high tea,' with a hot dish.

The sale of alcoholic liquor is subject to a complicated system of licensing regulations, as a result of which one is frequently in doubt as to when and where it is permissible to indulge in alcoholic liquor. A few districts have exercised their right of local option and gone 'dry.' These restrictions, however, do not affect travellers as far as their own hotels are concerned.

A fixed charge for attendance is not usually made in Scottish hotels. A fairly satisfactory plan is to distribute among the staff a sum equal to at least ten per cent of the total bill (more for one-night visitors), or to hand in a similar amount to the cashier for distribution.

Travellers of moderate requirements will save much money by staying in LODGINGS, even if only for a night or two. In villages likely addresses can often be obtained at the post office or garage, and lists are published in the holiday handbooks of the railway companies, the C.T.C. handbook, etc.

Scottish innkeepers and lodging-house proprietors are well known for their honesty, but it is advisable to arrange terms in advance. The standard of cleanliness in Scotland is high, and there is no need to worry about drinking water or sanitation.

Hikers and cyclists should enrol as members of the Scottish Youth Hostels Association (7 Bruntsfield Crescent, Edinburgh, 10), and thus become entitled to use any of the ninety-odd HOSTELS at a charge of 2s. (juveniles 1s.) per night. Most of the hostels provide meals at very low charges. Membership costs 10s., for those under twenty-one 5s., under sixteen 2s. The Scottish hostels may be used without formality by those holding membership cards of other national youth hostels associations.

Except in the largest towns, restaurants are rare, and for a substantial meal the traveller must betake himself to a hotel. Simple but daintily served luncheons and teas at moderate prices are obtainable at the wayside 'cafés' or tea-rooms, abundant in the tourist districts.

A SCOTTISH CALENDAR

(With acknowledgments to the Scottish Tourist Board)

January.	1 January: New Year's Day, a Bank Holiday. 'Burning the Clavie' (tar-barrel) at Burghead, accompanied by a sort of carnival. 25 January: Burns's birthday. Last week: Up-Helly-Aa at Lerwick, with the burning of a Viking galley.
February.	2 February: Candlemas (term or quarter-day). Candlemas Handba' at Jedburgh. 10 February: Salmon-fishing begins. 28 February: Trout-fishing begins.
March.	'Whuppity Scoorie' at Lanark. Kate Kennedy Pageant at St Andrews. 31 March: Deer-stalking (for hinds) ends. Good Friday: Bank Holiday.
April.	Summer Time (one hour in advance of Greenwich Mean Time) begins on the day after the third Saturday.
May.	Exhibition of the Royal Scottish Academy at Edinburgh, till beginning of September. First Monday: Bank Holiday. 15 May (fixed date): Whitsun term or quarter-day. Pilgrimage to the Wishing Well at Culloden. General Assembly of the Church of Scotland at Edinburgh.
June.	Opening of the tourist steamer services on the West Coast. Common Ridings (processions) at Hawick, Linlithgow, Selkirk, etc. Lanimer Day at Lanark. March Riding and Beltane Queen Festival at Peebles. Braw Lads' Gathering at Galashiels.

July.   Highland Games at Helensburgh, Kingussie,
         Luss, Tobermory, Inverness (Northern
         Meeting, founded 1788), Castlebay, etc.
         Regattas on the Clyde in the second half of
         July ('The Clyde Fortnight').
         'Guid Nychburris' Festival at Dumfries.
         Common Riding at Langholm.
         Second or third week: Glasgow Fair (no
         actual fair), when workers go on holiday.
         Third Wednesday: Rothesay Fair.

August. 1 August: Lammas (term or quarter-day).
         First Monday: Bank Holiday.
         12 August: Grouse-shooting and deer-
         stalking (for stags) begin.
         Highland Games at Lochboisdale, Glen-
         finnan, Lochmaddy, Edinburgh, Rothesay,
         Fort William, Kyleakin, Dunoon, Port-
         ree, etc.
         Lammas Fair at St Andrews.
         St James's Fair at Roxburgh.
         Regatta at Lerwick.
         Riding of the Marches and Marymass Fair at
         Irvine.

August–September (three weeks).   International Festival
         of Music and Drama at Edinburgh (cf.
         page 53).

September. Highland Games at Aboyne, Braemar
         (usually attended by a Royal party from
         Balmoral), Pitlochry, Oban, Mallaig, etc.
         'Mod' (festival of Gaelic music) of the High-
         land Association.
         15 September: Closing of the tourist steamer
         services on the West Coast.
         Autumn Golf Meeting at St Andrews, when
         the new captain plays himself in.
         Rood Fair at Dumfries.

October. Summer Time ends on the day after the first
         Saturday.
         12 October: Deer-stalking (for stags) ends.
         15 October: Trout-fishing ends.

October.   31 October: Hallowe'en (the one night in the
            year when ghosts wander), with dipping
            for apples, roasting of nuts, etc.

November.   1 November: All Saints' Day or Hallow-
            mas. Salmon-fishing ends.
            10 November: Deer-stalking (for hinds) be-
            gins.
            11 November: Martinmas (term or quarter-
            day). The previous Sunday is Remem-
            brance Day, with sale of artificial poppies
            in aid of disabled ex-service men.
            30 November: St Andrew's Day, the festival
            of the patron saint of Scotland.

December.   10 December: Grouse-shooting ends.
            25 December: Christmas Day, a Bank Holi-
            day.
            31 December: Hogmanay (bringing in the
            New Year).

GLOSSARY OF SCOTTISH PLACE-NAMES, ETC.

Aber, mouth of a river
Ach, *auch*, field
Allt, *ault* (genitive *uilt*),
  stream
An, of the (also a diminutive
  ending)
Ard, *aird*, height
Aros, dwelling
Ay, island

Ba, *bo*, cow
Bal, township
Balloch, *bealach*, pass
Ban, white
Bar, headland
Beg, *beag*, little
Beath, *beith*, birch

Ben, *beinn*, mountain
Bield, shelter
Blair, plain, moor
Bothy, hut, shack
Brae, *bruach*, slope, hillside
Breac, *vrackie*, speckled
Broch, *brough*, *Pictish tower*,
  a round tower of un-
  worked and uncemented
  stones, of the early Iron
  Age, chiefly found in North
  Scotland (cf. p. 201)
Buie, yellow

Cam, *cambus*, crooked
Cannich, cotton-grass
Car, bend

*B

Carn, cairn, heap of stones

Carse, alluvial claylands beside a river

Chulish, strait

Clach, cloich, stone

Clachan, hamlet

Close, passage leading to a 'land'

Clunie, meadow

Coille, wood

Coire, corrie, semicircular recess or hollow in the mountains

Craig, creag, crag

Crannog, lake-dwelling

Croft, agricultural smallholding

Cruach, stack

Cul, coul, back, behind

Culdee, member of a Scoto-Irish religious order, eighth century onwards

Dal, dail, field

Damph, ox, stag

Darach, oak

Dearg, red

Dour, water

Druim, drum, ridge

Dubh, dhu, black

Dun, hill fort

Eaglais, eccle, church

Earth-house, Picts' house, weem, a primitive drystone building constructed just under the surface of the ground

Eilean, island

Fail, phail, cliff

Feu, perpetual leasehold

Fionn, fyne, white

Firth, frith, arm of the sea, estuary

Garbh, garve, rough

Gair, gare, short

Gart, enclosure

Glas, grey or green

Goe, creek

Gorm, blue

Gowan, blacksmith

Haar, Scotch mist

Haugh, alluvial land by a river

Holm, islet

Hope, small bay, inlet

Howe, hollow

Howff, haunt, tavern

Inch, innis, island

Inver, mouth of a river

Kil, cell, church

Killie, wood

Kin, ken, head, headland

Kinloch, head of a loch

Knock, knoll

Kyle, strait

Lag, luig, hollow

Land, building divided into tenements

Larig, mountain pass

Law, conical hill

Learg, larg, hillside

Liath, leath, grey

Linn, pool, waterfall, ravine

Lub, loop

Machair, machar, low-lying meadowland by the sea

Mains, home-farm attached to manor house

Mam, rounded hill

Meal, *mull*, bare headland

Mod, an assembly held annually in a different place with the object of promoting the Gaelic cult and corresponding with the Eisteddfod in Wales

Monadh, moor

Mor, *more*, *mhor*, great

Muc, *muic*, sow

Na, *nan*, *nam*, of the

Ness, *-nish*, nose, headland

Ob, *oban*, bay

Ochter, upper, high-lying

Ord, height

Pend, archway

Pictish tower, see Broch

Picts' house, see Earth-house

Pit, township

Pol, pool

Policies, private grounds attached to a mansion

Quoich, cup

Rath, fort

Rhinns, peninsula

Roost, tidal current

Ross, peninsula, forest

Rudha, cape

Scuir, *sgurr*, scar, steep rock

Sgeir, *skerry*, sea rock covered at high water

Shieling, summer pasture, or hut occupied by herdsmen when cattle are driven to hills for summer grazing

Strath, wide valley

Struan, running water

Tacksman, tenant, lessee

Tarbet, *tarbert*, portage, isthmus

Tigh, *ty*, *tay*, house

Tir, *tyre*, land

Tober, well

Tolbooth, prison

Tom, hillock

Tor, *torr*, heap, hill

Tron, public weighing machine

Tulloch, *tully*, knoll

Uam, cave, weem

Uig, nook, corner

Uisge, *uisk*, *esk*, water

Val, fell

Vik, creek

Vitrified fort, see p. 134

Voe, bay, inlet, fiord

Weem, cave or earth-house (q.v.)

Wynd, narrow street or passage

BIBLIOGRAPHY

OUT of the vast field of literature dealing with various aspects of Scottish life, the following works, mostly published in recent years, have been selected as most suitable for the general reader. A 'Select Bibliography' of Scotland is obtainable from the National Book League (price 1s.).

The *Royal Commission on the Ancient and Historical Monuments and Constructions of Scotland* is compiling complete inventories of buildings in Scotland dating from before the year 1707. Since 1909 it has published elaborate and copiously illustrated volumes on the counties of Berwick, Caithness, Kirkcudbright, Sutherland, Wigtown, Dumfries, East Lothian, Fife, Kinross, and Clackmannan, Midlothian and West Lothian, the Outer Hebrides, Skye, and the Small Isles, and Orkney and Shetland. *The Castellated and Domestic Architecture of Scotland* (five volumes, 1887–92), and *The Ecclesiastical Architecture of Scotland* (three volumes, 1896–7), by D. Macgibbon and T. Ross, published by David Douglas, Edinburgh, are standard works. See also *Cathedrals of Scotland*, by I. G. Lindsay (Chambers, 1926). Newer architectural works include *Scottish Church Architecture*, by J. S. Coltart (Sheldon Press, 1936), and *Shrines and Homes of Scotland*, by Sir John Stirling Maxwell (Maclehose, 1937).

The classic descriptions of travelling in Scotland in the eighteenth and early nineteenth centuries are the Scottish portion of Daniel Defoe's *Tour through the Whole Island of Great Britain* (1724–6), Thomas Pennant's *Tour in Scotland, 1769*; Dr Johnson's *A Journey to the Western Islands of Scotland*, in 1773; James Boswell's *The Journal of a Tour to the Hebrides with Samuel Johnson, LL.D.*; Dorothy Wordsworth's *Recollections of a Tour made in Scotland, A.D. 1803*; and Robert Southey's *Journal of a Tour in Scotland in 1819*.

Among miscellaneous nineteenth-century works, Mrs Grant of Laggan's *Letters from the Mountains* (1773–1807), Hugh Miller's *The Old Red Sandstone* (1842), John Galt's

Annals of the Parish (Everyman's Library), and Dean Ramsay's *Reminiscences of Scottish Life and Character* (1858; new edition, Nelson, 1947) may still be read with interest.

The long list of modern travel and descriptive books includes *Scotland : A Description of Scotland and Scottish Life,* edited by Henry W. Meikle (Nelson, 1947), J. J. Bell's *The Glory of Scotland* (Harrap, 1932), and H. V. Morton's *In Search of Scotland* and *In Scotland Again,* published by Methuen in 1929 and 1933 respectively. The most comprehensive general guide is *The Blue Guide to Scotland* (Benn, 1949). *The Face of Scotland,* by Harry Batsford and Charles Fry (Batsford, 1948), George Blake's *The Heart of Scotland* (Batsford, 1951), G. S. Fraser's *Vision of Scotland* (Elek, 1948), and W. A. Poucher's *A Camera in the Cairngorms* (Chapman & Hall, 1947) have excellent collections of photographs. Two admirable books on Skye are *A Summer in Skye,* by Alexander Smith (1865), and *The Misty Isle of Skye,* by J. A. MacCulloch (Mackay, Stirling, 1905). Alasdair Alpin MacGregor writes mostly on the Hebrides: *Behold the Hebrides!* (Chambers, 1925), *A Last Voyage to St Kilda* (Cassell, 1931), *The Haunted Isles* (Maclehose, 1933), etc. Seton Gordon's books deal mostly with wild life: *Hebridean Memories* (Cassell, 1923), *The Cairngorm Hills of Scotland* (Cassell, 1925), etc. Four of Macmillan's Highways and Byways series deal with Scotland: *The Border,* by Andrew and J. Lang (1913), *Galloway and Carrick,* by C. H. Dick (1916), and *The West Highlands* (1935) and *The Central Highlands* (1948), both by Seton Gordon. Collins's Britain in Pictures series include *The Story of Scotland,* by F. Fraser Darling (1942), and *Life among the Scots,* by Janet Adam Smith. Two excellent books on *Edinburgh* are those by George Scott-Moncrieff in the British Cities series (Batsford, 1945), and by Sacheverell Sitwell and Francis Bamford (John Lehmann, 1948). Other outstanding works are those by George Scott-Moncrieff on *The Lowlands of Scotland* (Batsford, 1949), W. T. Palmer on *The Verge of the Scottish Highlands* (Hale, 1947), and J. R. Allan on the *North East Lowlands of Scotland* (Hale, 1952).

Ian Finlay covers the arts and crafts of Scotland in his *Art in Scotland* (Oxford University Press, 1948) and

Scottish Crafts (Harrap, 1948). Sir Thomas Innes deals with a Scottish speciality in *Tartans of the Clans and Families of Scotland* (Johnston, 1951).

For climbers the nine *Scottish Mountaineering Club Guides* (3 Forres Street, Edinburgh) are indispensable. See also *Mountaineering in Scotland*, by W. H. Murray (Dent, 1947), and his *Undiscovered Scotland* (Dent, 1951). The standard geological work is Sir Archibald Geikie's *The Scenery of Scotland* (1865; 3rd ed., Macmillan, 1901).

The best *Short Histories of Scotland* are those by P. Hume Brown (Oliver & Boyd, 1950), George Malcolm Thomson (Routledge & Kegan Paul, 1930), and Robert L. Mackie (Oxford, 1930). The standard work on *The Prehistory of Scotland* is by Professor V. Gordon Childe (Routledge & Kegan Paul, 1935). Those who are interested in the Young Chevalier should consult Andrew Lang's *Prince Charles Edward Stuart* (Longmans, 1903) and Compton Mackenzie's *Prince Charlie* (Davies, 1932). Scottish social life is dealt with in James Mackinnon's two interesting volumes on the *Social and Industrial History of Scotland*: From the Earliest Times to the Union (Blackie, 1920) and From the Union to the Present Time (Longmans, 1921). Elizabeth S. Haldane's *The Scotland of Our Fathers* (Maclehose, 1933) is a popular social history of Scotland in the last century, treated in a lively manner and from a liberal point of view.

A Literary History of Scotland, by J. H. Millar (Fisher Unwin, 1903), is still the best work of its kind. See also Agnes Mure Mackenzie's *Historical Survey of Scottish Literature* down to 1714 (Maclehose, 1933). The 'literary geography' of Sir Walter Scott is fully treated in *The Lands of Scott*, by James F. Hunnewell, an American writer (Black, 1871), and *The Scott Country*, by W. S. Crockett (Black, 1902). Similarly, *The Burns Country*, by C. S. Dougall (Black, 1904).

TOUR I: BERWICK TO EDINBURGH

Total distance by road: about 80 miles.

BERWICK—EYEMOUTH—COLDINGHAM—ST ABB'S HEAD—FAST
CASTLE — DUNBAR — TANTALLON CASTLE — BASS ROCK —
NORTH BERWICK — DIRLETON — HADDINGTON — MUSSEL-
BURGH — EDINBURGH — DALMENY — FORTH BRIDGE —
LINLITHGOW.

THERE could hardly be a more appropriate spot from which
to set out on a tour of Scotland than *Berwick-upon-Tweed*,
the northernmost town in England, situated on the Great
North Road from London (337 miles) to Edinburgh
(58 miles). It lies at the mouth of the 'silver Tweed,'
a turbulent stream that rivals the Clyde as the greatest
and most historic river of southern Scotland. Three
notable bridges span it at Berwick: the James VI Bridge,
of fifteen arches, dating from 1642; the Royal Tweed
Bridge, with four spans of reinforced concrete, 1928; and
the Royal Border Bridge, constructed for the railway by
Robert Stephenson in 1850. Berwick is the Border town
par excellence, having changed hands thirteen times before
1482, when Richard Crookback captured it for his brother
Edward IV, and finally made it an English possession.
Berwickshire, its county, still forms part of Scotland.

Berwick is a picturesque town, grey, with red roofs, but
its main architectural feature is its Elizabethan enceinte
of walls with their massive brick bastions. These date
from 1558, and are among the earliest examples of military
engineering in the new Italian style introduced in conse-
quence of the invention of artillery. Portions of the older,
Edwardian walls survive also, chiefly on the west side
of the town, and include a picturesque watch-tower.
The Castle, where, according to tradition, Edward I
imprisoned the Countess of Buchan in a cage hung from
the walls for her offence in crowning Robert Bruce, was
pulled down by Stephenson to make a site for the railway
station. The Parish Church of Holy Trinity is one of the
few built—or in this case rebuilt—in the time of the

Commonwealth. Before leaving Berwick you may try the sweets known as 'Berwick cockles.'

The main road north from Berwick is traversed by frequent motor-coaches and buses on their way to Edinburgh, some of which take the old road through Coldingham. On the left rises Halidon Hill, where, in July 1333, Sir Archibald Douglas, Regent for the youthful David II, engaged Edward III's archers in an attempt to raise the siege of Berwick. Six Scottish earls fell on that fatal day. The top of the hill affords a view westward of the Merse (i.e. marsh), the largest plain in Scotland. The road runs high above the sea and enters Scotland after 3 miles—look out for the notice by the roadside. This is Lamberton Toll, once, like Gretna Green, the goal of eloping couples. Burnmouth, 5½ miles from Berwick, is tucked away at the base of the cliffs, and can easily be missed by travellers on the main road. It is a primitive fishing village of whitewashed, red-roofed cottages, clustering against a background of grass-grown cliffs of red sandstone. The whole of the Berwickshire coast, like that of Northumberland, is well worth exploring on foot.

Here the St Abbs buses leave the Great North Road and the main railway line on the left, and pass through *Eyemouth*, terminus of a branch line from Burnmouth. A prosperous fishing centre, with a fleet of trawlers and a rocky harbour, it is also a quaint and unconventional holiday resort. Its kippers are excellent. *Coldingham*, a sleepy village 8 miles from Burnmouth, and 1 mile from the sea, has a church incorporating the important early-Gothic remains (north and east choir walls) of a Benedictine priory. Coldingham Bay, with its alluring golden sands and the fishing village of St Abbs, forms a delightful seaside resort, and there is an excellent two-mile walk thence along the cliffs to the lighthouse on *St Abb's Head*. The site of the nunnery of which Ebba was abbess about the middle of the seventh century is probably included in the scanty remains still to be seen here. The scenery, with cliffs of porphyritic trap and numerous caves, is very impressive. Four miles farther on are the meagre, battered ruins of *Fast Castle*, which can be reached also direct from Coldingham by a road that eventually degenerates into a footpath. The Castle, once the property of the Home family, is the reputed original of Wolf's Crag, the home of Ravenswood and his faithful steward, Caleb Balderstone, in *The Bride of Lammermoor*—'the solitary and naked tower, situated on a projecting cliff that beetled on the German Ocean. . . . Tall and narrow, and built of a greyish stone, [it] stood glimmering in the moonlight, like the sheeted sepulchre of some huge giant. A wilder, or more disconsolate dwelling, it was perhaps difficult to conceive.'

The buses from Coldingham to Cockburnspath (10 miles) run only in summer, and infrequently at that. (Otherwise you can go to Ayton and change there.) The road attains a height of 758 feet, and commands fine views of the heathery moorlands. It then descends to rejoin the Great North Road and the Edinburgh railway at the charming Pease Dean.

Cockburnspath (pronounced 'Cóburnspath') has a small fishing harbour, an old market cross, and a church with a curious circular tower of the turn of the sixteenth century in the centre of its west gable. The road then nears the sea and crosses the Dunglass Burn into the county of East Lothian. In the grounds of Dunglass House is a ruinous but beautiful little collegiate church, dating from 1443. On the left is Cocklaw (1,046 feet), an outlier of the Lammermuirs. The coast is seldom out of sight, and the tall white lighthouse at Barness is a prominent feature of the landscape. Shortly before reaching Dunbar (8 miles from Cockburnspath) we cross the Broxburn, scene of Cromwell's victory over Leslie on 3rd September 1650— 'The Lord hath delivered them into our hands!'

Dunbar (accent on second syllable), by-passed by the main road, is a small seaport and holiday resort, with golf, swimming-pool and boating-lake, etc. The low rock above the harbour is crowned with the shapeless sandstone ruins of the Castle, which was a favourite refuge of Mary Queen of Scots. The church has a sumptuous monument to George Home or Hume, Earl of Dunbar (*d.* 1611). The Town House is a harmonious Renaissance composition of about the year 1620.

At a point 4 miles beyond Dunbar motorists turn sharp right, while bus passengers go on to East Linton

and change there for the North Berwick bus.   The railway
junction for North Berwick is Drem.   On the left of East
Linton is the isolated hill of Traprain Law (710 feet),
where the famous hoard of Roman silver now in the
National Museum of Antiquities at Edinburgh was found
in 1919.   Near its foot is Whittingehame ('g' soft), where
Lord Balfour was born and buried.   The North Berwick
road crosses the flat seaward portion of East Lothian,
which is reputed to be the best-farmed land in Europe, and
is called the 'Garden of Scotland.'   Its coast is lined with
a succession of famous golf links.   North Berwick Law, a
basalt cone 613 feet high, dominates the plain.   Whitekirk, a village where you turn sharp right, has a fine
fifteenth-century church that was destroyed by the
Suffragettes in 1914, but has since been reconstructed.

The road reaches the sea near the impressive ruins of
Tantallon Castle, which is approached by a footpath.
Once the fastness of the Douglases, built by 'the grim'
third Earl in 1374, 'Tantallon's dizzy steep, hung o'er the
margin of the deep,' consists of a great screen wall thrown
across the promontory, with a central gatehouse, corner
towers, and a treble ditch.   Though considered impreg-
nable—'Ding down Tantallon and build a brig to the
Bass'—it was destroyed by General Monk in February
1651.

The celebrated *Bass Rock*, with its lighthouse, $1\frac{1}{4}$
miles off shore, consists of a stock of trachyte, with
350-foot cliffs on all sides except the south, and is a
haunt of gannets and other sea birds.   With its sixteenth-
century defences it was one of the 'strengths' of Scotland,
frequently used as a prison for English captives and
(after 1671) for Covenanters.   The most notable incident
in its history was in 1691, when four Jacobite officer
prisoners got rid of their keepers and held the rock against
all comers for nearly three years.   David Balfour, in
Catriona, was detained here: 'just the one crag of rock,
as everybody knows, but great enough to carve a city
from . . . the straight crags painted with sea-birds'
droppings like a morning frost, the sloping top of it green
with grass, the clan of white geese that cried about the
sides, and the black, broken buildings of the prison
sitting close on the sea's edge.'

North Berwick, 14 miles from Dunbar by this route,
is probably the most fashionable seaside resort in Scotland. Golf is the chief attraction, and the only other
amusements are tennis and bathing. There are remains
of a twelfth-century Cistercian nunnery, in private grounds
near the station. The next village, a very pretty one, is
Dirleton, with a spacious green and the ruins of an important thirteenth-century castle of the De Vaux, Haly-
burton, and Ruthven families. Monk captured it from
the moss-troopers and 'slighted' it in 1650. Gullane
(pronounced 'Gillan,' with hard 'g') and Aberlady, 7½
miles from North Berwick, are golfing resorts. Adjoining the former is Muirfield, the course of the Honourable
Company of Edinburgh Golfers.

From Aberlady make straight inland (buses available)
for Haddington, 5 miles, passing close to an obelisk
on Garleton Hill that commemorates the Earl of Hope-
toun (pronounced 'Hopton'), a Peninsular hero. *Haddington* is the county town and the alleged birthplace of
John Knox—the site of the house is supposed to be marked
by a tree in Giffordgate. Its most interesting building
is the Parish Church, which was formerly the Collegiate
Church of St Mary, and dates from the end of the fourteenth century. Its choir and transepts are roofless.
The south wall bears marks of bullets fired in the siege
of 1548, when the English held Haddington against the
French and the Scots. Note the tombs of the Earl of
Lauderdale (1638) in the north choir aisle, and of William
Seton (1682) in the north transept. Jane Welsh, Carlyle's
wife, was a native of Haddington, and is buried here.
This church is commonly known as 'The Lamp of Lothian,'
but that appellation properly belonged to the choir of the
church of the Friars Minor, which Edward III destroyed
in 1356. The estate of Lennoxlove, south of the town,
was originally called Lethington, and once belonged to
'La belle Stuart,' Duchess of Richmond and Lennox,
who sat for the original figure of Britannia on the coinage.
She left it, with a request that it should be called 'Lennox
love to Blantyre,' to her nephew the Earl of Blantyre,
and it is now the seat of the Duke of Hamilton (premier
peer of Scotland) and open to visitors on summer afternoons.

As you proceed by the Great North Road or the railway
from Haddington to Edinburgh (17 miles) you pass
between the battlefield of Prestonpans, on the right—
a victory for Prince Charlie over General Cope on
21st September 1745—and that of Pinkie, where the
Protector Somerset routed the Scots in 1547. Farther
south is Carberry Hill, where Mary Queen of Scots surrendered to her nobles in 1567. *Musselburgh*, in the
county of Midlothian, is an old-world town at the mouth
of the River Esk, now engaged in industry. The old
bridge near the station dates partly from the sixteenth
century and is reserved for pedestrian traffic. Portobello, the seaside resort of the Edinburgh operatives, is
mercifully by-passed. As it approaches Edinburgh the
road leaves Arthur's Seat on the left.

Edinburgh (pronounced 'Ed'nbŏrŏ'), 'the heart of
Scotland, Britaine's other eye,' has been the capital city
since the mid fifteenth century, although its population
(466,000) is less than half that of Glasgow. It has
earned its title of the 'Modern Athens' both on account
of its history as a cultural centre, and because of many
similarities in the natural setting of the two cities. Like
Athens, 'stately Edinburgh' is 'throned on crags,' with
the Castle as its Acropolis, Leith its Piraeus. 'Auld
Reekie,' a more affectionate appellation, refers to the
smoke-veil discharged from the innumerable chimneys.

In contrast to the large area covered by the modern
city, historic Edinburgh, built almost entirely of the local
sandstone, is confined within a small compass. The Old
Town, 'jagged, picturesque, piled up,' occupies a long
ridge that descends from the Castle Rock to the Palace
of Holyrood. The New Town, or more modern part of
Central Edinburgh, consists of 'airy, open, coldly-sunny'
streets and squares, built for the most part in the latter
half of the eighteenth century.

'Few places, if any, offer a more barbaric display of
contrasts to the eye. In the very midst stands one of the
most satisfactory crags in nature—a Bass Rock upon dry
land, rooted in a garden, shaken by passing trains, carrying a crown of battlements and turrets, and describing its
warlike shadow over the liveliest and brightest thorough-
fare of the new town. From their smoky beehives, ten

stories high, the unwashed look down upon the open squares and gardens of the wealthy; and gay people sunning themselves along Princes Street . . . see, across a gardened valley set with statues, where the washings of the old town flutter in the breeze at its high windows.' (R. L. Stevenson, *Edinburgh : Picturesque Notes.*)

The main street of modern Edinburgh, 'noblest of earthly promenades,' is the far-famed Princes Street, which is open to the south and commands a marvellous view of the Castle and the outline of the Old Town across gardens laid out on the site of a lake-bed, the old Nor' Loch. This gorge to some extent supplies Edinburgh's chief deficiency—a river. Princes Street connects the two principal railway stations of Edinburgh: the Waverley Station at the east end and the Princes Street Station at the west end, each with its great hotel. Opposite the former is the Register House (i.e. Public Record Office), a fine design of Robert Adam's, 1772. The Princes Street Gardens contain numerous memorials to eminent Scotsmen, including the conspicuous Scott Monument, erected in the very centre of 'mine own romantic town.' Ruskin likened it to 'a small, vulgar Gothic steeple,' and Dickens to 'the spire of a Gothic church taken off and stuck in the ground.' It was designed by George Meikle Kemp, an architect who started life as a shepherd and was drowned in the Edinburgh Canal shortly before the inauguration of the monument in 1844. The statue of Sir Walter, with his dog Maida at his feet, is by Sir John Steell. There is a museum of Scott relics inside the monument. In the west part of the gardens is the exceedingly beautiful Scottish-American War Memorial, raised by American subscriptions in 1927, and designed by Professor R. Tait McKenzie of Philadelphia.

The best route from Princes Street to the Castle is by the Mound, past a floral clock and classical edifices housing the Royal Scottish Academy and the National Gallery of Scotland. Both were designed by the same architect, William Henry Playfair (who was responsible for so much of 'Modern Athens' and the New Town), though thirty-six years separated their dates of opening, 1823 and 1859. The National Gallery has an excellent general collection of pictures, in which the Scottish school

(Raeburn, Wilkie, Allan Ramsay, etc.) is naturally well represented.

The final approach to the Castle is by the Castle Esplanade, with its military monuments and a car park, and a drawbridge over the dry moat. The Castle is open freely to visitors from 10 a.m. onwards. Sunday, when it is open from 11 a.m., is a bad day for a visit, as the historic apartments are closed to the public. Edinburgh, or in early times Dunedin, is supposed—quite erroneously —to derive its name from a military post established on the Castle Rock by Edwin, King of Northumbria (*d.* 633). The Castle was captured by Edward I in 1296, but Sir Thomas Randolph, Earl of Moray, retook it for Bruce in 1314 by a famous escalade. Edward III held it from 1337 to 1341. Cromwell captured the Castle in 1650, after the Battle of Dunbar, but in 1745 it somewhat mysteriously held out against Prince Charles Edward when he occupied Edinburgh.

Beyond an outer gateway you pass through the Portcullis Gate below the Argyll Tower, where the Marquis of Argyll was confined before his execution in 1661. The roadway ascends past the Governor's House to the top of the hill, whence you obtain a glorious view of the city, with the Firth of Forth and the Highlands in the background. The first building encountered is St Margaret's Chapel, the oldest structure in Edinburgh, dating from the eleventh or twelfth century. St Margaret, who introduced the Roman use into Scotland, was the sister of Edgar Atheling and wife of Malcolm Canmore. She died in the Castle in the year 1093, and was buried at Dunfermline. The great fifteenth-century cannon behind the chapel is known as Mons Meg, and according to one tradition was cast at Mons in Belgium. At the east end of the rock, beyond the back of the National War Memorial, is the Half-Moon Battery, where a time gun is fired at 1 p.m. on weekdays.

You now enter Crown Square or Palace Yard, a quadrangle surrounded by buildings mainly of the fifteenth century. On the north side is the Scottish National War Memorial, designed by Sir Robert Lorimer and opened in 1927. Its external aspect is somewhat severe, but the interior is a work of consummate beauty. E. V. Lucas called it 'the most beautiful and moving of the recent works of man.' It consists of a Gallery of Honour with memorials to Scottish regiments, etc., and an octagonal Shrine with stained-glass windows by Douglas Strachan, and a bronze frieze by Morris Meredith-Williams. Even parts played by animals in the First World War are commemorated. The altar bearing the silver casket with the roll of honour (over a hundred thousand names) stands on an outcrop of living rock—'a stroke of architectural inspiration.' There is a naval and military museum in connection with the memorial.

In the south-east corner of Crown Square are Queen Mary's apartments, with the room in which she gave birth to James VI (James I of England) on 19th June 1566, and the Crown Room, where the Regalia ('Honours of Scotland') are kept. The Old Parliament Hall, or Banqueting Hall, on the south side of the square, was the meeting-place of some of the earlier Scottish parliaments. This was the scene of the 'Black Dinner' of 1440, when a black bull's head was served at a banquet given by James II in honour of the young sixth Earl of Douglas and his brother David, a grim intimation of their impending execution. The hall now contains a collection of arms and armour. The remains of King David's Tower, the castle keep, built by David II and battered down by the English in 1573, are shown by a guide, together with the dungeons under the Banqueting Hall.

The long street that leads from the Castle to Holyrood Palace under various names—Castle Hill, Lawnmarket, High Street, Canongate—is often called the 'Royal Mile.' It intersects the oldest part of Edinburgh and, like the 'closes' and 'wynds' that adjoin it, is lined with tall tenement houses or 'lands.' Once the abode of rank and fashion, they are now inhabited by the poorer classes. In the Lawnmarket are Gladstone's Land (National Trust) and Lady Stair's Close, with Lady Stair's House, which bears the date 1622, the initials of the builder and his wife, and the inscription 'Feare the Lord & Depart from Evill.' This was the scene of the remarkable incident described by Scott in his story of *My Aunt Margaret's Mirror*. The house is now used as a branch of the City Museum. On the other side of the Lawnmarket is Brodie's Close, once the abode of the famous Deacon Brodie, who was a respectable citizen by day and the leader of a gang of burglars at night, and was hanged in 1788. Just beyond the statue of the Duke of Buccleuch (pronounced 'Bŭclóo') in the High Street is the 'Heart of Midlothian,' marked in stones in the pavement on the site of the portal of the Old Tolbooth or prison.

St Giles's Church, the principal church in Edinburgh, is still often styled Cathedral, though it was actually such only for two short periods in the seventeenth century. The present structure was begun about the year 1387, and completed by the mid fifteenth century except for the central tower, surmounted by its famous Crown, which was finished in 1495 and is one of the open stone coronals that are almost peculiar to Scottish architecture. From the south-east door one enters an antechapel, on the left of which is the small and highly ornate Chapel of the Thistle, designed by Sir Robert Lorimer and completed in 1911. The Most Ancient and Most Noble Order of the Thistle, revived by James VII (James II of England) in 1687, consists of the Sovereign and nineteen Knights (K.T.).

The interior of St Giles's, dark and impressive, was shorn of much of its beauty by the Reformation and unhappy restorations. Until 1872 it was divided up into two, three, or four churches. The vaulting and the memorials are of particular interest. Colours of Scottish regiments hang from the nave pillars. The stained glass is modern, of course. From the antechapel you first enter the beautiful Preston Aisle, on the left of which are the Royal Pew and the Chepman Aisle, a chantry founded by Walter Chepman, the first Scottish printer (*d.* 1538?). Here is a modern monument ('Montrose 1661') to the Marquis of Montrose, Covenanter and Royalist, who was hanged in the Grassmarket in 1650, and is buried in the vault below. Beyond the organ is the Side Chapel of the nave, with a floor tablet marking the spot whence, in 1637, according to the story, Jenny Geddes threw the cutty stool at Dean Hannay as he was reading from Laud's service book. A monument in this aisle, by Augustus Saint-Gaudens, the American sculptor, commemorates Robert Louis Stevenson. 'Is it not a pathetic thought that this

Scottish genius, so pre-eminently Scottish, should have laid his bones, not in the Lothians that he loved so well . . . but in the far-distant islands of the Pacific?' (Lord Rosebery).

The Albany Aisle, in the north-west corner of the nave, contains the font, after Thorwaldsen, and a bronze statue of John Knox, who died as minister of St Giles's. St Eloi's Chapel, on this side of the north door, has a modern monument to the Marquis of Argyll, Montrose's great rival, himself beheaded in 1661 after the Restoration.

The Mercat Cross, outside the east end of the church, is a modern restoration carried out at Gladstone's expense in 1885. Parliament Square, the open space on the south side of St Giles's, once formed part of the churchyard. It contains an equestrian statue of Charles II in lead (1685), and a brass plate in the roadway inscribed 'I. K. 1572' and marking the grave of John Knox. The frontage of Parliament House, on the south side of the square, dates from 1829, though the body of the building was erected in 1632-40. The Scottish Parliament met here from 1639 till the Union in 1707, and the building is now used by the Court of Session, or supreme law courts of Scotland. The Great Hall is a noble Gothic chamber with an open timber roof and a window of nineteenth-century Munich glass depicting the Institution of the Court of Session by James V in 1532. The National Library of Scotland, adjacent, was founded in 1682 by Sir George Mackenzie of Rosehaugh, King's Advocate (called 'Bloody' Mackenzie from his treatment of the Covenanters), and was presented to the nation in 1924 by the Faculty of Advocates. It is one of the six libraries entitled to a free copy of every work published in the United Kingdom, and now comprises about three-quarters of a million volumes. Over the lobby door hangs a standard carried at Flodden. A selection of interesting manuscripts, etc., is exhibited in a room below the Great Hall, together with Greenshields's statue of Sir Walter Scott.

The Council Chambers, or municipal offices, are on the other side of the High Street, and under the central arch is the City Cenotaph, or Stone of Remembrance. Farther on, at the point where the High Street crosses the 'Bridges,' stands the Tron Church, named after the public weighing beam. Next, on the left, John Knox's House, open to visitors, and inscribed 'Lufe God abufe al, and thi nychbour as thiself.' Its association with the great Reformer, however, is doubtful.

Then comes the Canongate, now a squalid street, but once occupied by the Canons of Holyrood Abbey. Moray House (pronounced 'Murray'), on the right, was built in 1628, and occupied by Cromwell in 1648 and 1650. It is now a training college and open to visitors. The ceilings are noteworthy. Here, in a summer-house in the garden, the Treaty of Union ('ane end of ane auld sang') was negotiated—perhaps signed—in 1707. Huntly House, close by, has a half-timbered front of 1570, and the interesting City Museum is now installed here. In Bakehouse Close, adjacent, is Acheson House (1633), restored by the Marquis of Bute and open for inspection. Opposite Huntly House are the Canongate Tolbooth (1591), with a projecting clock, and the Canongate Church (1688). Adam Smith, of *Wealth of Nations* fame, and Robert Fergusson, the poet, are buried in the graveyard. White Horse Close, on the same side, is worth a glance.

The Palace of Holyroodhouse, at the foot of the Canongate, was begun by King James IV about the year 1500, but all of it, except the north-west wing containing the Historical Apartments, was burnt down in 1544, and the greater part of the present buildings was erected in 1670–9 for Charles II, whose architect was Sir William Bruce of Kinross, King's Surveyor in Scotland. Mary Queen of Scots spent six years here (1561–7), but since James VI left to ascend the English throne in 1603 it has only occasionally been occupied by royalty. Prince Charles Edward made Holyrood his headquarters from 17th September to 31st October 1745. The Lord High Commissioner is in residence at Holyrood for a fortnight in May, while representing the Sovereign at the General Assembly of the Church of Scotland.

The palace is open to visitors daily, but it is closed on Sunday mornings. The Historical Apartments include a picture gallery with a hundred and ten imaginary portraits of Scottish kings, executed by Jacob de Witt for Charles II in two years (1684–6). The artist was paid a salary of £120 per year, which works out at a portrait every six and a half days, at 43s. 8d. each. There are also a few valuable early Flemish paintings. Queen Mary was married to Bothwell with Protestant rites in this gallery in 1567, three months after the murder of Darnley. Darnley's rooms, adjacent, communicate by a private staircase with those of Queen Mary on the floor above. A brass plate in the vestibule of the queen's audience chamber marks the spot where the body of David Rizzio, the queen's Italian secretary, was left by his murderers. The State Apartments contain a sumptuous collection of furniture, portraits, and tapestry.

At the back of the courtyard is the entrance to the ruined Chapel Royal, which is the only relic of Holyrood Abbey. Several of the Stuart kings were crowned, married, or buried here. The Abbey was founded by David I in 1128, on the spot where he was saved from the attack of a hunted stag by the miraculous agency of the Holy Cross.

Return by the Canongate to the Tron Church and turn left along South Bridge. This brings us to the University, or rather the old University building, a splendid design of Robert Adam's (1789). Founded in 1583, this is now the only British university produced by the Reformation. Part of the building covers the site of the house in Kirk o' Field occupied by Queen Mary and Darnley in February 1567, and mysteriously blown up on the 9th during the queen's temporary absence, Darnley's dead body being found in a neighbouring garden. Adjacent, in Chambers Street, is the Royal Scottish Museum of science, natural history, applied art, and antiquities. A tablet on No. 8 Chambers Street states that near this spot stood Sir Walter Scott's birthplace in the vanished College Wynd (15th August 1771). The Greyfriars Church near the farther end of Chambers Street, a plain building, consists of Old Greyfriars, built in 1612 and re-erected after a fire in 1845, and New Greyfriars, 1721; the two churches and congregations, however, were united in 1937. The churchyard contains a Martyrs' Memorial and the graves of many well-known Scotsmen; Sir Walter Scott's father, and several of his brothers and sisters, are buried here, and a tablet on the west wall of the church commemorates Allan Ramsay, the poet. The National Covenant of 1st March 1638 was signed inside the church—the more

enthusiastic signatories using their own blood as ink—
and not, as an exploded tradition has it, on the tomb of
a Boswell of Auchinleck at the south-east corner of the
church. Hence, Forrest Road leads south past Lauriston
Place to various new University buildings, the Royal
Infirmary (the largest voluntary hospital in Great Britain,
founded in 1729 and rebuilt since 1870), and George
Square, No. 25 in which was Sir Walter Scott's home
from soon after his birth until his marriage in 1797.
Heriot's Hospital in Lauriston Place is a very attractive
building of 1650. Candlemaker Row leads from the
Greyfriars gate in the other direction to the Grassmarket, where a cross in the pavement near the east end
indicates the site of the gallows where so many Covenanters
suffered for conscience' sake in the seventeenth century.
A few yards along the Cowgate, a street that runs east
from the Grassmarket, is the highly interesting Magdalen
Chapel, founded in 1547 and containing some pre-
Reformation glass.

You should now return to Princes Street by way of
Victoria Street, George IV Bridge, Bank Street, and the
Mound, and explore the New Town, as the solidly built
quarter to the north of Princes Street is still called. Take
a walk along George Street, which, with a statue at every
cross-street, leads from Charlotte Square on the west to
St Andrew Square on the east. No. 39 in Castle Street
(the first cross-street) was Sir Walter Scott's town house
from 1802 until his commercial crash in 1826, and most of
his works were written there. Previously he had lived at
108 George Street—to rooms on the second floor of which
he brought his bride (née Charlotte Charpentier) in 1797—
and at 10 Castle Street, from 1798 to 1802. St Andrew
Square contains the Melville Monument, a 150-foot column,
and just north of it, housed in a single building in Queen
Street, are the Scottish National Portrait Gallery and the
National Museum of Antiquities, both of them intensely
attractive to anybody interested in the history of Scotland.

The next thing to do is to follow Waterloo Place, the
eastern continuation of Princes Street, past the huge new
Government Buildings, and climb Calton Hill to get what
is probably the best view of Edinburgh, and to see its
interesting monuments and buildings: the monument to

Dugald Stewart, the philosopher, in the form of a copy of the Monument of Lysicrates at Athens; the City Observatory; the picturesque National Monument, in the style of the Parthenon, intended to commemorate the Napoleonic wars, but left unfinished; and the Nelson Monument, which can be ascended and has a time ball that functions at 1 p.m. Greenwich Mean Time.

'A thousand years of history are here crystallised within the circuit of a single glance. . . . There, in the centre, towers the great crown of St Giles. Hard by are the quaint slopes of the Canongate,—teeming with illustrious, or picturesque, or terrible figures of Long Ago. Yonder the glorious Castle Crag looks steadfastly westward,—its manifold, wonderful colours continuously changing in the changeful daylight. Down in the valley Holyrood, haunted by a myriad of memories and by one resplendent face and entrancing presence, nestles at the foot of the giant Salisbury Crag; while the dark, rivened peak of Arthur's Seat rears itself supremely over the whole stupendous scene. Southward and westward, in the distance, extends the bleak range of the Pentland Hills; eastward the cone of Berwick Law and the desolate Bass Rock seem to cleave the sea; and northward, beyond the glistening crystal of the Forth,—with the white lines of embattled Inchkeith like a diamond on its bosom,—the lovely Lomonds, the virginal mountain breasts of Fife, are bared to the kiss of heaven.' (William Winter, *Gray Days and Gold*.)

Another popular excursion is by a Corstorphine (pronounced 'Costórfin') bus or tram to the Scottish Zoological Park, with an aquarium. The Dean Bridge, spanning the Water of Leith and reached from the west end of Princes Street via Queensferry Street, is an attractive spot, and on the way back you can digress by Melville Street to have a look at St Mary's Episcopal Cathedral, a vast Gothic church built by Sir Gilbert Scott in the eighteen-seventies.

The event of the year at Edinburgh from the tourist point of view, is the *International Festival of Music and Drama*, which was first held in 1947 and lasts for three weeks in August and September. In addition to events of purely Scottish significance (such as the Highland Games immediately preceding the Festival itself) there are performances of plays both old and modern, symphony concerts and recitals, operas, and ballets, by British, European, and American companies and artists, besides exhibitions of painting and other arts and an International Film Festival.

Leith, the port of Edinburgh, has the venerable Trinity House to show, besides the usual sights of a dockyard town, while Newhaven, which adjoins it on the west, and was founded by James III in 1488, is inhabited by a fisherfolk with many old customs and a distinctive dress for their fishwives. Farther west is Granton, a fishing harbour created by the Duke of Buccleuch in 1835.

Those who want to make Edinburgh a centre for excursions will find no lack of railway facilities and motorbus and motor-coach services: e.g. to Roslin, the Pentland Hills, Melrose, etc.

One excursion that had better be done from Edinburgh, as it can otherwise hardly be fitted in, is to Dalmeny (pronounced 'Dalménny'), South Queensferry, and Linlithgow (pronounced 'Linlíthgo'). The buses from Edinburgh to South Queensferry (8¾ miles) pass Fettes College (pronounced 'Féttis'), a well-known public school, and cross Cramond Bridge. It was at the older Cramond Brig—fifteenth century, but partly rebuilt—lower down the River Almond, that James V was rescued from an affray by Jock Howieson. He rewarded him with a gift of the Braehead estate under the condition of presenting a basin, ewer, and towel for the king to wash his hands whenever he passed the bridge. This service was last performed by the representative of the Howieson-Craufurd family on the occasion of King George V's visit in 1927. The bus then passes Dalmeny Park, seat of the Earl of Rosebery, on the right, and leaves to the left the road to *Dalmeny Church*, which dates from the latter part of the twelfth century, and is the most complete Romanesque parish church in Scotland. Nave, chancel, and stilted apse all survive, but the west tower has gone. The zigzag decoration of the arches and the interlaced arcading over the south door are noteworthy. The Rosebery Chapel is an incongruous addition. South Queensferry is a picturesque little town with the old Hawes Inn, which figures in *The Antiquary* and *Kidnapped*. A ferry (motor-

cars 3s.–6s. 6d., motor-cycle 1s. 2d.) plies across the Firth
of Forth to North Queensferry in Fife, while the railway is
carried over by the *Forth Bridge,* just over a mile long, and
one of the engineering marvels of the world. It was constructed in 1883–90 by Sir John Fowler and Sir Benjamin
Baker.

From South Queensferry you can go by bus (change at
Winchburgh) or train to *Linlithgow* (9½ miles), the county
town of West Lothian, and an ancient little place that
lives in the past. 'Glasgow for bells, Linlithgow for wells,
Falkirk for peas and beans.' Linlithgow is sometimes
called the Windsor of Scotland on account of its Royal
Palace, birthplace of Mary Queen of Scots. The precincts
of the Church and the Palace are entered by a fine gateway.
The Parish Church of St Michael, begun in the latter part
of the fifteenth century, and completed by 1559, is one of
the grandest in Scotland, and shows the influence of
French architecture. The Palace, set on the bank of a
loch, dates in its present form from the fifteenth to
seventeenth centuries: the west side from 1424–37, the
east from about 1469, the south from about 1500, the
north from 1616–33. It has been ruinous since 1st
February 1746, when it was set alight by the carelessness
of Cumberland's troops. In the centre of the courtyard
is a richly carved fountain of about the year 1535. The
graceful stair-towers in the corners of the quadrangle were
built in the early sixteenth century. On the east side is
the Great Hall, containing a monumental triple chimney-
piece, on the south the Chapel, on the west the Royal
Apartments. The room in which Queen Mary was born,
on 7th December 1542, is shown. Queen Margaret's
Bower is so named from a tradition that James IV's
queen there sat awaiting in vain the king's return from
Flodden. The Regent Moray died in the Guard Room in
1570, after being shot in the streets of Linlithgow by James
Hamilton of Bothwellhaugh. The road from Linlithgow
to Stirling passes through Falkirk, famous for its iron-
works, and for two battles: Wallace's defeat by Edward I,
1298, and a victory of Prince Charles's over General
Hawley on his northward retreat, 17th January 1746.

The rolling mills of the British Aluminium Co. Ltd at
Falkirk were installed during the Second World War to

give the increased output of aluminium and alloy required by the aircraft industry. Here the ingot metal is cast into rolling slabs of up to two tons in weight. These pass to hot and cold rolling lines which yield continuous strips of up to six feet in width. The aluminium plate is used also in shipbuilding, for roofing, and in the construction of road vehicles.

Most tourists will want to avoid the industrial districts —coal, iron, steel, shale oil, etc.—between Edinburgh and Glasgow. There is a splendid arterial road between the two cities, 44¼ miles in length, free from steep gradients, and by-passing all the important centres of population.

TOUR II: EDINBURGH TO MELROSE
AND CARLISLE

Total distance by road: about 140 miles.

CRAIGMILLAR CASTLE —— ROSLIN —— PEEBLES —— NEIDPATH
CASTLE —— INNERLEITHEN —— GALASHIELS —— ABBOTSFORD —
MELROSE —— DRYBURGH ABBEY —— KELSO —— ROXBURGH
CASTLE —— JEDBURGH —— HAWICK —— SELKIRK —— ST MARY'S
LOCH — MOFFAT —— LOCHMABEN —— ECCLEFECHAN —— GRETNA
GREEN—CARLISLE.

LEAVING Edinburgh by the 'Bridges,' you take the
Peebles road — buses Edinburgh–Peebles–Galashiels —
straight on if you are going direct to Roslin (7¼ miles),
or bear left by East Preston Street and the Old Dalkeith
Road if you want to visit the lonely ruins of *Craigmillar
Castle* en route. Craigmillar, whose massive tower dates
from the last quarter of the fourteenth century, was an
occasional residence of Mary Queen of Scots, and there is a
celebrated view from the top of the tower. Thence you
can either take a cross-road and rejoin the Peebles road
at Liberton, or make a detour via Dalkeith and Lasswade.
Dalkeith House, a former seat of the Duke of Buccleuch
(pronounced 'Bŭclóo'), was built by Vanbrugh for Anne
Duchess of Monmouth and Buccleuch. The house and
park are not at present open to the public. At Lasswade
is Sir Walter Scott's first country home, occupied by him
from 1798 to 1804, and much enlarged since his time. It
lies on the left of the Loanhead road, near the top of the
hill.

An alternative road from Edinburgh to Roslin is from
the west end of Princes Street, via Lothian Road and
Leven Street. You pass near Merchiston Castle (pronounced 'Merkiston'), the birthplace in 1550 of John
Napier, inventor of logarithms, of 'Napier's bones' (an attempt at a calculating machine), and of a forerunner of the
battle 'tank.' By turning right at Fairmilehead and then
left, you can visit Swanston, a charming hamlet 'lapped

in a fold of the Pentlands,' where for several years the young R. L. Stevenson spent the summer months.

To reach Roslin from the main road to Peebles, you turn left at Bilston. *Roslin* (or *Rosslyn*) *Chapel* is the choir of a collegiate church begun in 1446 by Sir William Sinclair, Earl of Orkney and Caithness, and is remarkable for the 'crazy, half-Asiatic richness' of its sculptural decoration, unapproached in this country and possibly the work of Spanish craftsmen. An army of workmen is said to have been employed on it for thirty-four years. Among the subjects represented are the Seven Deadly Sins, the Seven Cardinal Virtues, the Dance of Death, and a great variety of foliage decoration. The celebrated Prentice Pillar derives its name from the story—paralleled else-where—that an apprentice produced it in the absence abroad of his master, who on his return slew him with his mallet in a fit of jealousy. The large sacristy below the chapel and east of it seems to have been used at one period as a priest's dwelling. Rosslyn Castle, the remains of which overlook the North Esk close by, belonged to the Sinclairs (or St Clairs) and dates from the fifteenth and sixteenth centuries. It was destroyed by General Monk in 1650.

The road to Peebles, which is 22¾ miles from Edinburgh, then ascends southwards to Penicuik (pronounced 'Pénny-cook'), where it is joined by the railway. A digression may be made hence to Carlops, 5½ miles south-west, to see Habbie's How, the scene usually associated with Allan Ramsay's pastoral comedy *The Gentle Shepherd*.

> Gae farer up the burn to Habbie's Howe,
> Where a' the sweets o' spring an' simmer grow:
> Between twa birks, out o'er a little lin,
> The water fa's and make a singan din,
> A pool breast-deep beneath as clear as glass,
> Kisses, wi' easy whirls, the bord'ring grass.

Beyond Leadburn the Peebles road passes from Mid-lothian into Peebles-shire, and attains its highest point, 931 feet. It then descends again through Eddleston.

Peebles is a county town, but not now so small and sleepy as to justify the facetious saying 'Peebles for pleasure.' The Cross Keys (dated 1653) is considered to represent the Cleikum Inn in *St Ronan's Well*, where Meg

Dods reigned supreme. There is little else to see save the ruined Cross Church and the Chambers Institution, presented to the town by William Chambers, the publisher. The latter incorporates the mansion where 'Old Q,' the notorious Duke of Queensberry, Wordsworth's 'Degenerate Douglas,' was born. Peebles is described under the name of Priorsford in *Penny Plain*, by Miss Anna Buchan (O. Douglas), and Neidpath Castle is Peel Tower in the book. But it is useless looking for the Rigs and Bella Bathgate's home. The surrounding country, like the town itself, is very pleasant, and a mile up the Tweed, in a delightful spot, are the ruins of *Neidpath Castle*, which was once owned by the Frasers and the Earls of Tweeddale. Note the strawberries carved over the gate—*fraises*, Frasers.

Between Peebles and Melrose (22¼ miles) main road and railway mostly follow the north bank of the Tweed, and pass *Innerleithen* ('th' as in 'then'), a pleasant little spa, that is reckoned to be the original St Ronan's Well. The south bank road passes Traquair House, reputed the oldest inhabited mansion in Scotland (open to visitors on Wednesday and Sunday afternoons in summer), and—just before you cross the river to regain the main road—Ashestiel, the house tenanted by Sir Walter Scott from 1804 to 1812, before moving to Abbotsford. *Marmion* was composed there. Galashiels (pronounced 'Gallăsheéls,' or 'Gala' for short), with its cluster of mill chimneys, is situated on the Gala Water near its junction with the Tweed, and is noted for its cloths and woollens, like most of the other Tweed towns. 'Tweed' cloth is said to derive its name from the inspired error of a London clerk, who misread the word 'tweel' (twill). The stirring War Memorial here is one of the best in the kingdom. On the eastern outskirts of the town is a wall tablet recording how, in 1832, on his way back from Italy to die at Abbotsford, Sir Walter Scott gazed on this scene for the last time. Galashiels is in Selkirkshire, and soon after leaving it you enter Roxburghshire. Buses run from Galashiels to Kelso via Melrose and Newtown St Boswells.

On this side of Melrose, beyond the bridge over the Tweed, a road goes off on the right to *Abbotsford* (2½ miles from Melrose), the large turreted mansion in the baronial

style erected by Sir Walter Scott in 1817–25, as the
realization of his life's dream, but at the expense of his
hard-earned savings. Financial ruin overtook him in
1826, but the house and estate were given back to him by
his creditors in 1830. It is now owned by his great-great-
grandson in the female line, Major-General Sir Walter
Maxwell-Scott. From April to October visitors can see
over part of the house, which contains Scott's magnificent
collection of Scottish historical relics, as well as mementoes
of Scott himself. The dining-room, in which Scott died on
21st September 1832, is not shown. On the Abbotsford
estate is the Rhymer's Glen, where Thomas of Ercildoune
met the Fairy Queen.

After rejoining the Galashiels–Melrose road you pass
Darnick Tower, an old Border peel, now a tea garden.
Melrose (accent on first syllable), situated in the middle of
the Scott country, is the chief tourist centre in the Lowlands. To the south—'Three crests against the saffron
sky, Beyond the purple plain'—rise the Eildon Hills (pronounced 'Eéldŏn'), the highest of which, 1,385 feet,
commands a view that includes 'more than forty places
famous in war and verse.' There is a view indicator. The
Eildons owe their singular shape to an evil spirit who split
them into three at the command of Michael Scott, the
'Wizard of the North.' Melrose Abbey, a monument of
consummate beauty, is the church of a Cistercian house
founded by David I in 1136 with monks from Rievaulx.
Though wrecked by the Earl of Hertford in 1544, it owes
its ruined state to its use as a stone quarry and to the
ravages of wind and weather. The remains, of reddish-
grey sandstone and in a continental modification of the
Perpendicular style, date for the most part from the turn
of the fifteenth century. Every part will repay close
inspection, notably the capitals of the columns, carved
with the leaves of the curly kale and other intricate pat-
terns—see especially the south-west pier at the crossing—
the vaulting, or what is left of it, and the window of the
south transept with its lace-like flamboyant tracery. The
ugly piers and arches in the nave date from the time
when it was used as a parish church, in the seventeenth
and eighteenth centuries. Bruce's heart is believed to be
interred beneath the east window, and Alexander II was

buried a few yards farther west. On the north side are tombs of the Douglases; on the south, at the entrance to the sanctuary, the tomb of Michael Scott. It was *The Lay of the Last Minstrel* that brought fame to Melrose:

> If thou would'st view fair Melrose aright,
> Go visit it by the pale moonlight;
> For the gay beams of lightsome day
> Gild, but to flout, the ruins gray. . . .
> And, home returning, soothly swear,
> Was never scene so sad and fair!

You next take the road to Kelso (13¾ miles), which runs near the south bank of the Tweed, but soon diverge left at Newtown St Boswells to visit *Dryburgh Abbey*, 1¼ miles away, on the Berwickshire side of the Tweed. You can leave your car at the footbridge a few minutes' walk from the Abbey. Bus travellers alight at Newtown St Boswells, railway passengers at St Boswells Station, where in any case they must change for Kelso. Dryburgh was a Premonstratensian house of White Canons, founded in 1150 by Hugo de Morville, Constable of Scotland, and colonized from Alnwick. The ruins, presented to the nation by Lord Glenconner in 1918, show a chaste Decorated style less ornate than that of Melrose, but are both picturesque and important. They include parts of the church (west and south doorways, transepts, gable of south transept, etc.), sacristy, chapter house, calefactory, refectory (rose window), and other domestic buildings. The setting of lawns and old trees—which include cedars and a very ancient yew—is remarkably beautiful. Sir Walter Scott, whose ancestors the Haliburtons of Newmains once owned Dryburgh, is buried in St Mary's Aisle, together with his wife, his son, and his son-in-law and biographer, John Gibson Lockhart. Close by rests Field Marshal Earl Haig of Bemersyde (*d.* 29th January 1928). Bemersyde (pronounced 'Beemerside'), a neighbouring estate held by the Haigs for over seven centuries—'Tyde what may betyde, Haig shall be Haig of Bemersyde' (there are several variants)—was purchased by public subscription in 1921 and presented to Earl Haig, a scion of the family. The view of Tweed and Eildons from Bemersyde Hill delighted Sir Walter Scott.

Kelso is a captivating grey Roxburghshire town on the

north side of the Tweed, with a spacious, cobbled market-place. The bridge, built by Rennie, and said to have been his 'try-out' for Waterloo Bridge, commands a celebrated view of the Abbey. Kelso Abbey was founded by David I in 1128 for Tironensian monks from Picardy, and though it was small its mitred abbots claimed precedence over the rest of the Scottish hierarchy. The ruined church is a grand example of later Norman architecture in red sandstone, and the tower, its chief feature, is quite castle-like in aspect. The Market Square, with its Court House, is picturesque. Floors Castle is the Duke of Roxburghe's seat.

The main road and bus route from Kelso to Jedburgh (11¼ miles)—railway passengers sometimes change at Roxburgh—runs on the east bank of the River Teviot, a tributary of the Tweed. If the alternative road on the west bank is chosen, you pass the meagre relics of *Roxburgh Castle*, once a royal residence with an important town beside it that, after giving its name to the county, has entirely vanished. James II was killed by the bursting of a cannon during the siege of the castle, which was held at the time by an English garrison, in 1460.

Jedburgh, now the county town of Roxburghshire, is small and wears an air of antiquity. The Border courts were held here, and 'Jeddart justice' was proverbial: Hang first and try after. The Abbey was founded by David I in 1118 for Canons Regular from Beauvais, and its ruined church, with a magnificent nave and two massive Norman doorways, is a mixture of the Romanesque and Pointed styles. The north transept, in the Decorated style of the fourteenth century, is still whole. In Queen Street stands the picturesque old house—now a museum of relics—in which Mary Queen of Scots lay ill for ten days in 1566, of a high fever brought on by a ride to visit the wounded Bothwell at Hermitage Castle, forty miles or more there and back in a day. Prince Charlie lodged in Jedburgh on his way south, 6th November 1745—traditionally at a house still standing at the foot of Castlegate (Nos. 9 and 11). The Gatehouse in the Market Place contains the town clock and bells.

The next objective, Selkirk, is reached by bus, changing either at Hawick or Galashiels, or by railway, with changes at Roxburgh, St Boswells, and Galashiels. *Hawick* (pronounced 'Háw-ick' as in 'saw') is the chief centre of the woollen tweed industry of the Border, and is noted also for its hosiery. It has an ancient tumulus known as the Moat and a monument to the 'Callants' (young men) of Hawick, who defeated an English force here soon after Flodden. If motoring from Jedburgh to Selkirk, go via St Boswells, where you join the Kelso–Selkirk road, or try a more direct route over the hills.

Selkirk, another woollen tweed town, is the capital of Selkirkshire, and is situated at the junction of the Ettrick and Yarrow valleys. The Selkirkers like to be called 'Souters,' i.e. shoemakers, and delectable bannocks are baked here. Among the town's monuments are statues of Scott and Mungo Park, the African explorer, and a memorial for Flodden—'O Flodden Field!' Ettrickdale is celebrated from the poetry of James Hogg, the 'Ettrick Shepherd,' who was born in Ettrick village and buried in Ettrick churchyard.

The main road to Moffat (34 miles)—buses but no railway—crosses Ettrick Forest, a region of mountain, moor, loch, and burn, celebrated for its ballads, the most touching of which, *Flowers of the Forest*, is a lament for Flodden. From Selkirk the road ascends the valley of the Yarrow, a brown shallow stream rippling over a stony bed. Wordsworth, Scott, Hogg, and many minor poets have sung its praises. The valley is wooded at first, but bare higher up. On the way we pass (right) Philiphaugh, where Montrose's career of victories in aid of Charles I was brought to an end in 1645 by a crushing defeat at the hands of Leslie's Covenanters. The ruined Newark Castle, on the opposite bank of the stream, lies within the Duke of Buccleuch's domain of Bowhill. Newark was built by James II in the mid-fifteenth century, and it was here that the Last Minstrel sang his Lay to Anne Duchess of Monmouth. Farther on, Yarrow Church, small and very pretty, is passed. *St Mary's Loch*, three miles long, is the 'lone St Mary's silent lake' of *Marmion*.

> A silvery current flows
> With uncontrolled meanderings;
> Nor have these eyes by greener hills
> Been soothed, in all my wanderings.

And, through her depths, St Mary's Lake
Is visibly delighted;
For not a feature of those hills
Is in the mirror slighted.

WORDSWORTH, *Yarrow Visited*.

Dryhope Tower, near the beginning of the lake, to the right, was the home of Mary Scott, the 'Flower of Yarrow.' On the lake bank are the Rodono Hotel and Tibbie Shiel's Inn, the latter once kept by Mrs Isabella Richardson, who used to entertain here the literati of Edinburgh, and died in 1878 at the age of ninety-six. Hard by is a monument to James Hogg. Next comes the Loch of the Lowes. The road ascends to a height of 1,105 feet, enters Dumfriesshire, and then descends Moffatdale, at the head of which, to the right, is a ravine with the Grey Mare's Tail, a waterfall over two hundred feet in height, the finest in the Lowlands. Above it lies Loch Skeen, an eerie tarn.

Moffat, in Annandale, is a favourite summer resort, with bracing air, golf, fishing, and sulphur waters that taste like rotten eggs. It is an excellent centre for walks and motor drives among the hills and dales of the Border country. The High Street is remarkable for its width. You should take a five-mile run up the Edinburgh road, by bus if you like, to see the Devil's Beef Tub, 'a d——d, deep, black, blackguard-looking abyss of a hole,' as the Laird of Summertrees called it in *Redgauntlet*. The River Annan's head waters are here, and a mile or two farther on, beyond the watershed (1,349 feet), the sources of the Tweed lie on the right of the road, while that of the Clyde is a little west, at the foot of Clyde Law. Three counties meet at the divide: Dumfries, Peebles, Lanark.

Those tourists who do not wish to visit the not particularly interesting district between Moffat and Carlisle can go direct to Dumfries, 22 miles (buses available). On the way they can inspect the pretty Raehills Glen.

The main road (40½ miles) and railway from Moffat to Carlisle run via Lockerbie. Motorists will find the by-road to Lockerbie via Lochmaben preferable. Bus travellers change at Lochmaben for Lockerbie, or go on to Annan and change there for Carlisle. *Lochmaben* (pronounced 'Lockmáyben') is almost an island, being surrounded by five lochs. Castle Loch is noteworthy as the sole habitat of the vendace (*Coregonus vandesius*), a small fish of the salmon family, which is netted in August. On a peninsula projecting into the loch are the very ruinous remains of a castle of the Maxwells, founded in the fifteenth century, and once an important Border fortress. The older castle, which disputes with Turnberry the honour of being Robert Bruce's birthplace, was mainly constructed of timber, and is now represented by a mound at the north end of the strip of land between the Castle Loch and the Kirk Loch. Buses run to Carlisle from Lockerbie, which is noted for its August lamb fair. The saying 'A Lockerbie lick' commemorates a fight between the Johnstones and the Maxwells in 1593.

Ecclefechan's title to fame is its connection with Thomas Carlyle. The house where he was born in 1795 is now National Trust property, open on week-days. He died at Chelsea in 1881, and is buried ('Humilitate') at the far end of Ecclefechan churchyard. Archaeologists will make their way to the Burnswork or Birrenswark, a hill about 3 miles north. It has two Roman camps, on the south and north slopes, perhaps constructed by Agricola in order to besiege the British stone-built fort on the summit. The three circular mounds in front of the southern camp were thrown up to defend the gates and are locally known as the Three Brethren. This was possibly the scene of the Battle of Brunanburh in 937, at which Athelstan defeated the Danish pirate kings, the Scots, and the British of Strathclyde. Hoddam Castle, 3 miles south-west of Ecclefechan, on the opposite bank of the Annan, was built by John Maxwell, Lord Herries, in the late sixteenth century, and is still occupied; it is thought to be the original of 'Redgauntlet.'

Gretna Green, like other Border villages, was formerly the haven of runaway couples from England, as by Scots law a declaration before even unofficial witnesses is a valid marriage ceremony. Since 1856, however, one of the parties must have lived in Scotland for twenty-one days. One or more of the blacksmith's cottages where the ceremony was often performed is now a 'museum.' The actual boundary between Scotland and England is the little River Sark. On the right lies the Solway Firth, where the tide comes in at amazing speed—'He who dreams in the bed of the Solway will wake up in the next world.' On the left is Solway Moss, where the Scottish army of James V was routed in 1542. The 'Debatable Land' between Sark and Esk was neutral territory till 1552, and a notorious refuge for malefactors.

Carlisle, the county town of Cumberland, is important as a railway junction and for its growing industries. It lies on the River Eden, 8 miles from the Scottish border. In spite of its antiquity—Carlisle was the Luguvallium of the Romans, and the Roman Wall ran through its northern suburb of Stanwix—the city has only two monuments that are likely to detain you long: the Castle and the Cathedral. The former served for many centuries as a bulwark against the Scots, and its outstanding feature is a Norman keep dating from the time of William Rufus. The dungeons are shown, and souvenirs of Mary Queen of Scots' brief detention in the Castle in 1568, when she took refuge in England after the Battle of Langside. The Cathedral, one of the smallest in England, was once attached to an Augustinian priory established in 1123. Of the Norman nave only two bays survive, the rest having been pulled down by the Scots during the Civil War. The south transept is Norman, the north transept and central tower early fifteenth century. The beautiful choir, with its great east window, was rebuilt in the Decorated style in the mid-fourteenth century. The stalls and roof are noteworthy.

Americans may care to have a look at the tablet on the Congregational Church in Lowther Street, recording the pastorate of Thomas Woodrow, President Wilson's grandfather. The President's mother was born at 83 Cavendish Place, Warwick Road, and the President himself was made a Freeman of the City in 1918.

The public-houses of Carlisle and district are under State management—a relic of the First World War when munition factories were established here and at Gretna.

TOUR III: CARLISLE TO STRANRAER, AYR, AND GLASGOW

Total distance by road: about 370 miles.

ANNAN — RUTHWELL — CAERLAVEROCK CASTLE — DUMFRIES —LINCLUDEN ABBEY—NEW ABBEY—DUNDRENNAN ABBEY — KIRKCUDBRIGHT — GATEHOUSE OF FLEET — NEWTON STEWART—LOCHTROOL—WIGTOWN—WHITHORN—GLENLUCE — STRANRAER — MULL OF GALLOWAY — GIRVAN — CROSS-RAGUEL ABBEY — TURNBERRY — ALLOWAY — AYR — PREST-WICK — TROON—ARDROSSAN — WEMYSS BAY—GREENOCK—PAISLEY.

MOUNTING the Dumfries bus or your car, you leave Carlisle by the way you came—that is if you came from Scotland—and take the Gretna Green road as far as Sark Bridge, beyond which you are in Dumfriesshire and Scotland. Then bear left at the fork for Annan, 17½ miles from Carlisle. Annan is a neat little town, but interesting solely, if at all, as the birthplace of Edward Irving, the founder of the Catholic Apostolic Church. He is honoured by a statue in the main street. There are two main roads from Annan to Dumfries. Follow the example of the buses and take the one that runs via Ruthwell (pronounce 'u' as in but, and 'th' as in then). *Ruthwell* is famous on account of its Cross, which has been set up for safety inside the church—you may have to ask at the manse for the key. Some 17½ feet high, and made of the local red sandstone, the Cross is covered with carvings of biblical figures, interlaced foliage, and inscriptions in Latin and (on the sides) Anglo-Frisian runic characters. The runes on the lower panels consist of verses from an Anglo-Saxon poem, *The Dream of the Rood*. The figure of Christ has a moustache but no beard. The transverse arm is modern. There is a companion cross at Bewcastle in Cumberland, and both are believed to date from the late seventh century. Comlongon Castle, near Ruthwell, is a well-preserved ruin with a fifteenth-century tower and its original iron gate.

You should leave the bus route and the railway at Ruthwell and take the road that runs, near the shore of the Solway Firth at first, to Bankend. Hard by is Caerlaverock (or Carlaverock) Church, where, if you are interested, you can see the grave of Scott's 'Old Mortality' (Robert Paterson), whose sole occupation for forty years was recutting the inscriptions on Covenanters' tombstones.

Turn south here for *Caerlaverock Castle*, by the shore, one of the most striking examples of early fifteenth-century military architecture in Scotland. It belonged to the Maxwells, Earls of Nithsdale, and is a triangle in plan, with a double moat, a gatehouse flanked with drum towers, and a drum tower at each of the other two corners. Over the gateway are the Maxwell arms and motto: 'I bid ye fair.' In the courtyard are domestic buildings of the fifteenth and early seventeenth centuries. The castle capitulated to the Covenanters in 1640 after a thirteen weeks' siege.

You proceed to Dumfries by a road that skirts the estuary of the River Nith and passes Glencaple. By this route it is 21 miles from Annan to Dumfries.

Dumfries (pronounced 'Dumfreéss'), the county town, is situated on the east bank of the River Nith, which is spanned by an important six-arched bridge, built in 1431 and now used for foot traffic only, and by two other bridges. The former Town House (1707), with the Midsteeple, is quaint, but the chief interest of the town is its associations with Robert Burns. He spent the last five years of his life as an exciseman at Dumfries, and his house in Burns Street, where he died on 21st July 1796, may be inspected. His remains rest in a classical mausoleum in the churchyard of St Michael's, close by, together with those of his wife and other members of his family. Note also the Covenanters' tombs, with typical inscriptions. There are more Burns relics at his two favourite 'howffs' (the best memorials of all), the Globe and the Hole i' the Wa', both of which are in the High Street. The name of the modern Greyfriars Church commemorates the church of the Franciscan friary, before the high altar of which Robert Bruce (or his followers) stabbed the 'Red Comyn' in 1306 in revenge for his submission to Edward I.

A room at the County Hotel is by tradition pointed out as Prince Charles Edward's lodging on 21st December 1745, on the retreat from Derby.

Now take a walk along the west bank of the Nith, north from Maxwelltown, to see the ruins of *Lincluden Abbey*. Once a priory of Benedictine nuns, founded in 1164 by Uchtred, Lord of Galloway, Lincluden was converted into a college for a provost and prebendaries at the beginning of the fifteenth century. The church was one of the finest examples of the Decorated style in the country. The tomb of Princess Margaret, daughter of Robert III and wife of the fourth Earl of Douglas, is one of the principal features.

> Yonder Clouden's silent towers,
> Where at moonshine midnight hours,
> O'er the dewy bending flowers,
> Fairies dance sae cheery.

Ellisland (pronounced 'Ellis-land'), in the same direction, 6 miles from Dumfries and attainable by bus, was farmed by Burns, unsuccessfully of course, from 1788 to 1791, before his removal to Dumfries. Motorists might return via Irongray, where Helen Walker, the prototype of Scott's Jeanie Deans, is buried.

[For motorists who want to see what Dumfriesshire has to show in the way of scenery, the following 80-mile drive is suggested. Up Nithsdale to Thornhill, fork right at Carronbridge, and ascend the grand Dalveen Pass (1,105 feet) to Elvanfoot. Then west via Leadhills and Wanlockhead, two lead-mining villages, the latter the highest in Scotland (1,380 feet), and over the Mennock Pass (1,409 feet) to rejoin the Glasgow road 2 miles south of Sanquhar. Descend Nithsdale to Carronbridge and then strike off to the right, through Penpont, to Moniaive (pronounced 'Monni-iv'), reputed the prettiest village in the Lowlands. On the way back to Dumfries, Maxwelton House, the home of 'Annie Laurie,' is passed.]

On the west bank of the Nith, opposite Dumfries, you are in the Stewartry of Kirkcudbright, so called because after the dispossession of the Baliols the shire was administered by a royal steward. The counties of Kirkcudbright and Wigtown together form Galloway, a beautiful region noted for its mild climate and for its dairy-farms and black cattle. S. R. Crockett's Galloway novels were once very popular, but his history is much blown upon nowadays. *The Raiders* was his best book. John Buchan's exciting tales, *The Thirty-Nine Steps*, *Huntingtower*, and *Castle Gay*, and Miss Dorothy L. Sayers's *The Five Red Herrings*, are mainly localized in Galloway.

New Abbey, served by frequent buses, is situated 7¼ miles south of Dumfries, at the foot of Criffel. This Cistercian abbey, colonized from Dundrennan (the Old Abbey), was founded in 1275 by Devorgilla, daughter of Alan, last Lord of Galloway. Devorgilla ordered the heart of her husband, John de Baliol, to be placed in her tomb—thence the alternative name, Sweetheart Abbey. She and her husband were the joint founders of Balliol College, Oxford. The church, roofless but otherwise in fair preservation, is in the Pointed style of the early fourteenth century, with admirable rose and other windows. Criffel, owing to its height (1,866 feet) and its isolation, commands magnificent views in all directions, and may be scaled in a couple of hours. One of its spurs is crowned with a Waterloo monument. Bus-and-railway travellers must return to Dumfries and go thence to Dalbeattie and Castle Douglas, but motorists proceed round Criffel from New Abbey, via Kirkbean, to Dalbeattie (18 miles), a clean little granite-quarrying town. Arbigland, on the shore near Kirkbean, was the birthplace of Paul Jones, the famous American privateer. The Mote of Urr, three miles north of Dalbeattie, is the most notable Anglo-Norman earthwork in Scotland. It is formed on a natural circular hillock, a truncated cone with its own encircling trench, situated at one end of a base court or bailey. It was once a river-island.

Castle Douglas is a modern town, built on the bank of the Carlingwark Loch. Threave Castle, the stronghold of the Douglases from 1369 to 1455, built by the 'Black Douglas'—Archibald the Grim, third Earl—and subsequently the headquarters of the Stewards of Kirkcudbright, is situated on an island in the River Dee, 2½ miles west of Castle Douglas. It is now National Trust property. Note the 'gallows knob, which never wanted its tassel,' and the sockets in the walls constructed for the support of a brattice or projecting platform of timber. [The bus route from Castle Douglas to Ayr, 51 miles, past Loch Ken and via New Galloway, Dalry, Carsphairn, and Dalmellington, provides a short cut for those who have no time for Wigtownshire, and incidentally traverses some of the most picturesque valley-and-mountain scenery of Galloway. The Dee and the Ken have been harnessed to provide electricity for the Galloway Power Scheme.]

An alternative, and perhaps more interesting, route from Dalbeattie to Kirkcudbright (18 miles—bus available) is via the round tower of Orchardton, a mile off the road, to the left—dating from the mid fifteenth century and unique in Scotland—Auchencairn, which has good bathing, and the grand ruins of *Dundrennan Abbey*, which was founded in 1142 for Cistercian monks from Rievaulx. Here Mary Queen of Scots spent her last night on Scottish soil (15th May 1568), sailing next day from Port Mary to take refuge in England. The chief relics of the abbey are the transepts and the north and south walls of the choir, in the Transitional style of the late twelfth century. The chapter-house doorway and the abbots' tombs are notable. This part of the coast is very fine, but (or because) somewhat inaccessible.

Kirkcudbright, the county town, situated on the east bank of the River Dee, is pronounced 'Kirkoóbry' and means Church of St Cuthbert. A group of artists of the Glasgow school has settled here. The Castle of the Maclellans, now in ruins, is not older than 1582. The Tolbooth, dating from the first half of the seventeenth century, has a fine tower and spire, the latter said to have been built with stones fron Dundrennan. The Stewartry Museum is interesting. St Mary's Isle, a peninsula projecting into Kirkcudbright Bay, with a heronry, is private property; the house, at that time the seat of the Earl of Selkirk, was raided by Paul Jones in 1778.

To get from Kirkcudbright to Newton Stewart by railway, a long detour, you have to return to Castle Douglas. The road and bus route (28 miles) leads via the pretty little town of *Gatehouse of Fleet*, and then skirts the shore of Wigtown Bay, the scenery of which is very fine. The fifteenth-to-sixteenth-century castles of Cardoness, Barholm, and Carsluith (pronounced 'Carslúóth')

are passed, and Cairnharrow (1,497 feet) rises on the
right. Ellangowan in *Guy Mannering* seems to be a
combination of either Barholm or Carsluith with Caerlaverock. 'The front of the old castle . . . consisted of
two massive round towers. . . . The esplanade in front
of the castle commanded a noble prospect. The sea-coast
in some places rose into tall rocks, frequently crowned with
the ruins of old buildings, towers, or beacons, which,
according to tradition, were placed within sight of each
other, that they might communicate by signal for mutual
defence and protection. Ellangowan was by far the most
extensive of these ruins.' Gatehouse is probably Kipple-
tringan, and Creetown Portanferry. At Creetown Cairnsmore of Fleet, one of the tallest mountains in these parts
(2,331 feet), comes into sight.

Newton Stewart is an old town beautifully sited on the
west bank of the River Cree, which separates the Stewartry
of Kirkcudbright from the Shire of Wigtown. The view
from Rennie's bridge is one to linger over. This is a
centre for several excellent excursions, the one of capital
importance being to *Loch Trool*, a scenic gem, 13½ miles
north. Pedestrians should prefer the road on the east
bank of the luxuriant valley of the Cree. The finest
scenery is among the cirque of hills at the east end, where
Bruce won a skirmish by rolling down boulders on English
troops marching along the lake side. Merrick (2,764 feet),
the highest mountain south of the Clyde and Forth, rises
about 4 miles north, at the head of the valley of the
Buchan Burn. Merrick means 'hand,' and its five peaks
have been called the 'Five Fingers of the Awful Hand.'
East of it are Loch Enoch and the Cauldron of the
Dungeon, with its Long Loch, Round Loch, and Dry
Loch, one of the wildest scenes in the British Isles.
Another favourite excursion from Newton Stewart is to
Murray's Monument, a beauty spot on the road to New
Galloway.

From Newton Stewart you can either go direct by rail
or bus to Glenluce (15½ miles), or make the long and
scenically not very exciting detour southwards, by bus or
branch line, through the Machars, the flat, bare peninsula,
celebrated for its dairy-farms, that lies between Wigtown Bay and Luce Bay. In the latter case you pass

through Wigtown, a sleepy, picturesque little county town. The Wigtown Martyrs were Margaret Maclachlan and Margaret Wilson (the latter a girl of eighteen), who, for refusing to conform to episcopacy, were in 1685 tied to a stake at the mouth of the River Bladenoch, and left to drown in the rising tide. They are commemorated by their tombstone in the parish churchyard and by a monument on Windy Hill. Beyond Garliestown, a diminutive seaport on a small bay, you come to *Whithorn* (pronounced 'Whit-horn'), the terminus of the railway, and once a great place of pilgrimage, for here or hereabouts, in the year 396, St Ninian, a Romano-Briton, who had been consecrated bishop in Rome, built the first stone church in Scotland—the White House or Candida Casa—dedicating it to St Martin of Tours. The Christian community that he founded did not, however, long survive his death. This was the first entrance obtained by Christianity to any part of the isle of Britain. What is left of the old Priory Church—founded for Premonstratensians or White Canons by Fergus, Lord of Galloway —is interesting, notably the Norman south-west doorway and the sculptured stones in the crypt. The bus goes on to Isle of Whithorn, a village on the rocky coast, 3¾ miles from Whithorn and 21½ from Newton Stewart. A ruined chapel here disputes with Whithorn Priory Church the honour of covering the site of the Candida Casa. Burrow Head is the extremity of the peninsula, and beyond it—4 miles from Whithorn—is St Ninian's Cave, with crosses incised on its rocks and stones, indicating that it was a place of pilgrimage in the Middle Ages. From Isle of Whithorn (and Whithorn) buses run to Glenluce (24½ miles), skirting the east shore of Luce Bay, past Monreith, a developing little resort, and Port William. Monreith House is noted for its lovely gardens.

Glenluce lies prettily at the head of Luce Bay, in a district of sand dunes, moorland, and copses. Glenluce Abbey, a mile to the north, was founded in 1190 for Cistercians by Rollard, Lord of Galloway, and its remains comprise the cloister and chapter-house, together with a fragment of the south transept.

The road from Glenluce to Stranraer, a ten-mile bus ride, keeps company with the railway—motorists bound for the

Mull of Galloway diverge left after 3 miles—and passes
close to the White Loch and the Black Loch, on the neck
of land between which are Lochinch Castle, seat of the
Earl of Stair, and the ruins of Castle Kennedy, an early
seventeenth-century mansion. The grounds, open on
application at the estate office, are the finest in this part of
Scotland; the pinetum and the species associated with
Hooker's journey to the Himalayas are deservedly famous.

Stranraer (pronounced 'Stranrár' or 'Stranráwer'),
situated at the head of Loch Ryan, is the starting point
for the shortest sea passage to Ireland—to Larne, 35 miles.
It is the chief town of the curiously shaped double peninsula known as the Rhinns of Galloway, which enjoys a
singularly mild climate, thanks to the Gulf Stream, and is
a stronghold of dairy-farming.

The railway goes on to Portpatrick ($7\frac{1}{2}$ miles), on the
west coast, a summer resort with a first-class hotel and
impressive cliff scenery in its environs. It is only 21 miles
from Donaghadee in Ireland. A bus from Stranraer will
take you as far as Drummore ($17\frac{1}{4}$ miles), which is $4\frac{3}{4}$ miles
by a rough road from the *Mull of Galloway*, a rugged
headland, the most southerly point in Scotland. The
parish is Kirkmaiden, and 'Frae Maidenkirk to Johnny
Groats' is 280 miles. Sandhead, on the bus route, is a
very attractive spot with splendid sands, and near it is
the deserted church of Kirkmadrine, with eight sculptured
stones, two of which, inscribed in Roman characters of
the fifth or sixth century, are the oldest inscribed Christian
monuments in Scotland. At Port Logan, on the west
coast, farther south, there are world-renowned sub-
tropical gardens and a curious pond with pet codfish,
accessible to the tides.

The railway from Stranraer to Ayr runs inland, and the
bus route is far preferable as the road (52 miles), one of the
finest in Scotland, hugs the coast for most of the time.
It leads at first along the east shore of Loch Ryan, near
the mouth of which it enters Ayrshire in crossing the
Galloway Burn. Ayrshire, as befits the homeland of
John Loudon McAdam, boasts the best-engineered roads
in Scotland. Carrick, the southern division of the county,
was the domain of the Bruces. Duke of Rothesay,
Earl of Carrick, and Baron of Renfrew are the Scottish

titles of the eldest son of the Sovereign. You ascend Glen
App (1 in 16), a delightful wooded valley, and descend
again to the sea at Ballantrae. Mrs Stevenson says: 'In
January, 1876, my husband, while on a tramp through
Carrick and Galloway, spent a night at Ballantrae.
Names always had a great fascination for him . . . the
flowing, mellifluous sound of "The Master of Ballantrae"
he felt gave an impression of elegance and smooth duplicity
that should suggest the character he meant to depict.'
The scene of the novel—'Durrisdeer, near St Bride's, on
the Solway shore'—is identified as Borgue, near Kirkcudbright.

The road from Ballantrae to Girvan hugs the Carrick
coast, with grand marine views and imposing cliff scenery.
The rocky islet conspicuous out at sea is Ailsa Craig, which
rises to a height of 1,114 feet, and is a great breeding place
of gannets and other seafowl. The lighthouse-keepers are
the only inhabitants.

Girvan is a fishing town and seaside resort. The main
railway line and the buses that come from Stranraer leave
the coast here and run inland to Ayr via Maybole, 2
miles from which, on the Turnberry road, are the ruins of
Crossraguel Abbey (pronounced 'Crossráygel'). Founded
before 1240 for Cluniac monks from Paisley, it retains
its church, aisleless and transeptless, and its chapter-
house. The coast road, with a bus service from Girvan
to Ayr (22 miles), goes on, in company with a branch
railway, to *Turnberry*, which consists of little more than
its golf course, a good hotel, and a fragment of the Castle
in which Robert Bruce was born (if not at Lochmaben).
The liberation of Scotland from the English yoke began
with Bruce's night landing here from Arran in 1307.
Farther on is the farm of Shanter, where Douglas Grahame,
the original of Tam o' Shanter, lived. He and Souter
Johnnie (John Davidson) are buried at Kirkoswald
Church. Souter Johnnie's house has Burns relics.

Culzean Castle (pronounced 'Cullàne'), on the edge of
the cliff, is next passed. Formerly the seat of the Marquis
of Ailsa, with beautiful gardens, it is now a National Trust
property and open to visitors. An apartment has been set
aside for the use of Mr Eisenhower, who has stayed here
twice. On this side of Dunure is the 'Electric Brae,' a

freak hill on which you imagine your car is ascending
when in fact it is going downhill.   Dunure resembles a
Cornish fishing village, with a little harbour cut out of the
rock and a ruined cliff-castle.

Either before or after crossing the River Doon, you
should turn right to visit *Alloway*, birthplace of Robert
Burns, Scotland's national poet.   Alloway is approached
also by a direct road from Ayr, a two-mile bus ride that
follows the line of Tam o' Shanter's famous ride from the
Tam o' Shanter Inn in Ayr High Street, a quaint and still
unspoilt hostelry, to the Auld Brig of Alloway.   The
cottage in which Robert Burns was born on 25th January
1759 is a clay biggin built by the own hands of his father,
William Burns, who farmed seven acres here.   Two of the
four rooms were occupied by the cattle.   Attached to the
cottage is an interesting museum of souvenirs and relics.
The poet's father is buried in the graveyard of the ruined
Auld Kirk—the kirkyard where Tam o' Shanter saw the
'warlocks and witches in a dance,' and roared out 'Weel
done, Cutty-sark' to winsome Nannie.   The gravestone is
modern, for the original one was destroyed by souvenir-
hunters.   The Burns Monument, in a garden overlooking
the peaty waters of the Doon, consists of a round Greek
temple, and there are two amusing sculptures of Tam o'
Shanter and Souter Johnnie in a summer-house.   The
natural beauty of the Doon valley is not improved by these
various somewhat naïve tributes to the poet.   The Doon
is crossed by two bridges, the famous Auld Brig consisting
of a single slender arch.

Ayr, a grey old place of some size, is the county town, a
seaport, and a holiday resort on the Firth of Clyde—

Auld Ayr, wham ne'er a town surpasses
For honest men and bonny lasses.

The River Ayr is crossed by the two bridges between
which took place Burns's celebrated dialogue: the Auld
Brig, dating from the thirteenth century ('Your poor,
narrow footpath o' a street, Where twa wheelbarrows
tremble when they meet'), and the New Bridge, rebuilt in
1877 ('Conceited gowk! puffed up wi' windy pride').
In the High Street are the fine Town Steeple and the tall
Wallace Tower, which replaces an old tower in which

Wallace is said to have been imprisoned. Burns fans should certainly visit Mauchline (pronounced 'Móchlin'), a small town 11 miles east of Ayr, with which the poet had intimate associations during his life on the neighbouring farms of Lochlea (1777–84) and Mossgiel (1784–8). There is a Burns Memorial and Museum too at Kilmarnock, where the first edition of his poems was published in 1786.

There are various bus and rail routes from Ayr to Glasgow, but motorists should choose the coast road (48½ miles from Ayr to Greenock), with its string of seaside resorts and its grand views of the Firth of Clyde. There is at present no through bus service by this route, but you can get through to Glasgow eventually by several changes. You pass Prestwick, a pleasing little town with its famous transatlantic airport, and Troon (by-passed by the main road), a coal-shipping harbour and holiday resort with the usual equipment of swimming pool, etc. This part of the coast is one of the best natural golfing grounds in the world. Irvine is a coal-mining, iron-working, and chemical-manufacturing place. It is believed, with little certainty, that Irvine is the scene of *The House with the Green Shutters*, written by George Douglas Brown as a counterblast to the Scottish rural novels of the 'Kailyard School' and generally acknowledged to be the finest modern Scottish work of realistic fiction. John Galt, the Ayrshire novelist, whose works— *The Ayrshire Legatees, Annals of the Parish*, etc.—are having a revival, was born at Irvine and buried at Greenock, in the Inverkip Street kirkyard. Between Irvine and Kilwinning, on the right, are the grounds of Eglinton Castle, former seat of the Earl of Eglinton (now a hospital), where a celebrated revival of the medieval tournament was held in 1839. Kilwinning Church incorporates the remains of a priory church. Among the desolate sandhills near the mouth of the River Garnock are the Nobel (I.C.I.) explosives works.

The road regains the coast at Saltcoats and *Ardrossan*, two seaside resorts that can be by-passed, the former very plebeian, the latter the starting point of steamer services to Arran, Belfast, and the Isle of Man. Beyond Seamill and West Kilbride, two unspoilt spots, you come to Fairlie, with Fife's shipbuilding yard and a ruined castle in a pretty glen. *Largs* is another popular resort, with yachting as its main interest. It is worth while ascending the hill on the Kilbirnie road in order to be rewarded by a magnificent view of the Firth, with the islands of Little Cumbrae and Great Cumbrae and the mountains of Arran in the background. Largs was the scene in 1263 of one of the decisive battles of Scottish history. The land forces of Haco or Haakon IV of Norway appear to have repulsed the Scottish army of Alexander III, but his fleet was scattered and destroyed by storms, and the Norwegians had to relinquish the Hebrides and Man, which they had held for four centuries.

Beyond Skelmorlie (accent on first syllable) and Wemyss Bay (pronounced 'Weems'), where Renfrewshire is entered, you can take a road direct to Greenock, but it is better to keep to the shore of the Firth, with its views and its shipping. The Cloch Lighthouse is passed, and then comes Gourock, a populous resort.

Greenock (pronounced 'Grínnŏck'), founded in 1707 as the outer port of Glasgow, is frankly industrial, with shipyards, foundries, and miscellaneous factories. The building known as the Watt Monument commemorates James Watt, Greenock's greatest son. Captain Kidd, the pirate, and John Davidson, the poet, were likewise natives of Greenock. Most of Mr George Blake's novels are based more or less on Greenock, his birthplace, which he calls 'Garvel.' Beyond Port Glasgow, a shipbuilding place, but no longer a port, you pass Newark Castle, a sixteenth-century ruin on the bank of the Clyde.

Hereabouts you should leave the main Glasgow road and diverge right via Kilmacolm, a pleasant spot with a hydro, Bridge of Weir, Johnstone, Elderslie (the reputed birthplace of William Wallace), and *Paisley*, which is 17½ miles from Greenock and 7 from Glasgow. The object of this detour is the Abbey Church at Paisley, a magnificent Gothic structure in the Mid Pointed style, completed between 1384 and 1459. It was founded in 1169 by Walter FitzAlan, ancestor of the royal house of Stuart, for Cluniac monks from Wenlock in Shropshire. The round-arch triforium is noteworthy, and the triforium passage is corbelled out round the piers, a feature unique in this country but paralleled at Rouen Cathedral. The choir and central tower have recently been rebuilt after lying in ruins since 1560. The south transept, St Mirrin's Chapel (1499), contains sculptures portraying the life of the saint, who settled at Paisley in the year 548, and a recumbent effigy believed to be that of Marjory, daughter of Robert Bruce and mother of the Stuart dynasty. Paisley, with the Coats-Clark mills, is the greatest thread-making place in the world, and Brown & Polson's starch and cornflour, and Robertson's marmalade and jam, are other well-known products. The Museum in the High Street contains a collection of Paisley shawls, which were woven on the hand-loom here in the nineteenth century. They were made of silk and wool or cotton, with a Cash-mere pattern. No. 8 Castle Street was the birthplace of Robert Tannahill, the weaver-poet, who drowned himself at the age of thirty-six and ranks among the greatest of Scottish song-writers. His 'Braes o' Gleniffer' rise south of Paisley, beyond the old keep of Stanely Castle.

Motorists who wish to avoid Glasgow can go north from Paisley to Erskine and cross the Clyde there by ferry to Old Kilpatrick (car 1s. 6d.).

TOUR IV: GLASGOW AND THE CLYDE

DUNOON — ROTHESAY — ARRAN — CAMPBELTOWN — PASS OF
MELFORT—ISLAY—JURA—LOCH LOMOND—LOCH KATRINE
—TROSSACHS—FALLS OF THE CLYDE.

Glasgow (pronounced 'Gláasgo'), the second city of
Great Britain and Scotland's principal seaport, has nearly
1,100,000 inhabitants, almost one quarter of the total
population of Scotland. It is far and away the chief
shipbuilding centre in the country, and its cotton, coal,
iron, and chemical industries are also of prime importance.
The harbour and docks extend for four miles or more
along the River Clyde, which, fordable less than a hundred
years ago, has been deepened and widened sufficiently to
accommodate the largest ships. A good view of the port
is obtainable from the lowest and newest of Glasgow's
eleven bridges—the concrete George V Bridge, opened
in 1928. Just below it lies the Broomielaw, the quay
where most of the Clyde steamers berth.

Glasgow's phenomenal growth is quite a modern affair,
dating from the Union, and the city has almost no ancient
buildings to show, with the exception of its Cathedral.
The episcopal see was founded A.D. 560 by St Mungo
or Kentigern, and until the Reformation the city was
a 'burgh of barony' dependent on the bishops. The
Cathedral is a creation of the thirteenth century, in the
Early Pointed style, and is the finest Gothic church in
Scotland. It is the only cathedral in Scotland (except
that at Kirkwall) which remained uninjured at the
Reformation. As Andrew Fairservice says in *Rob Roy*:
'Ah! it's a brave kirk—nane o' yere whigmaleeries and
curliewurlies and opensteek hems about it—a' solid, weel-
jointed mason-wark, that will stand as lang as the warld,
keep hands and gunpowther aff it.' The spire, 220 feet
high, the Lady Chapel, and the Chapter House were added
in the fifteenth century. The transepts do not project
beyond the line of the nave and choir, which are separated
from each other by a fine stone rood-screen—a rarity in

Scotland—of the fifteenth century, with representations of the Seven Deadly Sins. Steps descend from the south transept to the Fergus or Blackadder Aisle. But the special pride of the Cathedral is its crypt beneath the choir, which is held to be one of the best examples of Gothic architecture in Europe. It contains the supposed tomb of St Mungo and the saint's well, the tomb of Bishop Wishart, who espoused the cause of Robert Bruce and officiated at his coronation at Scone, and 'Rob Roy's Pillar,' from behind which the mysterious stranger conveyed a warning to Frank Osbaldistone. The Necropolis, east of the Cathedral, with its memorials, towers, and obelisks, is a remarkable sight.

No. 3 Castle Street, hard by the Cathedral, is Provand's Lordship, the only surviving pre-Reformation house in Glasgow, dating from about the year 1470. It is now occupied by a club, but visitors are admitted. The interior is interesting, with its collection of Scottish armchairs and other furniture, besides portraits.

Most tourists will wind up their visit to Glasgow by an inspection of the Corporation Art Galleries, in Kelvingrove Park, one of the best collections of pictures in the kingdom, especially rich in Dutch works and in examples of the modern Glasgow School: Sir John Lavery, Sir James Guthrie, E. A. Walton, James Paterson, W. Y. McGregor, etc. On the hill north of the park are the modern buildings of Glasgow University, which was founded in 1451. The School of Art in Renfrew Street, near Sauchiehall Street, is notable as the chief work (1898) of C. R. Mackintosh, the precursor of modernist architecture. The Royal Botanic Gardens and the Victoria Park at Whiteinch, with its fossil grove, can occupy the tourist's spare time.

Mr J. J. Bell's *Wee Macgreegor* is a picture of working-class family life in Glasgow; and readers of Mrs Catherine Carswell's fine Glasgow novel, *Open the Door*, will be interested to know that the original of the Collessie Street house is 172 Renfrew Street, while the La France Quadrant house is 27 Hamilton Park Crescent, Hillhead.

Glasgow is 'an excellent place to get away from,' and almost on its very doorstep is some of the most superlatively beautiful scenery—mountains, sea-lochs, and islands—in the British Isles. Motorists are somewhat restricted in their movements among the peninsulas of the Firth of Clyde and have of course no chance of visiting the islands unless they are prepared for the expense of shipping their cars from place to place by steamer. They are recommended therefore to park their cars for a few days and to make two or three at least of the following steamer excursions. The beauty of the Clyde scenery can only be fully appreciated from the water.

Among the bewildering variety of one-day excursions and circular tours by steamer, motor-coach, and railway the following are the best patronized. When you have once travelled down the Clyde estuary by steamer, it will save time to travel by railway to Gourock, whence indeed nearly all the steamers start. Rothesay or Gourock makes a more convenient headquarters than Glasgow itself. Full details of the services are obtainable in Murray's Time Tables or from the offices of David MacBrayne Ltd (44 Robertson Street, Glasgow, C.2) and British Railways. The services are restricted in winter.

(1) By train to Craigendoran, Helensburgh, Rhu, Shandon, and Garelochhead. Motorists take the new Western Boulevard via Duntocher to Bowling, or the road along the north bank of the Clyde via Partick, Whiteinch, Clydebank (with the yards of John Brown & Co., where the *Queen Mary* and *Queen Elizabeth* were built), Dalmuir, Old Kilpatrick (the reputed birthplace of St Patrick), Bowling, Dumbarton, and Cardross, where Robert Bruce died—it is believed of leprosy—in 1329. Dumbarton, once the chief port in the west of Scotland, has its historic Castle strikingly situated on a rock at the mouth of the River Leven. Dr A. J Cronin's powerful novel, *Hatter's Castle*, is centred in Dumbarton, to which he gives the name of 'Levenford.' 'Garshake,' mentioned in the book, is Cardross, his birthplace, while 'Darroch' is Balloch, 'Ardfillan' Helensburgh, and 'Markinch' Luss. 'Ardfillan' figures also in *Three Loves*, and 'Markinch' in *The Provost's Tale*, etc.

Helensburgh is a pleasant town and watering place laid out in chequerboard fashion at the end of the eighteenth century by Sir James Colquhoun (pronounced

'Cohoon') of Luss, who named it after his wife. There is an obelisk in memory of Henry Bell, who made the engines for the first practical steamboat to appear on any European river—the *Comet*, which plied on the Clyde from 1812 to 1820. J. L. Baird, inventor of television, was born at the manse of Helensburgh. The road then hugs the east bank of the Gareloch (i.e. Short Loch), which is much used for laying up steamers. Beyond Rhu and Shandon, with a hydro, a by-road goes off on the right to Glen Fruin, the 'Glen of Weeping,' where a clan battle took place between the Colquhouns and the MacGregors in 1603, resulting in the outlawry of the latter and the proscription even of their name. Garelochhead is 30 miles from Glasgow. A road doubles back along the west bank of the loch to Clynder and Roseneath (opposite Rhu), whence it goes on to Kilcreggan (opposite Gourock) and to Cove and Coulport, on the west bank of Loch Long, where it ends, 14 miles from Garelochhead.

(2) Frequent steamers from Gourock to *Dunoon*, on the peninsula of Cowal (pronounced 'ow' as in now), and *Rothesay* (pronounced 'Róthsy'), on the Isle of Bute. These are the two principal holiday resorts on the Clyde. Dunoon has a statue of Burns's 'Highland Mary'—Mary Campbell, born at the farm of Auchamore, near Dunoon, and buried at Greenock. Glen Morag should be seen and Bishop's Seat (1,651 feet) climbed. Rothesay is a fishing port and yachting centre. The Castle, where Robert III died in 1406, is a ruin. Buses ply past Mount Stuart, seat of the Marquis of Bute, to Kilchattan Bay (pronounced 'Kilcáttan'), a quieter resort. Motorists can reach Dunoon from Glasgow by a detour (76 miles) via Luss, Tarbet, and Arrochar (see page 89), the east bank of Loch Fyne, Strachur, and Loch Eck, a lonely freshwater loch 6 miles long, west of which rises Ben More (2,433 feet), a state forest. From Strachur a road leads to Colintraive, whence a ferry plies hourly to the Isle of Bute, for Rothesay: car 7s. 6d., over 14 h.p. 9s. 6d., motor-cycle 2s. 6d.

(3) By train or motor-coach to Arrochar, and thence by motor-coach to Lochgoilhead and Carrick Castle, on Loch Goil. The latter is a ruined quadrangular fastness of the Argylls. From Lochgoilhead you can visit the Ardgoil estate, which was presented to Glasgow by Lord Rowallan.

Arrochar (accent on first syllable), in the Macfarlane country, is a beautiful spot on Loch Long, one of the grandest fjords in Scotland, separating Dunbartonshire from Argyllshire. Ben Arthur (2,891 feet), called also the Cobbler from its fantastic shape, rises to the west and should be climbed for the sake of the view. Arrochar is 36½ miles by road from Glasgow via Tarbet (cf. page 89); return via Whistlefield Hill (1 in 7, up and down) and Helensburgh, 40 miles.

(4) To the isle of *Arran*: steamers from Ardrossan to Brodick and Whiting Bay, and from Fairlie to Lochranza, going on to Campbeltown. No Sunday services. Arran, which combines with Bute and the Cumbraes to form the county of Bute, is a mountainous island, mostly wild and uncultivated—especially in the north, where the knife-edged granite mountains are enclosed as a deer park— and is of great geological interest. It forms a wholly delightful summer resort, though as it is almost entirely 'undeveloped' accommodation is both limited and simple. There are no railways, charabancs, cinemas, trippers, or 'Trespassers will be Prosecuted' notices—but keep out of Glen Iorsa, the deer's breeding-ground. Adders are common.

The usual port of entry is Brodick (pronounced 'Bróddick'), on the east coast. Brodick Castle is a seat of the Duke and Duchess of Montrose, and the latter owns most of the island. The highest mountain in the island is Goat Fell (2,866 feet), an easy three hours' climb. A hundred and twenty-six mountains are visible from the summit, which is provided with an indicator. The finest walk in the island is from Brodick up the bewitching Glen Rosa—west of which tower Ben Nuis (pronounced 'Noosh') and Ben Tarsuin over the Saddle, and down the wild Glen Sannox to Corrie. Or, better still, a strenuous all-day walk, for climbers only—from the head of Glen Rosa, via Cir Mhor (pronounced 'Keer Vore') and the 'Castles,' which afford finer views than those from Goat Fell—to Lochranza.

The coast road round the island, rough in parts, with dangerous hills, is 55¼ miles in length, and there are numerous bus services. It costs £3-4 each way to bring a car over from Ardrossan. Those staying some time in

Arran should make the circuit of the island, visiting as they go south from Brodick: Lamlash, the largest village on the island, whence you can ferry to Holy Isle, with its lighthouses, 'Fairy Hills,' wild goats, and the cave of St Molias, a disciple of Columba's; Glen Ashdale, with its waterfalls, near Whiting Bay; the ruins of Kildonan Castle; Bennan Head, the southernmost point of the island, with the Struey Cliffs and the Black Cavern; Lagg, a pretty spot; Blackwaterfoot, whence the 'String Road' provides a way back to Brodick; the King's Caves; the Standing Stones of Tormore; Machrie; Pirnmill; and Lochranza, with its beautiful sea-loch and fourteenth-century castle. The Cock of Arran, the northernmost headland of the isle, is 2 miles from Lochranza. The road runs inland for a while, returning to the coast at the mouth of the charming North Glen Sannox. Beyond the picturesque hamlet of Corrie the road regains Brodick.

(5) By steamer from Fairlie (or by air from Renfrew) to Campbeltown, on the long pendulous peninsula of Kintyre, the southern part of Argyllshire. The steamers (no Sunday service) call at Lochranza in Arran. Carradale, in Kintyre, lies near the base of Ben an Tuirc (1,491 feet), and about 4 miles south is the romantic glen of Saddell, with an old castle and the remains of an abbey. *Campbeltown* (pronounced 'Cámbleton') is an unprepossessing town, with distilleries and coal mines, and of no great interest apart from its Iona Cross, which dates from about the year 1500. Machrihanish, 6 miles away, on the west coast, is noted for its golf links. There is a magnificent cliff walk of about 12 miles from Machrihanish to the *Mull of Kintyre*, one of the Land's Ends of Scotland, with its lighthouse and a view of the Irish coast, 13 miles away.

Motorists can reach Campbeltown from Glasgow—there is a daily bus service—by an immense detour (134 miles) via Arrochar and Inveraray (cf. page 150), and thence by a very fine, undulating road along the west shore of Loch Fyne, past Furnace, with its granite quarries, Lochgilphead, and Ardrishaig, to Tarbert. The road then leaves Loch Fyne and runs above the bank of West Loch Tarbert (hairpin bend on Whitehouse Hill) to Clachan, with a 1 in 10 hill. Next you hug the west coast of Kintyre, in full view of the Atlantic rollers. From Tayinloan a ferry plies to the primitive island of Gigha (pronounced 'Geé-ă,' with hard 'g'). Some miles beyond Bellochantuy the road reaches an oasis of dairy-farms, and crosses the peninsula to Campbeltown. The main road goes on inland to Southend (16½ miles) and the sands of Dunaverty Bay. The road thence to the Mull Lighthouse (7 miles) is merely a rough cart track beyond Carskey, with gradients of 1 in 7 and 1 in 8. The east coast road from Southend back to Campbeltown (21 miles) is very attractive as regards scenery, but is rough, hilly, and narrow, with six gates to be opened and shut. Similarly, the east road from Campbeltown to Tarbert (38½ miles), along the coast of Kilbrennan Sound, is narrow and tortuous, with innumerable gullies and hairpin bends. The points of interest passed on the way are Peninver, Saddell, Torrisdale Bay, Dippen (for Carradale), and Grogport. The worst part of the road is between Saddell and Dippen.

(6) To Oban, by steamer and motor coach, returning by train on the same day if desired. The first part of this trip, as far as Ardrishaig (80 miles), is performed by a MacBrayne mail-steamer, which starts from Gourock daily (except Sunday) all the year round and calls at Dunoon, Innellan (opposite Wemyss Bay), and—beyond Toward Point (pronounced 'ow' as in cow)—Rothesay. It then threads the Kyles of Bute, a narrow, dog-legged channel separating Bute from the Cowal peninsula. Colintraive (pronounced 'Collintrĭv') and Tighnabruaich (pronounced 'Tinabrŏóăch'), two charming little places on the mainland, are passed, and between them the steamer picks its way through the Burnt Islands. After rounding Ardlamont Point we enter Loch Fyne, one of the largest of the Scottish sea-lochs, 40 miles in length, and famous for the quality of its herrings. After a call at Tarbert, where passengers bound for Islay disembark, the steamer is quitted at Ardrishaig (pronounced 'Ardrísheg'), where the motor-coach is in waiting.

The road from Ardrishaig to Oban—a delightful fortymile drive, accomplished in 2½ hours—traverses a thinly populated district of Argyllshire, winding among heathery rocks and low hills. It runs at first along the Crinan Canal (pronounced 'Crínnăn'), which was cut in 1801 to save small vessels the long detour round the Mull of Kintyre.

Beyond Kilmartin are the ruins of Carnassary Castle (left), built by the Bishop of the Isles in the mid sixteenth century, and afterwards a Campbell possession. The coach then climbs to 546 feet, and descends (1 in 10) to Kintraw, at the head of Loch Craignish, a sea-loch with wooded islets. Next comes a five-mile stretch along the shore of Loch Melfort to Kilmelfort at its head. A new road circumvents the *Pass of Melfort*, one of the most enchanting spots in the country, the road through which is now closed to vehicles owing to danger from falling rocks. You descend again to Kilninver, and follow the bank of Loch Feochan, another sea-loch, for 5 miles. Then another ascent (1 in 14), with a view of Ben Cruachan far off on the right, and finally a winding descent (1 in 18) to Oban, which is described on page 143. The return journey to Glasgow can be made by train via Callander, Stirling, and Falkirk.

Motoring routes from Glasgow to Oban. Via Bowling, Balloch, Luss, Tarbet, Ardlui, Crianlarich, Tyndrum, and Dalmally, 94 miles. Cf. pages 150, 142.—Via Tarbet, Arrochar, Inveraray, and Dalmally, 100 miles. Cf. page 149.—Via Inveraray, Lochgilphead, and Kilmartin (motor-coach daily), 120 miles. Cf. page 85.

(7) To Islay and Jura, the southernmost islands of the Hebrides, a two-day excursion. The route from Gourock is by the MacBrayne steamer as far as Tarbert on Loch Fyne. (There is also a daily air service from Renfrew Airport to Islay.). A brief motor-coach drive takes you across the isthmus to the head of West Loch Tarbert, whence, three days a week, another mail-steamer sails down the loch and across the Sound of Jura to the Small Isles Pier at Craighouse in Jura, and through the Sound of Islay to Port Askaig in Islay, which is connected by ferry with Feolin in Jura, only half a mile away. On the other three days in the week the steamer from West Loch Tarbert takes a more southerly course via the isle of Gigha to Port Ellen in Islay.

Islay (pronounced 'íla') is an island of peculiar charm, with sandy inlets and varied, but not mountainous, scenery. Apart from fishing and agriculture, there are many whisky distilleries. In the Port Ellen district are the first-class Machrie Golf Links (3 miles), on Laggan Bay, with a hotel, and the Oa (pronounced 'O'), a peninsula with fine cliffs. The American Memorial Tower on the Mull of Oa, 8 miles from Port Ellen, is a reminder of the torpedoing of the troopship *Tuscania* on 5th February 1918, when 400 American soldiers and seamen lost their lives. The victims were buried at Port nan Gallan, close by, at Kilnaughton Bay, near Port Ellen, and at Port Charlotte, on the west coast of Loch Indaal. Bowmore, the largest village on the island, is situated on the east coast of Loch Indaal, half-way between Port Ellen and Port Askaig, which are 20 miles apart. It makes a good centre for excursions to the attractive coast of the Rhinns of Islay and Loch Gruinart. At Machir Bay, on the west coast of the Rhinns, are the graves of the American troops who were drowned when the *Otranto* sank after a collision on 6th October 1918.

A regular steamer sails from Port Askaig to Colonsay (pronounced 'Cóllonsay'), an island that is noted for its rich pastures and is separated by a channel, dry at low tide, from the smaller island of Oronsay (pronounced 'Órronsay'). Oronsay has the ruins of a fourteenth-century priory and a fine graveyard cross dating from 1510.

Jura, a large but sparsely populated island, with scanty accommodation for tourists, has magnificent mountain scenery, culminating in the three conspicuous Paps of Jura, of which the highest is 2,571 feet. Like Islay it forms part of Argyllshire. Apart from the one road, which runs from Feolin, opposite Port Askaig, past the Craighouse Inn, to Lagg (17 miles), Jura is almost trackless.

(8) The Trossachs Tour—by railway, steamer, and motor-coach—is an indispensable item in every tourist agent's programme. A train from Queen Street or Central Station conveys you to Balloch Pier at the south end of *Loch Lomond*, where you join the steamer. The houseboats moored in the River Leven (pronounced 'Leeven') at Balloch make a gay show, unique in Scotland. Loch Lomond is the largest freshwater lake in Great Britain. Here is Scott's description (in *Rob Roy*) of its varied charms: 'But certainly this noble lake, boasting innumerable beautiful islands, of every varying form and outline which fancy can frame,—its northern extremity narrowing until it is lost among dusky and retreating mountains,—while, gradually widening as it extends to

the southward, it spreads its base around the indentures
and promontories of a fair and fertile land,—affords one
of the most surprising, beautiful, and sublime spectacles
in nature.'

Inchmurrin, the first island passed and the largest in
the lake, has an old ruined castle of the Earls of Lennox.
The steamer calls first at Balmaha (accent on last syllable),
on the east or Stirlingshire bank of the lake.   Luss, on the
west or Dunbartonshire bank, is a particularly lovely spot,
with its trim little cottages.   Rowardennan, on the east
bank, is the usual jumping-off place for the ascent of Ben
Lomond, a grand mountain, 3,192 feet in height.   A stiff
climb of rather more than two hours is rewarded by
magnificent views.   The summit is furnished with a
view indicator.   The next stop is at Tarbet, on the west
bank, which is only 1½ miles from Arrochar at the
head of Loch Long.   Westwards appears the Cobbler.
Passengers for the Trossachs disembark at Inversnaid,
the next pier, on the east bank, but the steamer goes on to
Ardlui at the head of the loch.   The Arklet Water forms
a waterfall close to the Inversnaid Hotel.   Here Wordsworth met his 'Highland Girl':

> And these grey rocks; that household lawn;
> Those trees, a veil just half withdrawn;
> This fall of water that doth make
> A murmur near the silent lake;
> This little bay; a quiet road
> That holds in shelter thy abode—
> In truth together do ye seem
> Like something fashioned in a dream.

Coaches convey the party from Inversnaid to Stronach-
lachar on Loch Katrine, 5 miles away over the hills.
Garrison Farm, on the left at the top of the hill, preserves
the memory of a fort built in 1713 in order to suppress the
MacGregors and commanded for a while by Wolfe.
Farther on Loch Arklet, a Glasgow reservoir, is passed.

Loch Katrine (pronounced 'Káttrin'), ravishing in the
depth and delicacy of its hues, is situated almost entirely
in Perthshire, and is 340 feet higher than Loch Lomond.
Its level has been raised somewhat since the aqueduct
of the Glasgow Waterworks was constructed in 1859.   A
steamer takes you from Stronachlachar to the east end of

D

the lake, 'Where the rude Trosach's dread defile Opens
on Katrine's lake and isle.' The matchless beauty of the
lake is concentrated in the vicinity of Ellen's Isle, which
is named after the heroine of *The Lady of the Lake*, and is
passed shortly before the steamer journey ends at the
Trossachs Pier.

The *Trossachs*, i.e. 'bristling country,' is the valley,
partly filled by the small Loch Achray, between Loch
Katrine and Loch Vennachar. Nature made it an
exquisite spot, particularly beautiful in spring and
autumn, with its foliage of birch, hazel, and dwarf oak in
a setting of purple crags. In the height of the season,
however, it is congested—in spite of road-widening—
with cars and tourists, itinerant pipers, beggar children,
and the like. On the north rises Ben A'an (1,750 feet), on
the south Ben Venue (2,393 feet), the 'middle mountain,'
with the Bealach nam Bo, or Pass of the Cattle, on its
flank. A rough road skirts the north bank of Loch
Katrine, and you should take a walk along it if time
permits. The 'silver strand,' however, is now submerged.
The Trossachs Hotel is on the north bank of Loch Achray.
No longer can one say: 'Where shall he find, in foreign
land, So lone a lake, so sweet a strand!'

From the Trossachs you go by motor-coach to Callander
or to Aberfoyle, in either case completing the journey back
to Glasgow by train. The Callander road crosses the
Brig o' Turk at the east end of Loch Achray and then
runs along the back of Loch Vennachar, with Ben Ledi
(2,875 feet) towering on the north. At the farther
end of the loch is the Coilantogle Ford on the River
Teith, where Fitz-James fought the duel with Roderick
Dhu. The shortest way back to Glasgow from the
Trossachs, however, is via Aberfoyle, which is reached
by a motor-coach that crosses the hills on the south, passing the pretty little Loch Drunkie. Aberfoyle, the centre
of the *Rob Roy* country, is situated on the bank of the
Laggan, one of the head-waters of the Forth. The Bailie
Nicol Jarvie Hotel forms a striking contrast to the inn
at the 'Clachan at Aberfoil' which it replaces. To the
tree in front of the hotel is fastened the very coulter
with which the Bailie set the Highlander's plaid on fire!
Three miles east of Aberfoyle is the Lake of Menteith,

the only 'lake' in Scotland and much used for boating. The ruined priory of Inchmahome, on the largest of the three islands, served as a refuge for the five-year-old Queen Mary after the Battle of Pinkie. R. B. Cunninghame Graham is buried here.

Motorists rightly reluctant to undertake the set Trossachs Tour should drive from Glasgow via Balloch along the west shore of Loch Lomond as far as Ardlui (42½ miles). This, beyond Luss, is quite one of the most beautiful roads in Great Britain. Return to Balloch (24½ miles) and proceed via Drymen by the tricky road to Rowardennan, on the east bank of the lake, a cul-de-sac (18½ miles). Near Drymen (pronounced 'Drimmen') is Buchanan Castle, the Victorian property of the Duke of Montrose. Return from Rowardennan to Drymen (10½ miles), and go north to Aberfoyle (10 miles). Then west by a narrow, tortuous, switchback road past Loch Ard and Loch Chon to Stronachlachar and Inversnaid (15 miles), the abrupt descent to which requires the greatest care. Return to Aberfoyle (15 miles) and thence go northwards over the hills, with sharp bends but easy gradients, to the Trossachs (7 miles). Then drive east past Loch Achray and Loch Vennachar to Callander (10 miles). The best road back to Glasgow (42½ miles) is via Stirling. Total mileage about 200.

(9) To the Falls of the Clyde, not such an attractive excursion as it used to be. If you go to Lanark by road (25½ miles), you can see a good deal of the industrial suburbs of Glasgow: Rutherglen, Cambuslang, Stonefield, Hamilton. The best motoring route to Hamilton is via Uddingston and Bothwell. Bothwell Castle, which is open to the public daily, is a grand ruin of the thirteenth century, in beautiful grounds. Bothwell Bridge (rebuilt) was the scene of the rout of the Covenanters by the Duke of Monmouth in 1679. One of the bus routes from Glasgow to Hamilton passes through Blantyre (near Stonefield), where the birthplace of David Livingstone, a one-room tenement, is now the centre of a national memorial, with a museum of relics and a gallery of tableaux.

Hamilton was once celebrated for the Palace of the Dukes of Hamilton, which, however, has been pulled down. The ducal mausoleum in the grounds is noted for its echo.

The High Parks contain the ruins of Cadzow Castle and a herd of white park cattle.

The bus route from Hamilton to Lanark is over the Clyde to Motherwell, and thence by Wishaw and Carluke. Roman Catholics will want to visit the miracle-working Lourdes Grotto at Carfin, near Motherwell. Motorists keep to the west bank of the Clyde, traversing a fruit-growing district. Near Crossford is Craignethan Castle, the accepted original of Tillietudlem in *Old Mortality*. Farther on you pass Stonebyres Linn, the lowest of the *Falls of the Clyde*, below which is a power station.

Lanark is an unprepossessing county town. The New Lanark Mills, beyond it, were the scene in 1814–29 of the pioneer activities of Robert Owen, the great social reformer and advocate of a co-operative commonwealth. Hard by, in the grounds of Bonnington House, are two falls of the Clyde, Corra Linn and Bonnington Linn, the beauty of which is now impaired by hydro-electric installations.

TOUR V: GLASGOW TO ST ANDREWS, AND BACK TO STIRLING

Total distance by road: about 160 miles.

ROMAN WALL — BANNOCKBURN — STIRLING — ALLOA — CUL-
ROSS — DUNFERMLINE — KIRKCALDY — LEVEN — LARGO —
ELIE — CRAIL — ST ANDREWS — LEUCHARS — CUPAR —
FALKLAND — KINROSS — LOCH LEVEN — RUMBLING BRIDGE
—DOLLAR.

THERE are two distinct railway routes from Glasgow to
Stirling. The main road runs via Muirhead, Cumbernauld (in a detached part of Dunbartonshire), and Denny,
26½ miles. But there is a bus service also via Milngavie
(pronounced 'Millghī'), Strathblane, Killearn, Balfron,
and Kippen, 38 miles. The road via Lennoxtown,
Campsie Glen, a popular resort, and over the Campsie
Fells to Fintry, and then by Kippen, 35 miles in all, is the
most picturesque but has steep gradients (up to 1 in 11).
The vine at Firbank, Kippen, planted by Mr Duncan
Buchanan in 1891, is said to be the largest in the world.

At Castlecary, beyond Cumbernauld, the main road
enters Stirlingshire as it crosses the *Antonine Wall* and
the Forth and Clyde Canal. The former, which is known
also as Grim's or Graham's Dyke, was a turf and clay
wall on a stone foundation 14 feet wide, constructed about
the year 142 by Quintus Lollius Urbicus, legate of Antoni-
nus Pius, and linking up a line of forts previously established by Agricola in A.D. 81 to keep out the northern
tribes. It extended from Bridgeness on the Forth to
Old Kilpatrick on the Clyde, a distance of 37 miles, and
after being twice overrun it was finally abandoned in 185.
On the north side of the wall was a great ditch, the soil
from which was thrown up to form an outer mound. To
the south ran a military road, connecting the forts. As a
rule little of the barrier is now visible above ground, save
the ditch and parts of the outer mound, but six of the
nineteen forts have been excavated. The Castlecary fort
was destroyed in the construction of the railway, but

considerable remains of the Wall are to be seen in the neighbourhood, both westwards, on the way to Westerwood, and eastwards, especially in Seabegs Wood and the grounds of Bonnyside House.

At St Ninians, a village on the outskirts of Stirling, you will probably want to make the short digression to the left to see the battle-field of *Bannockburn*, where Robert Bruce vindicated the independence of Scotland by his crushing defeat of Edward II's army on 23rd and 24th June 1314—the only important battle ever won by the Scots over the English. A flagstaff marks the position of the Borestone, on which Bruce's standard was planted. The National Trust owns part of the battle-field.

Stirling is an ancient and rather grubby county town, with its famous Castle as the chief attraction. If benighted here, remember that Bridge of Allan is only 3 miles away.

Stirling Castle, sombre and dark-grey, is built on a dominating crag that is approached through a network of old streets. Scottish history has been said to rest on two rocks, Edinburgh and Stirling, which indeed bear a strong family resemblance to each other. The latter, guarded by the Forth estuary on the east and the mountains on the west, was the strong centre of Scotland, commanding the main route to the Highlands. It was the last fortress in Scotland to surrender to Edward I, and Prince Charles besieged it vainly in 1746. Edinburgh, Stirling, Blackness (on the Forth, near Linlithgow), and Dumbarton were the four fortresses that had to be kept in repair and garrisoned by the terms of the Act of Union. Stirling was the favourite residence of the Stuart kings, and both Queen Mary and her son, James VI, spent part of their childhood there. Visitors are escorted by a guide through the mutilated castle buildings, which are in use as barracks. Facing the lower courtyard are the Palace of James V, a fanciful structure with many grotesque figures, and the old Parliament Hall, built by James III, who was born at Stirling in 1451. The Chapel Royal, rebuilt by James VI, is in the upper courtyard. A passage leads from this courtyard to the Douglas Garden, whence a flight of steps ascends to the Douglas Room, now a small museum. Here William, eighth Earl of Douglas, after being inveigled into the Castle by James II, was stabbed by him and his followers for conspiring with Crawford and Ross against the throne. 'Queen Mary's Look Out,' on the ramparts, commands a glorious view of the Carse of Stirling, as flat as a pancake, with the Forth meandering through it, and the Grampians in the background. Seven battle-fields are pointed out by the custodian.

After viewing the Castle you should cross the graveyard to the splendid Church of Holy Rude, which till 1935 was divided into two churches. The nave, with its round columns, is thirteenth century, but with fifteenth-century windows and roof; the choir, much loftier than the nave, was built by James IV towards the turn of the fifteenth. Queen Mary was crowned here in 1543, when only eight months old, and James VI (by John Knox) in 1567, at the age of twelve months. Near the church are Cowane's Hospital, founded in 1639; Mar's Wark, a bizarre specimen of Scottish Renaissance architecture, begun in 1570 and left unfinished; and Argyll's Lodging (now a military hospital), a splendid example of a baronial town mansion, built in 1630 by Sir William Alexander, Earl of Stirling and founder of Nova Scotia.

Cambuskenneth Abbey, reached from Stirling by a ferry over the Forth, was an Augustinian house founded by David I in 1147. Its principal remnant, a splendid tower, affords an excellent view of Stirling and its environs. James III and Margaret of Denmark were buried in the Abbey Church; their tombstone was placed here at the expense of Queen Victoria.

The next stage, from Stirling to St Andrews, can be covered either by railway—there are various routes, e.g. via Dunfermline, Thornton Junction, Leven, and Crail— or by bus, changing at Kirkcaldy. It is 21–24 miles from Stirling to Dunfermline, according to the road chosen. You leave by Stirling Bridge, the last road-bridge over the Forth, which is adjoined by the Old Bridge (early fifteenth century), now used by pedestrians only. This was once the main pass over the Forth, the river that 'bridled the wild Hielandman.' The battle at which Wallace defeated De Warenne in 1297 took place higher up, as the English were crossing a wooden bridge that has long since vanished.

On this side of the Wallace Monument, which crowns a wooded crag, the Dunfermline road turns right and crosses the fertile levels on the north bank of the Forth— 'A lairdship o' the bonnie links of Forth Is better than an earldom in the North.' Clackmannanshire is entered as the Devon is crossed, and *Alloa* (pronounced 'Állŏă') is soon reached. By the park of Alloa House, seat of the Earl of Mar and Kellie, is the fifteenth-century tower where both Queen Mary and James VI spent part of their youth. Clackmannan is the tiny capital of the smallest Scottish county. The Tolbooth has a seventeenth-century tower, and beside it is an ancient stone known as the Clack-Mannan. Above the town is a fine tower of the late fourteenth and subsequent centuries, in a complete state of preservation. It once belonged to the Bruce family.

You next enter the county—vulgo 'Kingdom'—of Fife, which lies between the firths of Forth and Tay, and has well-marked characteristics. Its coast is lined with a string of ancient little burghs. Some buses take the higher road from Clackmannan to Dunfermline. The coast road passes through Kincardine (pronounced 'Kin-cárdin')—with its road-bridge (1936) across the Forth, ½ mile long with twelve 50-foot spans and a 200-foot swing-span—and *Culross* (pronounced 'Coóross'), but some buses by-pass Culross, which is 'as perfect as any Cotswold hamlet.' Many of its weather-beaten, pantiled houses have external stone staircases, and the National Trust has twenty-seven properties here. The Town House dates from 1626, and the delightful 'Palace' was built in 1597–1611 by Sir George Bruce of Carnock. Much of its mural decoration survives. The Parish Church, with its fine tower, is the choir of a Cistercian abbey church, and contains the notable monument of Sir George Bruce. The Abbey was founded in 1217 by Malcolm, Earl of Fife, and colonized from Kinloss.

Dunfermline (accent on second syllable), a town with a great history, is a sober-looking place that manufactures silk and linen, and has a great reputation for its damask napery. In the latter part of the eleventh century, under Malcolm Canmore and his sons by the saintly Queen Margaret, Dunfermline was the political capital of Scotland.

The principal building in Dunfermline is its Abbey Church of Holy Trinity, a relic of the Benedictine monastery, founded in 1128 by David I, with an abbot from Canterbury, on the site of Queen Margaret's church. Dunfermline and Arbroath were the two greatest abbeys in Scotland. The choir and crossing-tower were entirely rebuilt in the churchwarden Gothic of the eighteen-twenties, but the dignified, mid-twelfth-century nave, though marred externally by seventeenth-century buttresses, is one of the finest examples of the Scoto-Norman style. It has many affinities with Durham Cathedral, which antedated it by fifty years. The grand columns are adorned with chevrons, twisted bands, or fluting. The Abbey Church is the resting-place of seven Scottish kings —from Malcolm (III) Canmore to Robert Bruce, who is commemorated in the lettered balustrade of the tower. The site of his tomb, below the former high altar, is indicated by a modern brass tablet in the New Church. On the south side of the churchyard are the early-fourteenth-century ruins of the frater and dorter, connected by a gatehouse ('The Pends') in Monastery Street with the remains of the monastic kitchen and guest house (later a royal palace) in Pittencrieff Glen. Dunfermline Palace was the birthplace of Charles I in 1600.

Pittencrieff Glen, containing a mansion built in 1610 (now a museum), was presented to his native town, among numerous other benefactions (including three-quarters of a million in cash), by Andrew Carnegie, the Pittsburgh steel magnate, who gave away more than £70,000,000 in all. His birthplace, a handloom-weaver's humble cottage, is in Moodie Street (No. 4), and is adjoined by a Memorial Building. The offices of the Carnegie United Kingdom Trust are at Comely Park House, New Row, and those of the Carnegie Dunfermline Trust and the Carnegie Hero Trust Fund in Abbot Street.

The buses from Glasgow and Stirling take the direct road to Kirkcaldy, 13½ miles from Dunfermline, but the local services are via Rosyth, Inverkeithing, and the seaside resorts of Aberdour, Burntisland, and Kinghorn. Rosyth (pronounced 'Rosïth') is a naval station on the Firth of Forth, and has quite an attractive garden city. Inverkeithing is notable for its sixteenth-century Market

Cross, for its old houses, and for a late-fourteenth-century 'Palace' or hospitium of the Grey Friars, on the east side of Queen Street. Aberdour (pronounce to rhyme with 'flower') has a ruinous castle of the fourteenth and subsequent centuries, besides the plain Romanesque Church of St Fillan. Burntisland, with large docks, founded in 1541, exports coal, and has a factory of the British Aluminium Co. From bauxite, a red ore imported from overseas—France, British Guiana, the Gold Coast, India, etc.—oxide of aluminium (alumina) is produced here by a chemical process involving the use of large quantities of steam. The alumina is then dispatched by rail to Fort William, Foyers, and Kinlochleven, to be converted into aluminium in electric furnaces. The remarkable church of Burntisland, built in the Dutch style in 1592, is square in plan, with a central tower, and is one of the very few Scottish Reformation churches that have any pretensions to be more than mere congregational barns.

In the firth are the islets of Inchcolm and Inchkeith. On Inchcolm are the remains of an Augustinian Abbey, founded by Alexander I in or about the year 1123. It is unusually interesting for its cloister-buildings: chapter-house, warming-house, and undercrofts that form the cloister-walks.

Kirkcaldy (pronounced 'Kirkáwdy'), which has an interminable main street, is an unattractive coal-shipping port, with factories of linoleum, a Scots invention. Adam Smith was a native of the place, and retired thither in 1767 on a pension from the Duke of Buccleuch, to write *The Wealth of Nations*.

The direct bus route from Kirkcaldy to St Andrews (24½ miles) is inland via Cupar, but it is much more repaying to continue along the sea road (36½ miles), in accordance with Defoe's advice: 'He that will view the county of Fife must go round the coast.' Small towns follow each other in rapid succession: Dysart, with its pantiled and colour-washed houses, its Tolbooth (1576), and the great sixteenth-century tower of St Serf's; East Wemyss, with Wemyss Castle, the gaunt fragments of 'Macduff's Castle,' and five 'weems' or cliff caves with walls marked with ancient devices; Buckhaven; Methil—on this side of which you pass the Wellesley Coal Pit, the largest in Scotland—and *Leven* (pronounced 'Léeven'), a summer resort, where you change buses.

Next come Lundin Links and *Largo*. Alexander Selkirk, who was marooned on the desert island of Juan Fernandez from 1704 to 1709, and is generally considered the prototype of Robinson Crusoe, was the son of a Largo shoemaker. His house, near the harbour, has been replaced by a modern structure that is easily identifiable by the statue on the front of it. The conical hill north of the town is Largo Law (948 feet). The view therefrom is immense.

Leaving Kilconquhar (pronounced 'Kilcónkar') and its small loch on the left, you arrive at *Elie*, which, with Earlsferry, its western suburb, forms a favourite summer resort with good sands and golf. Garnets ('Elie rubies') may be found on the beach. St Monans, the chief fishing place in Fife and an artists' haunt, has a charming church built by David II in 1362–70—cruciform, but naveless and aisleless, with curvilinear tracery and a squat tower crowned by a blunt spire—and the ruins of Newark Castle, sixteenth–seventeenth century. Pittenweem, with the gatehouse and other remains of an Austin priory, Anstruther Wester, Anstruther Easter, and Cellardyke (the fishermen's quarter) practically adjoin each other, and all, in spite of their diminutive size, are Royal Burghs, i.e. burghs created on crown property by royal charter. Anstruther has the accent on the first syllable. Six miles off shore is the Isle of May, with a lighthouse, a bird-watching station, and a relic of an Austin priory.

Crail is a picturesque little decayed seaport and fishing town with crow-stepped gables, fine sands for bathing, an interesting Collegiate Church, thirteenth century but much altered, and a quaint Tolbooth (1517) with a Dutch-looking tower. It is 2 miles from Fife Ness, the easternmost point in the county, off which lie the Carr Rocks and their lighthouse.

St Andrews, a town of great character on the bracing north-east coast of Fife, has many claims on the traveller's interest. First emerging from the mists of the dark ages in 908 as the seat of the Bishop of Alba, it is one of the historic cities of Scotland, with the ruined Cathedral of the Archbishop of St Andrews, who from 1472 until the

Reformation was the Primate of Scotland. St Andrews, too, has an ancient University; it is a fashionable seaside place; and, above all, it has an unchallenged kudos as the leading golfing resort in the world.

The golf links are at the east end of the town. There are four courses, all belonging to the municipality and all open to the public without introduction and at very low fees: the classic Old Course, the New Course, the Eden, and (for learners) the Jubilee. The Old Course starts from in front of the club house of the Royal and Ancient Golf Club, which, founded in 1754, is the premier golf club in the world and the governing authority of the game.

From the club house a road called 'The Scores' (i.e. scaurs or rocks) leads past the Martyrs' Monument, which commemorates the four Reformers—Patrick Hamilton, Henry Forrest, George Wishart, and Walter Mylne— burnt as heretics at St Andrews. Hamilton's martyrdom on 29th February 1528 is reckoned as the birthday of the Reformation in Scotland: 'the reek of Master Patrick Hamilton has infected as many as it blew upon.' The ruined Castle on the cliff at the east end of the Scores was once the bishops' residence. James III was born in the Castle in 1445. Cardinal Beaton, who rebuilt the Castle in 1543–6, was murdered there on 29th May 1546 by the followers of George Wishart, who seized the Castle and held out until the next year, when, together with John Knox, they were carried off by a French fleet to slavery in the galleys. The Castle was then rebuilt once more by Archbishop Hamilton, 1550–71. The Sea Tower has a 'bottle dungeon' which is supposed to have been used as a prison for Protestants. A subterranean passage, which may also be explored, is a unique survival, being a mine and countermine tunnelled through the rock during the siege of 1546–7.

At the east end of the town is the early-sixteenth-century wall of the Augustinian priory, which is a mile in circuit, and preserves its towers and gates. Within it stand the fragments of the Cathedral, which was founded in 1160, consecrated in 1318, and sacked by John Knox's iconoclasts in 1559, and then allowed to decay. The 'Pends,' a roofless Gothic gatehouse of the fourteenth century, formed the main entrance to the precincts. All that survives of the Cathedral and Priory Church is portions of the west and east gables, the south aisle wall of the nave, and the west wall of the south transept. The church was 355 feet in length, and the nave had fourteen bays, being surpassed in that respect by the nave of Norwich Cathedral alone. There is a small museum by the remains of the Chapter House. Near the east end is the curious little twelfth(?)-century Church of St Rule or Regulus, with an archaic square tower, 108 feet high. This was the predecessor of the Cathedral and the first church of the Augustinian priory. The masonry is in a remarkably good state of preservation. St Rule is supposed to have brought the relics of St Andrew, Scotland's patron saint, to St Andrews. Andrew Lang and three famous golfers—Allan Robertson and Tom Morris, father and son—are buried in the cemetery. Still farther east are the Kirk Hill, with remains of the collegiate church of Blessed Mary of the Rock, on the site of a house of Culdees, and overlooking the small Harbour.

The main street of St Andrews is South Street, running westward from the Cathedral. Adjoining the Pends are 'Queen Mary's,' a house where Mary Queen of Scots and, later, Charles II are believed to have lodged, and St Leonard's School, a well-known school for girls, partly occupying the chapel and other buildings of St Leonard's College, which was founded by Prior John Hepburn in 1512. St Mary's College, farther on, on the same side of the street, was founded by Cardinal Beaton in 1538, and now houses the Faculty of Theology and the University Library. The charming quadrangle—the buildings on the west side are original—contains a sundial (1664) and a thorn-tree that is said to have been planted by Mary Queen of Scots. The University of St Andrews was founded by Bishop Wardlaw in 1411, and is the oldest but smallest in Scotland. It now comprises the United College of St Salvator and St Leonard, the College of St Mary, and University College, Dundee. The students, some 2,000 in number, wear red gowns. Opposite St Mary's stands the Town Church, a graceful edifice of 1412, entirely reconstructed in 1907–9. It contains the ornate monument (carved in Holland) of Archbishop James Sharp, who was dragged from his coach and

brutally murdered by the Covenanters on Magus Muir,
near St Andrews, 1679. The Blackfriars Chapel, in
front of Madras College, a school for boys and girls, is a
fragment of the church of a Dominican priory (1525).
At the end of South Street is a city gate known as the
West Port; it dates from 1589, but was renovated in 1843.

Parallel with South Street are Market Street and North
Street. The United College, in the latter, has a tall tower,
and houses the University Faculties of Arts and Science.
It occupies the site of St Salvator's College, with which
St Leonard's College has been amalgamated since 1747.
The College Church contains 'John Knox's pulpit,' a
composite production and not authentic, and the elaborate
tomb of Bishop James Kennedy (*d.* 1465), who founded
St Salvator's in 1450. The semi-octagonal heads of the
doorways are noteworthy. Close by is the Graduation
Hall.

The return journey from St Andrews to Stirling can
be made either by railway, via Leuchars Junction, Ladybank, Strathmiglo (for Falkland), Kinross, Dollar, and
Alloa, or by the direct, inland bus route via Guard Bridge,
Cupar, Auchtermuchty, Strathmiglo, Milnathort, Kinross,
Dollar, and Alva (52 miles). Guard Bridge was built by
Bishop Wardlaw and rebuilt by Cardinal Beaton, whose
arms it bears. *Leuchars* (pronounced 'Loóchars'), 2
miles north of Guard Bridge, and served by buses from
St Andrews, has a R.A.F. aerodrome, and its church
should by all means be seen, for, though the rest is modern,
its chancel and domed apse, with its double arcade and a
seventeenth-century bell-turret above, is the most beautiful piece of Romanesque (1183–7) work surviving in
Scotland—in fact, the only important example of its class
apart from Dalmeny. Between Leuchars and Cupar you
cross the River Eden by a sixteenth-century bridge, near
the ruins of Dairsie Castle. *Cupar* (pronounced 'Coopar'),
the county town of Fife, is often known as Cupar-Fife to
distinguish it from Coupar Angus. A common saying is
'He that will to Cupar maun to Cupar,' meaning that
there is no arguing with an obstinate man. The parish
church has a Renaissance spire of 1620, and in the graveyard is the fine tombstone of Thomas Crichton (*d.* 1619).

An alternative road from Cupar to Strathmiglo, only

4 miles longer and with bus services, is by *Falkland*, which lies at the foot of the twin Lomond Hills. Falkland Palace, completed for James V and Mary of Guise between 1530 and 1541, is a stately château in the Renaissance style, and is remarkable for the richness of its architecture. It is now the property of the National Trust and may be inspected daily from April to October (winter on Wednesdays and Saturdays). The chapel has an oak ceiling (1633) and screen. The 'caichpule' or tennis court (1538) is unique in Scotland. The east wing is a picturesque ruin, on which wallflowers have taken root. James V died at Falkland in 1542, broken-hearted on hearing of the defeat at Solway Moss. Shortly before his death he was told of the birth of his daughter Mary, afterwards Queen of Scots—a piece of news that he received with the words: 'It came with a lass, and it will go with a lass.' The Palace replaces an old castle of the Macduffs, where the Duke of Rothesay, heir to the throne, was starved to death in 1402 by order of his uncle, the Duke of Albany, after Catharine Glover and the glee-woman—according to the story related in *The Fair Maid of Perth*—had discovered his prison and fed him with morsels of food at the end of a wand.

Rejoining the main road at Strathmiglo, near the foot of the Ochil Hills, you enter Kinross-shire at the hamlet of Burnside. At Milnathort you should bear left from the main road to Dollar and take the alternative road (about 4 miles longer) via Kinross and Rumbling Bridge. *Kinross* (accent on last syllable) is the small capital of a small county. Its chief building is Kinross House, the noble mansion built by Sir William Bruce in 1685–90 for his own occupation, a really fine example of the Italian Renaissance under French influence, with one of the best landscape gardens in Scotland. Kinross is situated on the bank of *Loch Leven* (pronounced 'Leeven'), a large lake once three times its present size. It is not particularly beautiful, but is famous for its trout and for its Castle of the fifteenth–sixteenth century, built on an islet and in good preservation (boats for hire). Queen Mary was imprisoned here by her lords after the Battle of Carberry Hill, from 17th June 1567 till 2nd May 1568, with Lady Douglas, who had been her father's mistress, as her jailer. Given the choice between divorce from Bothwell, a trial at which the Casket Letters were to be produced in evidence, and abdication, she chose the last. Finally she succeeded, with the help of the sixteen-year-old Willie Douglas, in making her escape from the Castle, only to be defeated a fortnight later at Langside and driven to take refuge in England. The story is told in Scott's novel, *The Abbot*. On another island in Loch Leven is the Priory of St Serf, with the ruin of a twelfth-century church.

Between Kinross and Dollar you continue to skirt the base of the Ochils, and pass close to *Rumbling Bridge,* a popular beauty-spot on the River Devon, somewhat resembling the Devil's Bridge near Aberystwyth. *Dollar,* in Clackmannanshire again, has a well-known school, the Dollar Academy, and above, on the right, the grand ruins of Castle Campbell. This romantically situated stronghold of the Argylls, dating from the third quarter of the fifteenth century to the beginning of the seventeenth, is said, without foundation, to have been burnt by Montrose in 1645. It is now National Trust property. Formerly known as 'Castle Gloom,' it is approached by the 'Burn of Care.' Near it the 'Burn of Sorrow' flows through a remarkable gorge called the Windy Pass.

From Tillicoultry (pronounced 'Tillicoótry') or Alva you can climb in a couple of hours to the top of Ben Cleuch (2,363 feet), the highest of the Ochil Hills, and commanding a glorious view. An indicator is provided. The Ochil glens are bonny: Glen Alva, Tillicoultry Glen, Menstrie Glen, etc. Stirling is regained by way of the Wallace Monument and Stirling Bridge.

TOUR VI: STIRLING TO PERTH AND ABERDEEN

Total distance by road: about 250 miles.

BRIDGE OF ALLAN—DUNBLANE—DOUNE—CALLANDER—LOCH
EARN—COMRIE—CRIEFF—HUNTINGTOWER CASTLE—PERTH
— SCONE — GLAMIS CASTLE — KIRRIEMUIR — FORFAR —
ARBROATH—MONTROSE—BRECHIN—DUNNOTTAR CASTLE—
STONEHAVEN—ABERDEEN—CRUDEN BAY—PETERHEAD.

THE railway and the main road (34 miles) used by the
through buses and coaches from Stirling to Perth run via
Dunblane and Gleneagles, but it is well worth while to
make the detour (41 miles longer) from Dunblane by bus
or railway, via Callander, Loch Earn, and Crieff. The
buses from Stirling to Dunblane (6 miles) cross Stirling
Bridge and turn left by the Wallace Monument for *Bridge
of Allan*, a pleasant little spa, well laid out in terraces on
the sheltered hillside. Its waters are unique in Great
Britain for their high percentage of calcium combined
with iodine and bromine. Perthshire is entered as you
cross the Allan Water.

The next town is *Dunblane*, a small place with a beautiful Cathedral founded by David I about the year 1140,
and now used as the Parish Church. The fine tower is
Romanesque; the rest of the church is in a chaste Gothic
style of the thirteenth century. The nave, long roofless,
was restored in 1893. The east end of the Lady Chapel is
the War Memorial. There are some interesting monuments, carved stalls of the fifteenth century, and good
modern woodwork. Ruskin wrote of the west window:
'I know not anything so perfect in its simplicity, and so
beautiful, as far as it reaches, in all the Gothic with which
I am acquainted. . . . Instead of putting a merely formal
dogtooth, as everybody else did at that time, he [the
designer] went down to the woody bank of the sweet river
. . . and took up a few of the fallen leaves that lay by it,
and he set them in his arch, side by side for ever.'

To the east of Dunblane, on the slopes of the Ochils,
was fought the indecisive Battle of Sheriffmuir, between

Argyll and the Jacobite Highlanders under the Earl of Mar, 13th November 1715.

[The main road from Dunblane to Perth passes Greenloaning, Blackford, and Auchterarder (pronounced 'Ochterárder'). At Braco (pronounced 'Bráyco'), a mile north of Greenloaning on the Crieff road, are the remains of the Roman military station of Ardoch, enclosed within the grounds of Ardoch House and visible by permission. It is considered to be the best-preserved example of Roman earthworks in the country. The fort, five acres in area, is defended by an inner rampart and, on the north and east sides, by five deep ditches and a strong outer rampart. Apart from this permanent fort, which was occupied in both the Agricolan and Antonine periods, there are traces of three large temporary camps to the north. Gleneagles, to the left of the main road, between Blackford and Auchterarder, is the most palatial hotel in Scotland. It has three golf courses and is open in summer only.]

The road from Dunblane to Lochearnhead (26 miles)—bus-passengers change at Callander for the Crieff bus—leads west to *Doune*, which has one of the finest castles in Scotland. Doune Castle, built in the first half of the fifteenth century by the Dukes of Albany, and recently restored by the Earl of Moray, lies on low ground, in the angle formed by the rivers Teith and Ardoch. The bridge over the Teith was built in 1535. Road and railway now follow the north bank of the River Teith to *Callander*, above which rises Ben Ledi. Callander consists largely of hotels and lodging houses, and is a popular tourist centre, being one of the chief starting points for the Trossachs Tour. Various motor-coach excursions are available. Walks may be taken to the Bracklinn Falls, on the Keltie Water, and in an hour and a half to the top of Ben Ledi (2,875 feet), the 'Hill of God,' which, from its position on the edge of the Highlands, commands varied views.

The road—one of General Wade's, constructed after the 'Fifteen—and the railway now mount the narrow and lovely Pass of Leny, through which the River Leny descends in cascades with a setting of birch and heather. Near the point where the river issues from Loch Lubnaig is a small graveyard marking the site of St Bride's Chapel where Angus, in *The Lady of the Lake*, handed the Cross of Fire to Norman, heir of Armandave, just after his marriage to Tombea's Mary. The road hugs the east bank of Loch Lubnaig for four miles, with some sharp turns, while the railway takes the west side. At Strathyre, and at the King's House Hotel, 2 miles farther on, by-roads go off on the left to Balquhidder (pronounced 'Balwhidder'), a village at the foot of Loch Voil. Rob Roy (*d.* 1734) is buried in the churchyard, but the three sculptured stones that are supposed to mark the graves of the outlaw and his wife and sons are really of much earlier date. The 'Braes of Balquhidder' are the hills on the north side of Loch Voil.

Beyond the King's House Hotel the main road descends to Lochearnhead, the pretty hamlet at the west end of Loch Earn (pronounced 'Ern'). The Killin road and railway go on north up the wild, boulder-strewn Glen Ogle, the former attaining a height of 948 feet, with 1 in 17–18 gradients on either side.

The Perth road and railway, however, turn east at Lochearnhead, and skirt the north shore of *Loch Earn*, a lovely hill-girt lake, seven miles long and half a mile wide. The hillier and more winding road on the south side of the lake passes the mouth of Glen Vorlich, by which Ben Vorlich (3,224 feet) is most easily scaled. From St Fillans, a delightful spot at the foot of the lake, road and railway descend in company with the River Earn to Comrie and Crieff, 20 miles from Lochearnhead. *Comrie*, a neat village, is sited on the geological fault between the Highland schists and the Midland sandstones, and is therefore liable to slight earthquakes. Dunmore Hill (837 feet), to the north, bears a monument to the first Lord Melville, and affords a good view. On the hill of Tomachastle, to the right of the road from Comrie to Crieff, is a prominent monument to General Sir David Baird, who stormed Seringapatam in 1799.

Crieff, a charmingly situated health resort, has a Runic market cross, and is an excellent centre for excursions. The Knock of Crieff (911 feet), an isolated hill to the north, is furnished with a view-indicator. A rough, steep road ascends Glen Turret past some waterfalls to

Loch Turret, behind which, at the head of the glen, rises
Ben Chonzie (3,048 feet). The chief among the many
country seats in the vicinity of Crieff is Drummond
Castle, seat of the Earl of Ancaster and famous for its
Italian gardens, which are open to the public on special
occasions only during the summer. Before leaving
Crieff for good you should drive up the Sma' Glen, a
highly picturesque road with two 1 in 17 hills, as far as
Amulree (12 miles) and back. The Crieff–Amulree–
Aberfeldy road is the only highway through the Central
Grampians.

On the way from Crieff to Perth (17½ miles)—both buses
and trains are at your disposal—you pass a turning on the
left for Fowlis Wester, most delightful of old-world
villages; the village of Methven; Almondbank Station,
where you should digress left to see Pitcairngreen, another
quaint village; and the ruins of *Huntingtower Castle*,
formerly called Ruthven. The first Earl of Gowrie and
other Protestant nobles invited the youthful James VI
to a hunting party here in 1582 and kept him a prisoner
for some months—an event known as the Raid of Ruthven.
The Maiden's Leap, between the two massive towers,
derives its name from a story that the Earl's daughter
jumped across to avoid being caught with her lover.

Perth, the county town, lies in a pleasant countryside
on the west bank of the fine River Tay. In John Buchan's
words, 'it played a resounding part in Scottish history:
it was the theatre of many famous episodes, the home of
kings and kings' councils, the gateway between North
and South, the meeting-place of Highlands and Lowlands.' In spite of all this, it now has very few old
buildings of any note. The Parish Church of St John,
however—whence Perth derived its former alternative
name of St Johnstoun— is a very stately edifice, dating
mainly from the fifteenth century. Until recently it was
split up between three different congregations, but a
reconstruction under the aegis of Sir Robert Lorimer has
restored its original aspect—a more satisfactory form of
County War Memorial than some others one might men-
tion. It was as the result of a sermon preached by John
Knox here in 1559, exhorting his hearers to purge the
church from idolatry, that a storm of iconoclasm spread

through all Scotland, destroying nearly all the pre-Reformation religious art of the country. John of Eltham died at Perth in 1336, slain—according to a baseless story—by his brother Edward III in front of the high altar of this church.

The most agreeable feature of Perth is its riverside boulevard, Tay Street, and its 'Inches' or riverside parks (literally 'islands'). The large building on the farther side of the South Inch is the General Prison for Scotland. A bronze tablet on the County Buildings by the Victoria Bridge bears a representation of Gowrie House. This was the scene of the mysterious 'Gowrie Conspiracy' of 1600, when Alexander Ruthven and his brother, the third Earl of Gowrie, were slain by James VI's attendants after an alleged assault on the king. Perth Bridge, at the beginning of the North Inch, is a handsome eighteenth-century design by Smeaton, and it commands a grand view of the Grampians. The fight between the Clan Chattan and the Clan Quhele, described in *The Fair Maid of Perth*, took place on the North Inch, and close by, in Curfew Row (which leads to Pullar's Dye Works), is the alleged 'Fair Maid's House,' which may be inspected. A tablet at the corner of Blackfriars Street, near at hand, commemorates the Dominican priory in which James I was murdered by Sir Robert Graham on 20th February 1437, in spite of the heroism of Catherine Douglas, as recounted in Rossetti's ballad *The King's Tragedy*.

> Like iron felt my arm, as through
>   The staple I made it pass:—
> Alack! it was flesh and bone—no more!
> 'Twas Catherine Douglas sprang to the door,
>   But I fell back Kate Barlass.

If you have time for an hour and a half's stroll, cross the river and climb Kinnoull Hill (729 feet) to enjoy one of the most beautiful prospects in Scotland.

From Perth you make for Forfar by way of Strathmore, the wide valley between the Sidlaw Hills on the south and the Grampians on the north. [This route has the advantage of avoiding Dundee, the third largest city in Scotland, and a considerable seaport, famous for its jute and marmalade factories, but of little interest to tourists except for the noble steeple of its Town Church and the view from Dundee Law. The Tay Bridge, a railway lattice-bridge, iron on brick piers, crossing the firth from Dundee to Fife, is one of the longest of its kind in the world—3,593 yards. It was opened in 1888, its predecessor having been blown down in a gale on 28th December 1879, carrying with it a train and its 75 or more occupants.] The main road and bus route from Perth to Forfar (31 miles), a part of the great highway to Aberdeen, leads via New Scone to Coupar Angus, while the railway route is via Cargill (for Meikleour).

Motorists should take the Blairgowrie road (3½ miles extra) by Old Scone and Scone Palace, a seat of the Earl of Mansfield. *Scone* (pronounced 'Scoon') is a place of historic interest, but a nineteenth-century mansion has completely replaced the Abbey and royal palace where the Scottish kings were crowned. The Stone of Scone, or Stone of Destiny, normally resting beneath the Coronation Chair in Westminster Abbey, was kept here from the time of Kenneth Macalpine, who brought it from Dunstaffnage in the ninth century, until Edward I carried it off in 1297 in token of the subjugation of Scotland. Beyond the bridge over the River Isla are the grounds of Meikleour (pronounced 'Meekle-ower,' to rhyme with 'flower'), with its celebrated Beech Hedge, 80 feet high and 600 yards long. For Coupar you take the next turning on the right.

At Coupar Angus, which in spite of its name is in Perthshire, bus travellers change into the Forfar bus. Meigle (pronounced 'Meegle') is celebrated for the ancient sculptured stones in its churchyard, which are thought to mark the grave of Queen Guinevere. Motorists should diverge to the left here, via Alyth (pronounced 'Aylith') in order to explore the valley of the River Isla, which flows through a remarkable gorge and forms two fine waterfalls: the Slug of Auchrannie and the Reekie Linn. Airlie Castle, below the former, is the residence of the Dowager Countess of Airlie. The head of Glen Isla (bus as far as Folda) is noted for its rare wild plants, e.g. the holly fern.

The next place of interest on the main road, which enters Angus (formerly Forfarshire) beyond Meigle, is *Glamis Castle* (pronounced 'Glaams'), the seat of the Earl of

Strathmore, nephew of H.M. the Queen Mother. Princess Margaret was born here in 1930. Glamis, seen from the Kirriemuir road, is one of the most romantic-looking castles in Scotland. In its present aspect, with its pepper-box turrets and other features of the 'Scottish baronial' style, it dates chiefly from the second half of the seventeenth century. Visitors are shown over the Castle on Wednesday and Thursday afternoons from June to September and also on Sunday afternoons in July and August. Macbeth (*d.* 1057) was Thane of Glamis, and the scene of his murder of King Duncan is traditionally placed here—likewise at Cawdor and Inverness. Glamis is popularly supposed to contain a secret chamber, attached to which is a mystery known only to the Earl, his heir apparent, and the factor.

Turn left at Glamis to visit *Kirriemuir* (5 miles), an appealing place in itself, noted as the birthplace of Sir James M. Barrie in 1860 (at No. 8 Brechin Road, a National Trust property) and the 'Thrums' of his novels. He was buried in the cemetery in 1937. The Auld Licht manse of *The Little Minister* 'looks down on the town from the north-east, and is reached from the road that leaves Thrums behind it in another moment by a wide, straight path.' The actual *Window in Thrums* survives at the top of the hill ascending to Southmuir—'On the bump of green round which the brae twists, at the top of the brae, and within cry of T'nowhead Farm, still stands a one-storey house, whose whitewashed walls, streaked with the discoloration that rain leaves, look yellow when the snow comes.' The excursion should be extended northwards over the hills to Cortachy Castle (accent on first syllable), seat of the Earl of Airlie, in Glen Quharity (pronounced 'Whaárity'), the beauty of which always held its dominie wondering: 'Like my own Glen Quharity on a summer day, when the sun is lingering and the clouds are on the march, and the glen is never the same for two minutes, but always so beautiful as to make me sad.' I have it on the best authority, however, that when Sir James wrote of Glen Quharity, he was mainly referring to Glen Clova and Glen Prosen. The road goes on up Glen Clova, the lovely valley of the South Esk. The Clova mountains are noted for their rare alpines: *Erigeron alpinum, Lychnis alpina,* etc.

Forfar (accent on first syllable) is the county town of Angus, with a small loch, but otherwise of little note, so you make rapidly, by bus or train, for the coast and Arbroath, 15 miles. *Arbroath* (accent on second syllable), formerly Aberbrothock, is the Fairport of Scott's novel, *The Antiquary*, which chiefly centres here. As a fishing port it is noted for its smoked haddocks ('smokies'). Its Abbey, once famous for its wealth and hospitality, is now a vast ruin. It was founded in 1175 for monks from Kelso, and was dedicated to St Thomas of Canterbury. William the Lion, the founder, was buried in front of the high altar. The remains, built of a friable red sandstone in the Transitional or Earliest Pointed style, comprise the Gatehouse, Church, and Chapter House. The rose window in the south transept is known as the 'O' of Arbroath. The cliff scenery north of Arbroath is equal to the finest on the east coast of Scotland. A few miles south is Carnoustie, with its famous golf links. Eleven miles out at sea from Arbroath is the Inchcape or Bell Rock, covered at high tide, and now marked by a lighthouse. The story attached to it is told in Southey's poem.

There is a good service of motor-buses and motor-coaches for the fifty-mile run northwards from Arbroath to Aberdeen. The main road mostly keeps near the coast, while the railway runs inland between Montrose and Stonehaven. Auchmithie, on the rugged coast between Arbroath and Montrose, is a very attractive fishing village, and farther on is Lunan Bay, with its wild cliffs and bright sands. *Montrose* (accent on second syllable) lies at the mouth of the South Esk, between the river and a large tidal basin that is not a pretty sight at low water. It is a pleasant-looking town, however, and a favourite summer resort, with excellent golf and bathing. The Marquis of Montrose was born here in 1612. After hearing the news of the Battle of Sheriffmuir, the Old Pretender and the Earl of Mar, who had landed at Peterhead in December 1715, secretly re-embarked from Montrose on 4th February 1716. Montrose appears to be the 'Garviekirk' of *The Interloper*, by Violet Jacob, most of whose novels and poems have a Forfarshire setting.

Before starting north for Aberdeen by road, take a run inland—by train, if no bus available—to *Brechin* (pronounced 'Breéchin'), 8½ miles. Brechin Cathedral, now the Parish Church, was founded by David I in 1150. It has lost its original transepts, but the choir, a comely example of Early Pointed, which was long left roofless, has been well restored. Of greater importance than the Cathedral itself, however, is the Round Tower attached to it, which dates from the tenth or eleventh century, and is one of the three that survive in Scotland, the other two being at Abernethy, 8 miles south-east of Perth, and at Egilsay in the Orkneys. They resemble the round towers of Ireland, and were probably used both as belfries and for defensive purposes. The Brechin tower is 86 feet high, and the inner diameter is 8 feet. The doorway is decorated with crude Celtic carvings of the Crucifixion, churchmen, and fabulous monsters. There was no stair-case, communication between the various floors being by means of ladders. Brechin Castle is the seat of the Earl of Dalhousie, and Kinnaird Castle, a short distance south-east, is that of the Earl of Southesk, in a large deer-park. The Caterthuns are two prehistoric hill-forts, about five miles north of Brechin.

If you are prepared to sacrifice a section of coast road, you can go from Brechin to Stonehaven (26 miles) by the main road via Laurencekirk, or, better, take the secondary road via Edzell and Fettercairn, 3 miles longer. Edzell, with a ruined castle of the Lindsays, is a holiday resort on the North Esk, the upper valley of which, Glen Esk, is worth a visit, though it is a cul-de-sac for cars (to Loch Lee 15 miles). Beyond the pretty village of Fettercairn, a side-road on the left leads to the ruins of Kincardine Castle (pronounced 'Kincárdin'), all that is left of the ancient county town of Kincardineshire. To the south stretches the flat, well-farmed district called the Howe o' the Mearns, scene of Lewis Grassic Gibbon's novels *Sunset Song* and *Cloud Howe*. The former is a tale of peasant life in an imaginary parish, 'Kinraddie,' apparently an amalgam of Arbuthnott, Fordoun, and Glenbervie, while the 'Segget' of *Cloud Howe* has been identified as both Auchinblae and Drumlithie, though its jute-mills suggest Inverbervie. In *Grey Granite*, which completes the trilogy, the town of 'Dundon' appears to be a compound of Aberdeen and Dundee.

The coast road running north from Montrose to Aberdeen soon crosses the North Esk into Kincardineshire, the alternative name for which is 'The Mearns.' The first places of any size are Gourdon, a live little fishing port, and Bervie, the cliff scenery near which is very imposing.

About 1½ miles on this side of Stonehaven *Dunnottar Castle* is passed, a grand ruin on a rock overlooking the sea and defended by a ravine on the landward side. It is one of the most impressive castles in Britain, the oldest (i.e. fourteenth century) parts being the square keep and the chapel. A previous castle was captured by Wallace from the English, on which occasion—so the story runs—the whole of the garrison, 4,000 men, perished in the flames. Dunnottar was held until 1715 by the Keiths, Earls Marischal of Scotland. The Scottish Regalia were kept here after the Battle of Worcester, and when the Castle was besieged in 1652 they were safely smuggled out. In the dungeon, or 'Whigs' Vault,' Covenanters to the number of 167, men, women, and children, were imprisoned in 1685. Those who died are commemorated in Dunnottar churchyard by the Covenanters' Stone, and it was this stone that 'Old Mortality' (page 68) was cleaning when Sir Walter Scott met him for the only time.

Stonehaven—Steenhive they call it locally—the capital of Kincardineshire, is a decayed fishing port and an unsophisticated seaside resort. The magnificent cliff scenery in the environs is best seen from a boat. For those who want to avoid Aberdeen the 'Slug Road' from Stonehaven to Banchory (16 miles) offers a useful short cut to Deeside. Farther on the Aberdeen road passes various villages, including Muchalls (pronounced approximately 'Muckles'), a primitive place with fine rocks and a small castle. Then Findon, which gave its name to Finnan haddocks, but is now practically derelict. The setting of Miss Agnes Mure Mackenzie's novel, *Keith of Kinnellan*, is mainly seaward Kincardineshire, the coast north of Stonehaven, and inland from that. The River Dee, on this side of Aberdeen, divides Kincardineshire from Aberdeenshire. The main road crosses it by the picturesque, seven-arched Bridge of Dee, which dates from the sixteenth century but has been widened. There are two other road-bridges lower down: the Wellington Suspension Bridge and the Victoria Bridge.

Aberdeen (accent on the last syllable), the 'City of Bon Accord,' situated at the mouth of the River Dee, has a population of 182,000 and is the principal seaport of the north, with over 300 steam trawlers and 'liners.' It is built almost entirely of granite, the local stone, which is now mostly used for making concrete. A visit to one of the quarries in the vicinity can be arranged. Aberdonians have a reputation for closefistedness of which they are rather proud than otherwise.

Union Street, with many handsome public buildings, is the main street of Aberdeen and the pride of the city. In Castle Street, at its east end, are the Municipal Buildings, which incorporate the old tower of the Tolbooth (1616), and the ornately beautiful City Cross, dating from 1686. Broad Street leads north to Marischal College, which was founded in 1593 by George Keith, fifth Earl Marischal. It houses the University Faculties of Law, Medicine, and Science. The buildings, modern and very imposing, and said to be the largest granite structure in the world after the Escorial, include the Mitchell Tower, 233 feet high, the Graduation Hall, and the Library. Over the inner doorway is the defiant Keith motto: 'Thay haif said. Quhat say thay? Lat thame say.'

The principal church of Aberdeen, on the north side of Union Street, is St Nicholas's, once the largest parish church in Scotland, but now divided into two, the East and West Churches. The West Church, which contains four seventeenth-century tapestries, was rebuilt in 1753 by James Gibbs, an Aberdonian. The transept, vestibule to both churches, is a good example of Transitional architecture. Union Bridge commands a view of the public gardens and railway in the valley below. Beyond it, turn right along Union Terrace and cross the railway again by the Rosemount Viaduct, in which are the Public Library, Her Majesty's Theatre, and a huge statue of Wallace. To the west, in Schoolhill, are the War Memorial and the Art Gallery and Museum, both worth seeing. A feature of the latter is a collection of self-portraits by modern artists. Adjacent is the entrance to Robert Gordon's Colleges (1739), with a statue of General Gordon.

Old Aberdeen, the quiet University quarter of the city, lies a mile or so from the centre, and is reached by bus from Union Street along Broad Street. King's College is the other constituent college of the University—for the Faculties of Arts and Divinity. The college buildings are modern, but the Chapel, with its fine lantern tower and crown, dates from the beginning of the sixteenth century. It contains an interesting pulpit, old stalls, and the modern tomb of Bishop Elphinstone, who founded the college in 1494. The Cathedral—St Machar's—farther north, is said to be the only ancient cathedral in the world that is built of granite. It is mainly the work of Bishop Lichton (1424–40), but the choir was rebuilt by Bishop Elphinstone (1488–1514), and Bishop Gavin Dunbar (1518–30) completed the west towers and constructed the splendid oak ceiling, with its forty-eight heraldic shields, showing the arms of Pope Leo X, the Emperor Charles V, the Kings and Princes of Christendom, and the Bishops and Earls of Scotland. The central tower collapsed in 1688, and the choir and transepts are still in ruins. In the south transept is the canopied tomb of Bishop Dunbar, in the north transept the effigy of Bishop Lichton. A half-mile farther north is the picturesque Bridge of Don or Brig o' Balgownie, a single-pointed arch built in 1320.

Before finally leaving Aberdeen, take a walk along the Docks, south of Castle Street, to the North Pier at the mouth of the Dee, and to the Town Links, now a sort of Blackpool, with a fine sandy bathing beach, scenic railways, dance hall, and the rest. The huge Fish Market on the north side of the Albert Basin presents busy scenes in the early morning, and all day during the herring season in July and August.

Aberdeenshire cannot be reckoned among the picturesque counties of Scotland as far as the interior—which is highly farmed and generally somewhat bleak and bare —is concerned, but the coast scenery of Buchan (pronounced approximately 'Búckăn'), its north-eastern division, is very fine. The bus route to Cruden Bay runs inland, but motorists should choose the coast road (23 miles), via Newburgh, at the mouth of the River Ythan, and Collieston, a primitive fishing village. There are fine cliffs from Collieston all the way to Peterhead, and on a promontory north of Collieston are the ruins of the Old Castle of Slains, destroyed by James VI in 1594.

Cruden Bay is a golfing resort created by the railway, with a hotel (Kilmarnock Arms) and a bathing beach of firm sand. The great walk is northwards along the cliffs to the Dun Buy Rock and to the famous Bullers of Buchan, a huge cauldron entered by a natural arch and presenting a magnificent sight in rough weather. Dr Johnson describes it in *A Journey to the Western Islands*—'If I had any malice against a walking spirit, instead of laying him in the Red Sea, I would condemn him to reside in the Buller of Buchan.' Boddam, a strange, red-granite village at Buchan Ness, the easternmost point of Scotland, is connected by bus with Peterhead, 3 miles farther.

Peterhead, the most easterly town in Scotland, is a great fishing port, and is built of the local red granite. The small harbours on either side of the projecting Keith Inch are connected by a canal, and Peterhead Bay has been converted into a harbour of refuge by a breakwater constructed by convicts from the neighbouring prison. A statue of Marshal Keith, presented by King William I of Prussia, stands in front of the Town House. Keith was born at Inverugie Castle, now a ruin, near Peterhead, and was exiled, together with his brother George Keith, tenth and last Earl Marischal, for his share in the Jacobite rising of 1715. After serving with distinction in the Spanish and Russian armies, he was made a Field Marshal by Frederick the Great, held high command in the Seven Years War, and fell at the Battle of Hochkirch.

TOUR VII: ABERDEEN TO BRAEMAR, PITLOCHRY, BANFF, AND INVERNESS

Total distance by road: about 350 miles.

BALLATER—BALMORAL CASTLE—BRAEMAR—THE CAIRNGORMS —DUNKELD—PITLOCHRY—LOCH TUMMEL—PASS OF KILLIE-CRANKIE—BLAIR ATHOLL—KINGUSSIE—AVIEMORE—GRAN-TOWN—HUNTLY—BANFF—ELGIN—PLUSCARDEN ABBEY—FORRES—FINDHORN GLEN—NAIRN—CAWDOR CASTLE—CUL-LODEN MOOR—INVERNESS.

THE first stage of this tour, which introduces some of the finest scenery in the Highlands, is from Aberdeen to Braemar, 58 miles—by motor-coach in the season, or by railway to Ballater and thence by motor-bus. The main road and the railway run all the way close to the north bank of the River Dee, the valley of which increases in beauty and graciousness, and takes on a more Highland character, the farther one proceeds. There is also a secondary road on the south bank of the river, narrow and hilly, but recommended to unhurried motorists. This tour traverses the district worst affected by the great gale of 31st January 1953, which is estimated to have destroyed five million trees in this corner of Scotland alone.

The main road, rather dull at first, leaves Aberdeen by Union Street, Holburn Street (left), and Great Western Road (right). Deeside, just west of Cults and Bieldside, provides the setting for Miss Agnes Mure Mackenzie's novels, *Without Conditions* and *The Half Loaf*.

On the left beyond Cults you have a glimpse of Blairs College, a Roman Catholic seminary, across the Dee. Peterculter (pronounced 'Peetercoóter') has paper works established in 1751. Farther on you see, on the right, Drum Castle, seat of the Irvines, built in 1619, with an earlier keep, and then Crathes Castle (pronounced 'Cráthiz'), completed 1596, with gardens open on Wednesdays and Saturdays. The valley grows more wooded, and the road becomes an avenue through pine forest. Banchory (pronounced 'Bánkŏry')—where you should see the Bridge of Feugh, a noted beauty spot, on the other side of the Dee—Kincardine O'Neil, and Aboyne (pronounced 'Abóyne') are pleasant summer resorts. Aboyne Castle is the residence of the Marquis of Huntly. The road crosses the Moor of Dinnet, a vivid purple in August, and passes Loch Kinord, a pretty wood-fringed lake. The stream that runs into the west side of the lake is called the Burn of the Vat, from the curious granite chasm through which it flows. The hill above it is Culblean (1,567 feet), behind which tower the bare slopes of Morven (2,862 feet).

Ballater (accent on first syllable), the railhead, is a trim modern village surrounded by wooded hills and more distant mountains. It has several good hotels and is a favourite holiday resort. Most of the shops display the Royal Arms over the door. The hill to the north, Craigandarrach (1,250 feet), is an excellent viewpoint. The chief excursion is the drive up the beautiful Glen Muick past Birkhall, residence of the Queen Mother, to Loch Muick (10 miles), and the ascent thence of Lochnagar, 4–5 hours' walk from Ballater.

The road from Ballater to Braemar ascends along the north bank of the Dee, through charming wooded landscapes. Abergeldie Castle, on the opposite bank, is leased by the Queen. Crathie Church, on the right, is a truly royal church. Queen Victoria laid the foundation stone in 1893; the Royal Family attends service here when in residence at Balmoral; and there are numerous royal memorials and gifts. John Brown, the devoted and faithful personal attendant of Queen Victoria, is buried in the graveyard by the river. The road on the south bank between Crathie and Braemar is closed to the public.

Balmoral Castle, the Scottish residence of H.M. the Queen, is about a mile farther on, on the opposite bank, and is screened by trees. It is best seen from the point where the Strathdon road diverges. The Balmoral estate was bought by Queen Victoria in 1852. The Castle is a white granite structure—'my dearest Albert's own creation . . . his great taste, and the impress of his dear hand, have been stamped everywhere.' The site was once occupied by a castle of the Farquharsons. The public is not admitted to the Castle, but in the absence of the Court the grounds are open on Mondays, Wednesdays, and Fridays, from 10 to 5.

Between Balmoral and the Inver Inn you pass, on the left, the Cairn of Remembrance, the rallying point of the Farquharson clan before a battle. Each man contributed a stone to the cairn—so the old story goes—and on their return each man took a stone away, the stones that were left representing the number of the slain. Farther on the Braemar road crosses Invercauld Bridge over the Dee, and runs below a prominent cliff called Craig Cluny. Ballochbuie Forest, the pinewoods on the south bank, is royal property, and closed to the public. Invercauld House, on the north bank, is the seat of the Farquharsons, and dates in part from the fifteenth century. Just outside Braemar you pass, on the right, Braemar Castle or Old Mar Castle, built in 1628, the seat of the Earls of Mar, then of the Earls of Fife, and now of Lord Tweedsmuir.

Braemar (accent on second syllable), or, if we give it its full title, Castleton of Braemar, is a bracing and fashionable little summer resort, with first-class—and not inexpensive—hotels. Situated amid the finest Highland scenery, it is a splendid headquarters for excursions among the mountains, although the tourist's freedom of movement is somewhat impaired by the proximity of the royal domains, and by the fact that much of the surrounding district is preserved as deer forest. In the stalking season (August and onwards) pedestrians are liable to be warned off any track that is not a public right of way. The foundations of the old castle of Braemar are to be seen by the bridge over the Clunie Water. A tablet marks the house—on the Glen Clunie road, beyond the church where R. L. Stevenson wrote *Treasure Island* in 1881.

The principal drive from Braemar is up the valley of the Dee, past the Linn of Corriemulzie and the hamlet of Inverey—where lodgings are sometimes to be had—to the Linn of Dee, 6½ miles. The Linn of Corriemulzie is a pretty waterfall to the right of the road, on a side-stream this side of the Victoria Bridge. The bridge (private) crosses the Dee to Mar Lodge, which was built by the late Duke of Fife. The road on the south bank ends at the

Linn of Dee, where the river pushes through a black, rocky fissure. After heavy rain this is a most impressive scene. There are some splendid Scots firs in the adjoining woods. An alternative return route to Braemar—but cars are not allowed—is by the north bank of the river, past Mar Lodge and the pretty Linn of Quoich, to Invercauld Bridge.

Morrone Hill (2,819 feet), which rises south of Braemar, between the Dee and the Clunie, should be climbed for the sake of its view. Three hours up and down should be allowed. Lochnagar (3,786 feet), the highest point of Balmoral Forest, is about 12 miles south-east, or four–five hours' walking. It derives its name from the small loch (Lochnagar, goat's lake) at the foot of the north-east precipices. Snow lies on this side all the year round. The ordinary route to the top is by Glen Clunie and Glen Callater to Loch Callater, 5 miles, to which point driving is practicable. The summit-plateau is covered with large patches of creeping azalea. The view is said to extend, in exceptionally clear weather, to the Cheviots, a hundred miles south.

> Years have roll'd on, Loch na Garr, since I left you,
>   Years must elapse ere I tread you again:
> Nature of verdure and flow'rs has bereft you,
>   Yet still you are dearer than Albion's plain.
> England! thy beauties are tame and domestic
>   To one who has roved o'er the mountains afar:
> Oh, for the crags that are wild and majestic!
>   The steep frowning glories of dark Loch na Garr.
>   BYRON.

The *Cairngorm Mountains*, north-east of Braemar, form the most extensive area in Great Britain at an elevation of over 3,000 feet, and include six peaks of over 4,000. There is not much rock-climbing, but innumerable hill-walking excursions are possible—until the stalking season starts, at least. Caution is called for, as fatalities have occurred through mist or snow, or from being benighted. Distances are vast, and there is an utter absence of accommodation or even shelter. The mountain slopes provide the best ski-ing in the country, and efforts are made to run a regular winter sports season at Braemar. The Cairngorms give their name to the brown or blue

E

quartz-crystals found in the granite. The golden eagle may be seen. The highest peak is Ben Muich-Dhui ('Mountain of the Black Sow'), or Ben MacDhui, which is 4,296 feet above sea-level—or only 110 feet lower than Ben Nevis—and a strenuous 18 miles from Braemar. The usual approach is by the Linn of Dee, whence a rough road ascends Glen Lui as far as Derry Lodge, to which point driving is possible. There is a cottage close by that sells refreshments. Thence Ben Muich-Dhui is scaled either by the pony track via Glen Derry and Loch Etcha-chan, or via Glen Lui Beg. The summit, a wilderness of red granite, is provided with a view-indicator. Below, in the hollow between Ben Muich-Dhui and Cairn Gorm, is Loch Avon, a lovely blue tarn, at the head of which is the Shelter Stone, with a natural chamber beneath it providing the only protection for miles around. A fairly level four-mile walk along the ridge north of Ben Muich-Dhui brings you to the top of Cairn Gorm (4,084 feet). Thence the descent may be made to Aviemore, 33 miles in all, via Glenmore Lodge and Loch Morlich. [The scene of Mr. Maurice Walsh's novel, *The Small Dark Man*, is laid from Loch Avon ('Loch Dhu') down Glen Avon to Inchrory, Tomintoul, and Glenlivet.]

The return journey (27 miles) may be made by the Larig Ghru (2,750 feet), a classic and excessively rough and stony walk. Beyond the trough-shaped pass, which is the wildest in Scotland, you come to the Pools of Dee, between Ben Muich-Dui on the left, and Braeriach (4,248 feet) and Cairn Toul (4,241 feet) on the right. Thence you either descend Glen Dee, or bear left for Glen Lui Beg and Derry Lodge.

The way from Braemar to Blair Atholl, a grand thirty-mile tramp, is by the Linn of Dee, Bynack Lodge, Glen Tilt, and Forest Lodge. Motors can go as far as White Lodge, and horse-drawn vehicles to Bynack Lodge, whence a bridle track, possible but not comfortable for cycles, brings you to Forest Lodge, the Duke of Atholl's shooting box, at the foot of Ben-y-Gloe (3,671 feet). The private road thence down Glen Tilt to Blair Atholl is open to cars and horse-drawn vehicles.

Having finished with the somewhat laborious delights of Braemar, you make your getaway southwards by car or motor-bus to Blairgowrie (35 miles), a splendid motor-ing route, reconditioned, but often snowbound in winter. It ascends Glen Clunie and at the Cairnwell Pass (2,199 feet), the highest main road pass in the country, leaves Aberdeenshire for Perthshire. Then comes a twenty-five-mile descent to Blairgowrie, beginning with the notorious, but now much improved, Devil's Elbow and its two 1 in 9 hairpin bends. On the left rises Glas Maol (3,502 feet). At the Spittal of Glenshee, once a refuge for travellers and now a hotel, the road reaches Glen Shee, and beyond the Bridge of Cally it runs high above the beautiful cañon eroded by the River Ericht in the conglomerate. Blairgowrie is a summer resort in the centre of a fruit-growing district, noted especially for its raspberries and strawberries.

At Blairgowrie you turn west for Dunkeld. Direct buses are available in the season; otherwise you can go via Perth, or by train via Coupar Angus and Stanley. The direct road (12 miles), very pretty and with stiff gradients, passes near a series of lochs: Loch Marlie, the Loch of Clunie, with its ruined island-castle, the Loch of Butter-stone, the Loch of Craiglush, and the particularly lovely Loch of Lows.

At Dunkeld you join the great trunk road and motor-coach route through the centre of the Highlands, from Perth to Inverness. It was originally one of the military roads constructed by General Wade in order to subjugate the clans after the Jacobite rising of 1715, and since its reconstruction it can claim to be the finest road in Scot-land. *Dunkeld* (accent on second syllable), on the east bank of the River Tay, is a small place, but it has an ancient Cathedral, approached by a charming old square, and placed in a lovely setting of shaded lawns beside the Tay. Founded in 1107, it has a choir of the fourteenth century, used as the parish church, and a roofless nave of the fifteenth, a venerable ruin converted, as so often in Scotland, into a burial ground. In the vestibule of the church is the recumbent effigy of the 'Wolf of Badenoch' —Alexander Stewart, Earl of Buchan and son of Robert II —whose career was one of unusual violence and savagery even for the fourteenth century. The Chapter House is the mausoleum of the Dukes of Atholl. Dunkeld House belonged to the Duke, and in its grounds are the foundations of a palace abandoned in 1830. The terraced walks are noted for their splendid trees: larches, firs, cedars, etc., and near the churchyard is a magnificent larch well over 100 feet in height. It was brought from the Tyrol and planted here in 1738.

Opposite Dunkeld, beyond Telford's stone bridge over the Tay, lies Birnam, a summer resort. Malcolm Canmore's soldiers hewed boughs from the trees of Birnam Wood (now vanished) and produced the appearance of a wood on the march, thus striking terror into the superstitious soul of Macbeth—

> I will not be afraid of death and bane
> Till Birnam forest come to Dunsinane.

Birnam Hill (1,325 feet) commands a glorious view. Dunsinane (pronounced 'Dunsínnan') is the westernmost of the Sidlaw Hills, 12 miles south-east, and is still crowned with the vestiges of Macbeth's castle. A delightful walk from Birnam is up the valley of the Bran to Rumbling Bridge, with pretty waterfalls, 2 miles; return by the road on the other bank, via Inver.

The road from Dunkeld to Pitlochry (12½ miles), served by the Perth–Struan and other buses, winds along the east bank of the Tay nearly to Ballinluig, near which you obtain a splendid view up the Tay valley, with Schiehallion in the far distance. The road then leaves the Tay valley for that of the River Tummel, on the east bank of which lies *Pitlochry*, one of the most fashionable of Highland summer resorts, with many palatial hotels. The environs are very beautiful, and Pitlochry is a great centre for motor-coach tours.

Robert Louis Stevenson spent the wet June and July of 1881—before moving on to Braemar—at Kinnaird Cottage, 2 miles north-east of Pitlochry, beyond the pretty village of Moulin. The cottage, where he wrote *Thrawn Janet* and *The Merry Men*, is near 'a little green glen with a burn—a wonderful burn, gold and green and snow white, singing loud and low in different steps of its career, now pouring over miniature crags, now fretting itself to death in a maze of rocky stairs and pots; never was so sweet a little river. Behind, great purple moorlands reaching to

Ben Vrackie.' The ascent of Ben Vrackie (2,757 feet), a splendid viewpoint, takes rather more than three hours, up and down. Craigour (1,300 feet), above Moulin, is much nearer and affords an equally lovely, though naturally more limited, view.

Two miles beyond Pitlochry the road to Kinloch Rannoch—buses ply thither from Pitlochry—diverges left from the Inverness road over the Bridge of Garry Walk across the bridge and take the path that descends left to the Falls of Tummel, an exquisite spot belonging to the National Trust, where the river forms a grand cascade. Four miles farther along the Kinloch Rannoch road—the scenery is varied and beautiful all the way—there is a rocky height on the left known as the Queen's View, which affords a splendid prospect of *Loch Tummel* and the least attractive flank of Schiehallion.

Beyond the Bridge of Garry the Inverness road and railway (Pitlochry–Blair Atholl, 7 miles) ascend, beside the River Garry, through the famous *Pass of Killiecrankie,* where, on 27th July 1689, William III's troops under General Mackay were routed by 3,000 Highlanders from Lochaber under John Graham of Claverhouse, Viscount Dundee. 'Bonnie Dundee,' however, fell mortally wounded in the moment of victory, and with him perished the cause of James II.

Blair Atholl, with the Tilt Hotel and a fine war memorial, is a bracing spot, 450 feet up, and is the last place of any size passed for many a long mile—to Dalwhinnie, 24 miles. Blair Castle is the seat of the Duke of Atholl, who owns over 150,000 acres. Both castle and grounds are open in summer, except on Fridays. The Murrays of Atholl have played a prominent part in Scottish history since the twelfth century, and the Atholl Highlanders, maintained by the Duke, are the only private standing army permitted in Great Britain. 'Atholl brose' is a mixture of whisky, cold water, and heather honey. Oatmeal, cream, or the yolk of an egg is sometimes added. Ben-y-Gloe (3,671 feet) rises on the north-east, and Ben Dearg (3,304 feet) on the north of Blair Atholl. The ascent of the former takes about seven hours up and down, and is rewarded by an uninterrupted view to the north and east.

A mile or so on this side of Struan the Inverness road

crosses the Bruar, an affluent of the Garry that flows for
a mile through a deep gorge, forming three waterfalls of
great beauty. It is an entrancing scene, on no account
to be skipped. The banks are now clothed with trees,
thanks to Burns's *Humble Petition of Bruar Water to the
Noble Duke of Athole*, written in return for ducal hospitality in the autumn of 1787.

> Let lofty firs, and ashes cool,
> My lowly banks o'erspread,
> And view, deep-bending in the pool,
> Their shadows' watery bed!
> Let fragrant birks, in woodbines drest,
> My craggy cliffs adorn;
> And, for the little songster's nest,
> The close embow'ring thorn.

The scenery becomes wilder and more desolate; from
Struan to Dalwhinnie there is hardly a single habitation
—only five houses in 19 miles. Near the station of
Dalnaspidal (accent on third syllable) road and railway
part company with the Garry, which issues from Loch
Garry, to the west. They then cross the bleak Pass of
Drumochter (1,484 feet), the highest point on any full-
gauge railway in the country. The two hills on the left
are the Atholl Sow and the Boar of Badenoch. At the
top of the pass Inverness-shire is entered.

As you approach Dalwhinnie you pass a war memorial
on the right, and a concrete dam built across the River
Truim, in connection with the electric power scheme
(page 153), to divert a portion of its flow into Loch
Ericht. Dalwhinnie, in Glen Truim, consists of two
hotels, a shop, and a few cottages. It is close to the head
of Loch Ericht, a wild and solitary lake, narrow but 15
miles long, and noted for its bull-trout. Its level has been
raised 12 feet, and its area slightly extended, by the construction of a dam on the River Ericht, near the south end
of the loch. Near the farther end, on the west, towers Ben
Alder (3,757 feet), where, in a thicket of holly on a southern
spur overlooking the loch, Cluny Macpherson had his
'Cage,' a two-storeyed structure of boughs, roofed with
moss. Prince Charlie lay hidden here from 5th to 12th
September 1746, until news of the arrival of the French
ship at Loch nan Uamh reached him. David Balfour and

Alan Breck, too, in *Kidnapped*, took refuge here after they had been hunted from the Moor of Rannoch by the dragoons.

At the exit from Glen Truim you find yourself in the much more fertile Glen Spey, a valley of woods and green fields. From Dalwhinnie to Aviemore is 26 miles. The Spey, famous for salmon, is the rapidest river in Scotland, and in spite of its length (90 miles) is totally unnavigable. The mountains to the north are known as the Monadhliath (pronounced 'Mŏnăleĕă'). On the left are the cliffs of Craig Dhu (2,350 feet), which provided the Clan Macpherson with a rallying cry. The Spey is crossed on this side of Newtonmore, a good touring centre; or motorists, if they prefer it, can take the secondary road on the south bank of the river. At Newtonmore you find a bus service for Kingussie, Aviemore, and Grantown.

Kingussie (pronounced 'King-yoóssie'), with an interesting Folk Museum, is a summer resort and centre for the exploration of this wild district of Badenoch. Craig Beg (1,593 feet), 1½ miles distant, and Croidh-la (2,099 feet), 4 miles, are good viewpoints. The road next passes an obelisk in memory of James Macpherson, author of the Ossianic poems, who built Balavil, the adjoining country house, and was born at Ruthven, opposite Kingussie. Then Kincraig and the pretty Loch Insh, with pike fishing by permit, at the mouth of the romantic Glen Feshie, which is noted for its Scots firs. Lynwilg Hotel, close to Loch Alvie, is a resort of climbers, for we are now in the vicinity of the Cairngorms, which rise on the east. The Tor of Alvie, on the right of the road, is surmounted by a Waterloo Cairn and a monument to the last Duke of Gordon.

Aviemore (pronounced 'Avvimóre') is as good a climbing centre for the Cairngorms as Braemar, and winter sports on a modest scale may be had. To the south-east stretches the tangled Forest of Rothiemurchus, the paths through which are notoriously confusing. On the west is the rock of Craigellachie (accent on the second syllable), the trysting place of the Grants, whose slogan was 'Stand fast, Craigellachie!' The clan territory extended down Strath Spey to the other Craigellachie, 40 miles away. The captivating little Loch-an-Eilean, 3 miles south of

Aviemore, is worth a digression.   On the island is a castle of the 'Wolf of Badenoch,' and water-lilies grow in the adjoining little loch at the north end.

At Kinveachy, beyond Loch Vaa, or at Carrbridge, an unspoilt, inviting resort a little farther on, you leave the Inverness road and take the road on the right for Grantown (14 miles from Aviemore), entering the county of Moray (pronounced 'Murray') at Dulnain Bridge.   Besides the railway from Aviemore, there are buses from Aviemore to Grantown via Kinveachy, Boat of Garten, Nethy Bridge, and Dulnain Bridge, and also from Carrbridge.   Motorists may prefer the secondary road ($17\frac{1}{2}$ miles) from Aviemore on the east or Inverness-shire bank of the Spey, via Nethy Bridge (pronounce 'eth' as in 'death').   Walkers should without fail choose the rough road from Aviemore to Nethy Bridge (16 miles) via Loch Morlich, Glenmore Lodge, the pretty little Green Loch, the Revoan Pass (1,197 feet), and Abernethy Forest, passing through some of the best scenery in the Highlands.   Castle Roy, beyond Nethy Bridge, was a stronghold of the Comyns.   Ian Macpherson's excellent novel of the Nethy region of Speyside—*Land of Our Fathers*—has a strong flavour of locality.

Grantown, in Moray county, was founded in 1766 by Sir James Grant, and Castle Grant, close by—compared by Queen Victoria to a factory—is the residence of the Countess of Seafield.   It is a pleasant, tidy little town, with beautiful trees in its square, and above all it is an excellent centre for expeditions in every direction.   Apart from those adumbrated above, the Loch-in-Dorb, 10 miles north, with another ruined island-castle of the Wolf of Badenoch, and the hilly road via the romantic Bridge of Brown to Tomintoul (pronounced 'Tommintówel'), $13\frac{1}{2}$ miles south-east, are particularly noteworthy. Loch-in-Dorb ('Loch Ruighi') is the main scene of Mr Maurice Walsh's novel, *The Key above the Door*.

The main road down the pretty valley of the Spey— to Craigellachie 25 miles, with a bus service—follows the east bank of the river, while a secondary road, no longer but with poor surface, runs near the west bank.   The Avon, a crystal-clear stream, the largest tributary of the Spey, is crossed near Ballindalloch Castle, a splendid baronial seat, modernized. The road to the right leads to the famous Glenlivet Distillery, founded by George Smith in 1824. This is the only distillery in the glen, although twenty-six of the Strathspey and Speyside distilleries use the name Glenlivet in a hyphenated form. From Ballindalloch nearly to Fochabers the Spey divides Moray on the west bank from Banffshire on the east. Ben Rinnes (2,755 feet) is prominent on the right. Aberlour (pronounce 'ou' as in 'our') has a linn on its burn.

At Craigellachie, a centre of the Speyside distilling industry, the Elgin road crosses the river by means of Telford's single-span iron bridge. Changing into the Dufftown bus, we quit Strathspey here and turn right above the fine gorge of the River Fiddich, through which the railway runs. The ruins of Balvenie Castle, fifteenth century, are passed. Dufftown, with 'Glenlivet' distilleries, was founded in 1817 by James Duff, fourth Earl of Fife. You then take the bleak moorland road eastwards to Huntly, 18 miles from Craigellachie, ascending the Fiddich valley, and attaining a height of 1,056 feet before dropping down into the valley of the River Deveron. The bus and/or railway route from Dufftown to Huntly is via Keith.

Huntly, in the angle between the Deveron and the Bogie, is built on a draughtboard plan, and makes a pleasant summer resort. A tablet in Duke Street indicates the birthplace of George Macdonald, a farmer's son, descendant of the Macdonalds of Glencoe. His novels, published in the sixties, include *David Elginbrod*, a mystical romance, and *Alec Forbes of Howglen*, descriptive of humble life in Huntly. Huntly Castle, once the seat of the 'Cock o' the North' Gordons—Earls of Huntly, then Marquises of Huntly, then Dukes of Gordon—was rebuilt in the second half of the sixteenth century, but is now a stately ruin, notable for its fine range of oriel windows.

From Huntly you make for the coast at Banff. The railway route is via Grange and Tillynaught. There are two roads of approximately equal length (21 miles), one —the bus route—via Aberchirder, the other via Glenbarry. Compared with what we have left behind us, the countryside is tame and uninteresting. *Banff*, the county town,

* E

with a number of old houses, is a small seaport and bathing resort at the mouth of the River Deveron. The sands are excellent. Duff House, a building of the mid eighteenth century, in the style of the Villa Borghese, was formerly the seat of the Duke of Fife but now belongs to the town; at the farther end of the park is the pretty bridge of Alvah. One of Smeaton's bridges, a seven-arch one, unites Banff with its less attractive sister-town Macduff, formerly Doune, but renamed in 1783 after James Duff, second Earl of Fife. It has a fine harbour and a considerable fishing fleet. The coast scenery east of Macduff, as far as Fraserburgh, is extremely fine, but the road (22 miles) is rough, with 1 in 6 hills. The finest point is Troup Head, with sheer cliffs 350 feet high, between the startlingly picturesque fishing villages of Gardenstown and Pennan. Gardenstown, founded by Alexander Garden of Troup in 1720, has a flourishing fishing industry in spite of its cramped situation. Pennan is all built of the local red sandstone, with red-tiled roofs. Fraserburgh is a busy fishing port, owing its name to Sir Alexander Fraser of Philorth, who built its first harbour in 1546. The novel to read in this district is William Alexander's *Johnny Gibb of Gushetneuk*.

We now follow the coast road westwards from Banff to Elgin, 34½ miles. The railway route is via Tillynaught and Buckie, and there is a good bus service: Macduff– Banff – Elgin – Nairn – Inverness. Portsoy, beyond the ruins of Boyne Castle, is noted for its 'marble,' i.e. serpentine, and other rocks. Cullen, the 'Portlossie' of George Macdonald's *Malcolm*, is a small fishing town with Cullen House, a seat of the Countess of Seafield, and a splendid view across Moray Firth to the mountains of Sutherland. The main road runs inland, direct to Fochabers, but the buses take the coastal road via Portknockie, Findochty, Buckie, and Portgordon (founded by the fourth Duke in 1797). All this rocky coast is very attractive, and most of the Moray Firth towns and villages are interested in the herring fishery. Fochabers (accent on the first syllable), in Moray, is a neat eighteenth-century village in a pine district. It is a creation of the Dukes of Gordon, who were formerly known as the 'Gudemen o' the Bog,' as Fochabers once stood on a morass called the Bog o' Gight. Gordon Castle, the former seat of the Duke of Richmond, adjacent on the north, was sold to the Crown in 1937, with 140 square miles of land. Spey Bay, at the mouth of the Spey, with a railway station, is a growing seaside resort.

The River Spey is crossed 4 miles from its mouth, and then, beyond Lhanbryde, you arrive at *Elgin* ('g' hard), the animated county town of Moray. It is an agreeable place, situated in the fertile 'Garden of Moray,' and is distinctly 'residential.' There is a spacious market-place, and a High Street with quaint houses and two crosses—the Little Cross and the Muckle Cross. On a height near the west end of the High Street is a tall column—which you can ascend—in memory of the last Duke of Gordon, who died in 1836. But the principal attraction of Elgin is its ruined Cathedral, once the 'Lantern of the North' and one of the finest churches in Scotland. Founded in 1224, it was rebuilt after being burnt by the 'Wolf of Badenoch' in 1390. The ruins, in the Early Decorated Gothic style, rival Melrose in impressiveness and 'atmosphere.' The chief features are the noble west front and its twin towers, the façade of the south transept, the east end of the choir, and the well-preserved Chapter House with its central clustered pillar. St Mary's Aisle was used as the burial-place of the Gordons. Lossiemouth, the port of Elgin, 4½ miles north, is a breezy seaside resort of increasing popularity, with good golf and bathing. On the way thither the ruins of Spynie Palace, the castle of the Bishops of Moray, are passed. Ramsay MacDonald (*d.* 1937) was born at Lossiemouth in a turf-thatched 'but and ben' (two-roomed cottage), and had a house there—'The Hillocks.'

The railway and main road from Elgin to Forres (11 miles)—the latter resembling an avenue through a pine forest—pass nothing of interest, unless you digress to the right on this side of Forres to see what little is left of Kinloss Abbey, one of David I's Cistercian foundations, situated on Findhorn Bay. On the west side of the bay are the Culbin Sandhills, which swallowed up a whole barony between 1670 and 1695. A more interesting route is the secondary road farther south (3 miles longer), which passes near the well-preserved remains of *Pluscarden Abbey* (accent on first syllable), occupying a beautiful site in a luxuriant valley. It was a Cistercian house, founded by Alexander II in 1230, and has recently been restored by the Marquis of Bute. The church, Early Pointed, has lost its nave. It contains a Flemish sacrament house, and the Chapter House is noteworthy.

Forres, noted for its sweet scenery and climate, is a very ancient town, scene of a part of *Macbeth*. Its most interesting 'sight' is Sweno's Stone, which stands just outside the town, on the left side of the road to Kinloss. This is a tall, slender shaft of sandstone, covered with sculptures—warriors, animals, and Runic knots. It is thought to date from the time of Malcolm II (*d.* 1034). Before leaving Forres pay a visit by all means to the Findhorn Glen, where the Findhorn, a rapid stream, has carved its way to the sea through red sandstone gorges of surpassing beauty. The best plan is to drive to Sluie, 5 miles along the Grantown road, and walk thence to Randolph's Leap, 3 miles or so higher up. Forres is the 'Muiryside' of Mr Maurice Walsh's novel, *While Rivers Run*, and the main scene of the story is laid near the mouth of the Findhorn ('The Leonach'), looking across the Culbin Sands. 'Larach na Gael' is the moor of Broadshaw behind Darnaway Castle, seat of the Earl of Moray, 4 miles or so from Forres.

The road from Forres to Nairn (10½ miles) crosses the River Findhorn by a suspension bridge and, in company with the railway, passes Brodie Castle, on the right, the stately seat of the Brodies, the park of which is open to the public. Macbeth's Hillock, a pine-clad knoll on the right of the road, a little farther on, is reputed to be the 'desert Heath' where Macbeth and Banquo interviewed the three witches. Immediately afterwards you cross the Nairnshire boundary. At Auldearn (pronounced 'Awldern') the Covenanters were routed by the Marquis of Montrose in 1645. *Nairn*, the county town, situated on the shore of the wide Moray Firth, at the mouth of the River Nairn, is a fashionable watering-place with good sands and golf. The harbour was constructed by Telford in 1820, and there is a separate fishermen's quarter known as 'Fishertoun.' The Highland line ran through the town,

English being spoken in the east part of the town, Gaelic in the west.

The main road and the railway run direct from Nairn to Inverness (16 miles), soon entering Inverness-shire, but motorists, by taking a secondary road parallel on the south, and 4 miles longer, can see Cawdor Castle and Culloden Moor *en route*. The former, 5½ miles from Nairn, is the picturesque seat of Earl Cawdor, and dates from 1454. Neither the castle nor its grounds is at present open to the public. Macbeth was Thane of Cawdor, and Shakespeare makes Cawdor Castle the scene of King Duncan's murder.

Just beyond the next bridge over the River Nairn is the entrance to Kilravock Castle, which has been owned by the Rose family from time immemorial. There is no admission without previous application by letter. The road that runs near the north bank of the Nairn crosses the railway and then reaches *Culloden Moor* (pronounced 'Cullōden' or 'Cullódden'), the little-changed setting of the battle of 16th April 1746, whereby the fate of house of Stuart was sealed. At 1 p.m. Prince Charles's five–seven thousand Highlanders, tired and hungry, were engaged by nine thousand government troops under the Duke of Cumberland, the third son of George II. All was over in twenty-five minutes. The Highlanders lost a thousand dead and another thousand in the subsequent flight. The number of English killed was only fifty. It is noteworthy that both commanders were only twenty-five years old. At the cross-roads is the Cumberland Stone, from which the Duke is said to have directed operations, and a little farther on is a large cairn, together with stones marking the graves of the various Highland clans. Culloden House, where the Prince spent the night before the battle, has been greatly altered. On the south bank of the River Nairn, close by, are the prehistoric Stones of Clava, which, like the battle-field, belong to the National Trust.

Inverness, with a population of 28,000, is the Capital of the Highlands, and in fact the only town of any size in the North of Scotland. It calls itself the Queen of the North, and prides itself on the purity of its speech. The River Ness, near the mouth of which it stands, connects

Loch Ness with the landlocked Firth of Inverness, or Inner Moray Firth, and is only 6 miles long. Inverness is an austere but lovable town, busy enough in the tourist season, though there is not really much to see. The base of the Old Cross in front of the Town Hall encloses the Clach-na-Cudainn, or Stone of the Tubs, the 'charter stone of the burgh.' The women of Inverness used to rest their pails on it when carrying water up from the river. The Public Library and Museum has a collection of Jacobite relics. The Castle is modern, with a south terrace commanding a lovely view. Macbeth's Castle occupied a different site. The chief things to see in Inverness, however, are the pretty Islands in the Ness, which are joined to each other and to each bank by foot-bridges, and the charming cemetery of Tomnahurich (Hill of the Yew Trees), above the Victoria Park. Craig Phadrig (550 feet), i.e. the Rock of St Patrick, 2 miles west of Inverness, is a good viewpoint. It is crowned with a vitrified fort, i.e. a prehistoric stronghold in which, apparently in order to strengthen the walls, the stones were fused into a solid mass by lighting brushwood fires around them. According to another theory the vitrification was accidental, caused by the constant lighting of beacon fires.

TOUR VIII: INVERNESS TO FORT WILLIAM AND OBAN

Total distance by road: about 170 miles.

CALEDONIAN CANAL—LOCH NESS—FALLS OF FOYERS—FORT AUGUSTUS—LOCH OICH—LOCH LOCHY—FORT WILLIAM——BEN NEVIS—BALLACHULISH—GLENCOE—PASS OF BRANDER—DUNSTAFFNAGE CASTLE—OBAN—LOCH AWE—MULL—STAFFA—IONA.

THIS route follows Glen More, the Great Glen of Scotland, a remarkable cleft along a line of fault running from northeast to south-west straight across the Highlands from sea to sea, and dividing the northern third of Scotland from the rest of the country. The *Caledonian Canal*, constructed in this 'wet trench,' is 60 miles in length, but only about a third (22 miles) of the total waterway is artificial, the rest being composed of Loch Ness, Loch Oich, and Loch Lochy, natural freshwater lakes of great depth, strung out along the valley. The Canal, with its twenty-nine small locks, now under the control of the Ministry of Transport, was surveyed by James Watt and constructed by Telford between 1803 and 1847 at a cost of over a million and a quarter pounds, its object being to save fishing vessels the slow and stormy passage through the Pentland Firth. It is now, however, little used for navigation, and the MacBrayne Co. has substituted for its pre-war steamers a daily service of motor-coaches running as far as Fort William, whence on three days a week in summer you can proceed to Oban on the same day by a MacBrayne steamer. The whole of the route, as far as Ballachulish, lies within Inverness-shire.

Seven miles out of Inverness you reach the north end of *Loch Ness*, which is 24 miles long, a mile wide, and in places over a hundred fathoms deep. Believe it or not, the loch is haunted by a Monster of the sea-serpent type, 30 to 50 feet long, with a long and slender neck —for it has been seen by more than fifty persons in recent

years and has even been filmed! The hills on either side
of the lake are well wooded, but the scenery, though
majestic, is perhaps a trifle monotonous.

The main road, with a bus service from Inverness to
Fort Augustus (34 miles) besides the Fort William service,
follows the north-west bank of the lake, and has been
reconstructed as part of the scheme for a great highway
from the south of Scotland to Inverness via Glencoe.

[There is also a narrow secondary road along the south-
east bank, via Inverfarigaig, with its fine gorge, as far as
Foyers (buses thus far), beyond which it curves inland,
ascends to 1,275 feet, with 1 in 6 hills, and then descends
(1 in 7) via Glen Doe, with a waterfall on the left, to join
the main road at Fort Augustus, 32½ miles from Inverness.
The *Falls of Foyers* have a 90-ft. drop and used to be
considered the grandest waterfalls in the country, but
they have had their volume diminished—especially in dry
weather—by the activities of the British Aluminium Co.
The factory here—the first large hydro-electric installation
in this country devoted to a metallurgical process—was
started in 1896 for the production of aluminium by the
Héroult method. The turbines (6,500 h.p.) are fed by a
tunnel and pipe-line from a point just above the falls.
When the natural flow of the River Foyers is insufficient,
water can be drawn from a reservoir that has been formed
at Loch Garth.]

A protruding spit of land on the north-west bank, near
the main road, bears the picturesque pink ruins of Castle
Urquhart (pronounced Érkert), which was built under
Edward I and was defended by a double wall. It is an
interesting structure, meriting careful inspection. Close
to it, at the mouth of Glen Urquhart (the road to Glen
Affric), is Drumnadrochit, with its well-known hotel, 2
miles south-west of which are the pretty Divach Falls.

The hill opposite Foyers is Mealfourvonie (2,284 feet), a
name that means the 'Lumpish Height of the Cold Moor.'
It serves as a sea-mark for mariners in the Moray Firth.
Beyond Invermoriston, at the mouth of Glen Moriston
(the road to Skye), you reach Fort Augustus, at the head
of Loch Ness.

Fort Augustus, a neat village, derives its name from a
fort originally built after the Jacobite rising of 1715, on

the forfeited estates of Lord Lovat, and named after William Augustus, Duke of Cumberland, the victor of Culloden. It now has a Benedictine Abbey and boys' school, the neo-Gothic buildings of which, including the handsome church, were begun in 1876 after the designs of Edward Welby Pugin. The church was completed in 1917. The five-mile stretch of the Caledonian Canal between Loch Ness and Loch Oich delays navigation considerably, as ships have to ascend through several locks, including five at Fort Augustus itself. The river running parallel with the canal is the Oich.

Loch Oich is narrow and only 4 miles long. The railway (disused) follows the south-east bank. The road—Fort Augustus to Fort William, 32 miles—runs along the opposite bank, past Invergarry Castle, once the seat of the McDonells, but burnt down by the Duke of Cumberland in 1746. Prince Charlie spent the day after Culloden here. This central portion of the loch, opposite the mouth of Glen Garry, is perhaps the most beautiful section of the whole route. The road then passes the Well of the Heads, a singular structure erected in 1812, with an inscription in English, Gaelic, French, and Latin. Ben Tee, or 'Glengarry's Bowling Green' (2,956 feet), is a conspicuous feature of the landscape.

Then comes a short section of canal, 1½ miles long, whence Laggan Locks lower vessels to the level of the mountain-girt *Loch Lochy*, which is 10 miles long by ¾ mile wide, and almost Norwegian in aspect. Road and railway hug the south-east bank for most of the way, then leave the lake and canal for a while, passing Spean Bridge (page 155) and Inverlochy Castle (page 138).

On the right, near the end of Loch Lochy, is the mouth of the Arkaig, a short, swift stream that issues from Loch Arkaig, passing Achnacarry, the seat of Cameron of Lochiel. The road from Gairlochy to Loch Arkaig leads through the 'Dark Mile,' a grand avenue of beeches planted by Lochiel before joining the rebellion of 1745. Miss D. K. Broster's Jacobite trilogy—*The Flight of the Heron, The Gleam in the North*, and *The Dark Mile*—has the Great Glen as its principal setting, and in all three books much of the action takes place at 'Ardroy,' an imaginary spot on the equally imaginary 'Loch na h-Iolaire' in the mountains north of Loch Arkaig.

At Gairlochy vessels descend by two locks into the final section of the canal, which runs between the road and the River Lochy, passing the foot of Glen Loy. Full view of Ben Nevis, with the aluminium works at its base, and of the other mountains of Lochaber—a name that signifies the district at the mouth of the lochs. To the left, on the river bank, is Tor Castle, with a ruined stronghold of the Mackintoshes. From Banavie (accent on first syllable) the canal descends to the sea at Loch Linnhe (pronounced 'Linny'), 93 feet lower down, by Neptune's Staircase (a flight of eight locks) and the three Corpachy Locks. Near the point where the River Lochy joins Loch Linnhe are the ruins of Inverlochy Castle, with its sturdy round towers. The Battle of Inverlochy, at which Argyll and the Covenanters were defeated by Montrose in 1645, is described in Scott's *Legend of Montrose* and Neil Munro's *John Splendid*.

Fort William, situated at the head of Loch Linnhe and owing its name to a vanished fort rebuilt under William III, is one of the great tourist centres of the Highlands, with a busy railway, steamer, and motor-coach traffic. It is not an attractive town in itself, and almost the only building of interest is the West Highland Museum with its arts and crafts collection and its Jacobite relics.

The premier excursion from Fort William is, of course, to the top of *Ben Nevis* (pronounced 'Névvis'), the highest mountain in the British Isles—4,406 feet—a vast, bare mass of pink granite surmounted by grey porphyry and agglomerates. The ascent takes $2\frac{1}{4}$ hours on the average, the descent 2 hours; the up-and-down record from the post office at Fort William and back, 14 miles, is 2 hours 12 minutes. The ordinary route is by a road starting at the bridge over the River Nevis, at the foot of the beautiful Glen Nevis (youth hostel), and becoming a pony-track at the farm of Achintee. The route via the Allt a Mhuillin, a stream descending from the north flank of Ben Nevis, is much longer and very strenuous, but quite safe. The rock scenery on this side (the greatest line of inland cliffs in the country) is superb. Snow lies all the year.

The observatory and hotel on the summit are derelict. The view—an indicator is provided—is naturally of enormous extent, covering in the clearest weather a radius of 100 miles and including the town of Inverness and the coast of Ireland. A narrow *arête* connects Ben Nevis with its north-eastern neighbour, Carn Dearg (4,012 feet).

Two of the most attractive steamer trips on the west coast of Scotland can be made from Fort William in summer (each once a week), namely to Staffa and Iona, and to Loch Scavaig in Skye. Detailed descriptions of these all-day excursions will be found on pages 144 and 163 respectively.

Between Fort William and Oban non-motorists have a choice between various means of transport: (1) MacBrayne steamer, simplest and best, but sailing two or three times a week only, in summer; (2) bus to North Ballachulish, cross the ferry, and proceed by train; (3) by the Glasgow motor-coach via North Ballachulish, Kinlochleven, South Ballachulish, and Glencoe to Tyndrum, and thence to Oban by motor-coach or railway; or (4) railway all the way. The steamer descends the beautiful Loch Linnhe, passes through the Corran Narrows, and calls at Kentallen (for Ballachulish), at the mouth of Loch Leven, and at Lismore, a long, low island opposite Port Appin and the mouth of Loch Creran. Beyond Dunstaffnage Castle, at the mouth of Loch Etive (pronounced 'Éttiv'), it enters the Sound of Kerrera and soon arrives at Oban. The railway journey is a long and roundabout one, involving a change of station at Tyndrum or Crianlarich, but it has the advantage of traversing one of the wildest and most roadless parts of Scotland, the Moor of Rannoch.

If motoring from Fort William to Oban, you take the road that hugs the shore of Loch Linnhe as far as Corran and then turns inland via the village of Onich and the north shore of Loch Leven (pronounced 'Leéven') to North Ballachulish, 12 miles. To reach Ballachulish on the opposite side of the loch—which separates Inverness-shire from Argyllshire—you either take your car across by ferry, at a cost of 5s.–7s. 6d. (motor-cycle 2s.), or make a 19-mile detour by the road made partly by German prisoners of war round the loch. The factory of the

British Aluminium Co. at Kinlochleven, at the head of the loch, was started in 1909 for the production of aluminium by the Héroult process in electric furnaces. The necessary oxide of aluminium is received from a sister-factory at Burntisland in Fife. The turbines (35,500 h.p.) are fed with water by a pipe-line and a 3½-mile conduit from the Blackwater Reservoir in the hills above, which is 8 miles long and was formed by the construction of a dam 3,110 feet long and 85 feet high. The carbon electrodes necessary for the process are also made at Kinlochleven. The factory is connected by an electric railway with a pier in the loch. The ingot metal is dispatched to the company's rolling mills at Falkirk and at Milton and Warrington in England.

Ballachulish (pronounced 'Ballahoólish') is a slate-quarrying village at the foot of the horseshoe-shaped Ben Vair (3,362 feet), on the south shore of the loch and a mile or so east of the ferry. As R.L.S. wrote in *Kidnapped*: 'There was a good deal of ferrying . . . the sea in all this part running deep into the mountains and winding about their roots. It makes the country strong to hold and difficult to travel, but full of prodigious wild and dreadful prospects.' A monument near the Balla-chulish Hotel stands on the spot where 'James of the Glens' (James Stewart of Duror) was hanged after being convicted by a Campbell jury at Inveraray on the charge of shooting Colin Roy Campbell of Glenure, the 'Red Fox.' The mystery of the Appin Murder (14th May 1752), the story of which is told, with variations, in *Kidnapped*, has never been solved.

There are two roads from Ballachulish to Oban. The direct road (39 miles), accompanied all the way by the railway, runs west from the ferry along the shores of Loch Linnhe and through the district of Appin—a name that signifies 'abbey lands.' After a detour round the head of Loch Creran (pronounced 'Creéran'), it passes Barcaldine Castle and, where you return to the sea, a knoll thought to be the Beregonium of Ptolemy and the capital of the Pictish kings. Loch Etive is crossed by the railway bridge at Connel Ferry (page 143), for which a fee of 4s.–6s. is charged (motor-cycle 1s. 3d.).

The roundabout route from Ballachulish to Oban via

Tyndrum, however, should be chosen—although it is nearly twice as far, viz. 73 miles—because it takes you through *Glencoe*, one of the most awesome passes in Scotland—most impressive in stormy weather—and scene of perhaps the most dastardly crime in its blood-stained annals. The National Trust owns 12,800 acres here. In 1691, as a measure for the pacification of the Highlands after Killiecrankie, an order was issued that every rebel chief must take the oath of allegiance to William III before the end of the year or suffer the utmost extremity of the law. In the last days of December Alexander or MacIan Macdonald, chief of the sept of Macdonald of Glencoe, who had fought with Claverhouse in 1689, made a vain attempt to find a magistrate at Fort William to administer the oath, and finally persuaded Sir Colin Campbell to do so at Inveraray, but five days late. Through the contrivance of Sir John Dalrymple, Master (later first Earl) of Stair, joint Secretary of State, and John Campbell, first Earl of Breadalbane, Macdonald's submission was ignored, and the extirpation of the 'damnable sept, the worst in all the Highlands,' was decreed. On 1st February a party of government troops, under Captain Campbell of Glenlyon, arrived at Glencoe with orders for quartering, and until the 13th they lived on friendly terms with the unsuspecting Macdonalds. The massacre began at 5 a.m. in the house of the chief, who was shot in his bed. Thirty-eight people in all were butchered, including two women and several children. The rest, about a hundred and fifty men, women, and children, fled into the mountains in a snowstorm, in which many of them perished.

The road from Ballachulish through Glencoe to Tyndrum (34½ miles), with bus service, has been completely remade, and the old road has in parts been replaced by a new highway, a section of the through route to Inverness. Charabancs ply in the season from Ballachulish Ferry Station to the top of the pass, or the Glasgow motor-coach may be used as far as Tyndrum (cf. page 139), but the most interesting trip is by motor-coach over the pass and then west down Glen Etive to the head of Loch Etive, whence a motor-launch takes passengers down the loch to Achnacloich, the rest of the journey to Oban being accomplished by train. You enter Glencoe at Garnach. About 300 yards to the left of the old road, near the Bridge of Coe, there is a monument commemorating the massacre. Mounds and scattered stones indicate the sites of the Macdonalds' cottages. On the left rises the Pap of Glencoe (2,430 feet), followed by the porphyry walls of Aonach Eagach (3,168 feet). On the right are the 'Three Sisters of Glencoe,' or 'Faith, Hope, and Charity': Aonach Dubh (2,849 feet), Gearr Aonach, and Ben Fhada (3,497 feet). Aonach Dubh has a cleft known as Ossian's Cave—Ossian is supposed to have been born on the shores of the little Loch Triochatan. Farther up the valley, on the left, is a ledge known as the Study (Scots for anvil), whence the best general view of the glen is obtained— 'that nightmare of gulf and eminence, of gash, and peaks afloat upon swirling mists . . . haunted for ever with wailing airs and rumours, ghosts calling in the deeps of dusk and melancholy, legends of horror and remorse.' —*John Splendid*.

Beyond the top of the pass (1,011 feet) the road descends, with the 'Shepherds of Etive' on the right—Buchaille Etive Beg (3,129 feet) and Buchaille Etive Mor (3,345 feet), the latter with famous rock-climbs, 'Crowberry Ridge' and 'The Chasm.' Beyond the point where the rough road down Glen Etive diverges stands the Kingshouse Hotel, on the old road, well known to climbers and anglers. It lies on the west edge of the Moor of Rannoch. The old road crosses Black Mount, one of the largest deer forests in Scotland, but the new road runs farther east, through a string of lochs and lochans, keeping west of Loch Bà and east of Loch Tulla. We reach the railway at Bridge of Orchy, where Ben Douran (3,523 feet) rises on the left. A short cut to Dalmally here diverges on the right down Glen Orchy, and motorists bound for Oban should make use of it. The new road from Bridge of Orchy to Tyndrum keeps to the west side of the valley.

At Tyndrum (pronounced 'Tynedrum') you are back in Perthshire for the moment. For Oban (38½ miles)— railway and motor-coaches available—you turn right and descend Glen Lochy, with Ben Lui (3,708 feet) on the left. Beyond the scattered village of Dalmally the road crosses the Orchy, and then the Strae. Kilchurn Castle (pronounced 'Kilhoórn'), a stately ruin at the head of Loch Awe, was a stronghold of the Campbells of Breadalbane. It was built in 1440 and enlarged in 1615. The inaccessibility of this and other fastnesses of the Campbells in the Loch Awe district gave rise to their proud boast: 'It's a far cry to Lochow!' Loch Awe Hotel, Station, and Pier are passed (cf. page 144), and then the Falls of Cruachan (accent on first syllable). This is the best point from which to ascend Ben Cruachan (3,689 feet), the dark mountain that towers above, three hours' stiff climbing, but rewarded by a wonderful view. 'Cruachan' was the rallying word of the Campbells.

The River Awe, accompanied by the road and the railway, then passes through the magnificent *Pass of Brander*. Taynuilt (pronounced 'Taynoólt'), beyond the pass, is a short distance from the south shore of Loch Etive, beside which the road runs farther on. At Connel Ferry, near its mouth, the loch is crossed by the railway bridge of the Ballachulish line, said to be the largest cantilever bridge in Europe after the Forth Bridge, of which it is a copy. The ebbing tide as it issues from the loch over a rocky bar forms rapids called the Falls of Lora, quite impressive at spring tides. Farther on a cart road on the right—cars not admitted—leads to Dunstaffnage Castle, which commands the entry to the loch. The Castle, in its present form, dates for the most part from the fifteenth century, and was ruined by fire in 1810, but Dunstaffnage was the seat of government of the Scots of Dalriada (Argyllshire) from the early sixth century until they were united with the Picts in the year 843. The Hereditary Keeper of the Castle is the Duke of Argyll, and Campbell of Dunstaffnage the Hereditary Captain. The chapel is a rare specimen of early-thirteenth-century architecture, notable for the beauty and richness of its detail. Among the ruins are two old guns, one of them raised from the Spanish galleon in Tobermory Bay. Flora Macdonald was kept here for ten days on her way to London as a state prisoner.

Oban, the principal town of the Lorne district of Argyllshire, is the most popular summer resort in the Western Highlands and the nodal point of a vast amount of tourist traffic by road, rail, and steamer. A century ago it was only a fishing hamlet. Its beautiful little land-locked bay, protected by the low island of Kerrera (accent on last syllable), is much frequented by yachts, and Oban is the headquarters of the Royal Highland Yacht Club. The best general view of the town is from the meagre remains of Dunollie Castle, to the north, which are adjoined by the residence of the Chief of Clan MacDougall. On the way thither you pass the Clach a Choin or Dog Stone, to which Fingal used to tie his dog Bran. On the hill above the town are the remains of an unfinished hydro and of McCaig's Tower, a circular structure that was intended to be a view tower, museum, and art gallery, but was likewise abandoned. Motor-boats ply to Ganavan, the best bathing beach, and to Kerrera. The Glencruitten golf-course is excellent.

The variety of excursions that can be made from Oban is almost bewildering. A favourite round is by motor-coach via the Pass of Melfort and Carnassary Castle (cf. page 87) to Ford, at the south end of Loch Awe, and thence by motor-launch on *Loch Awe*, a narrow freshwater lake, 24 miles in length, the scenery of which increases in grandeur as one progresses from the head towards the foot —an idiosyncrasy ascribed to the fact that its outflow was originally at the south end instead of into Loch Etive as it now is. A fair road, with some gates, skirts its east bank, leading to Dalmally (27 miles). On the same bank are the ruined castles of Fincharn and Ard-chonell, once belonging to the Macdonalds and the Campbells respectively. On the opposite side of the loch is the state forest of Inverliver. Towards the north end of the lake are the piers and hotels of Taychreggan, on the west bank, and Portsonachan, on the east, connected by a ferry (not for cars). From Loch Awe Pier, at the north end of the lake, you return to Oban by railway.

One excursion from Oban that must on no account be omitted is that to Staffa and Iona by MacBrayne steamer, a magnificent all-day trip costing 35s. The steamer—daily (except Sundays) in summer, in winter to Tobermory only—describes a circuit round *Mull*, an Argyllshire island, notable for its grand mountains and its broken coast-line, the length of which is estimated at 250 miles. Few visitors will agree with Dr Johnson's opinion of it

as 'a most dolorous country.' Tobermory and other
points are called at by the steamer, which every other day
encircles the island in the opposite direction to that
described below.

As it leaves Oban Bay the steamer passes an obelisk
erected on the north end of Kerrera as a memorial to
David Hutcheson, founder of the steamer services on
which the West Coast is now so dependent. Duart Point,
on Mull, opposite the isle of Lismore, bears a tower built
in honour of William Black, the novelist, much of whose
Macleod of Dare is set in Mull and off its coasts. Duart
Castle, on the point, has recently been rebuilt, and is now
again the seat of the Chief of the Macleans. Ben Nevis
comes into sight at the head of Loch Linnhe. The Sound
of Mull, 2 miles wide and 20 miles long, divides Mull
from Morven. On a promontory of the mainland are the
ruins of Ardtornish Castle, once the headquarters of the
Lords of the Isles, a proud title borne by the Macdonalds,
Earls of Ross, from about 1350 to 1500. Scott's poem,
The Lord of the Isles, opens in the 'rugged halls' of Ardtornish. Just beyond it is the mouth of Loch Aline (pronounced 'Allin'), meaning 'beautiful loch.' Behind Salen
(pronounced 'Saálen'), on Mull, rises Ben More (3,169 feet),
the highest mountain in the island. Aros Castle (pronounced 'Aáross'), a ruin at the entrance to Salen Bay,
was another fortress of the Lords of the Isles. Tobermory
—the name means 'Well of St Mary'—was founded in
1788 by the British Fishery Society, and is the chief place
in Mull. It has three hotels. The *Florida*, one of the
vessels of the Spanish Armada, sank in Tobermory Bay,
and attempts are still made from time to time to salvage
its treasure.

After rounding Ardmore Point the steamer leaves the
sheltered waters of the Sound. On the right you see the
mouth of Loch Sunart and the south coast of the peninsula
of Ardnamurchan ('Cape of the Great Seas'), with the
ruins of Mingary Castle (accent on first syllable, with
hard 'g'), once the stronghold of Clan MacIan, near
Kilchoan. Ardnamurchan Point, with its lighthouse, is
the most westerly point of the Scottish mainland. Farther
north are the islands of Muck, Eigg with its precipitous
Scuir, and Rum with its lofty mountains; behind them the

Coolins in Skye are discernible on a clear day. On the west, near at hand, are Coll and Tiree. The steamer then passes between the small Treshnish Isles on the right, the last but one of which is the 'Dutchman's Cap,' and Gometra, Ulva, and Little Colonsay (pronounced 'Cóllonsay'), on the left, with their basaltic cliffs. Beyond the latter opens Loch na Keal, a haunt of seals. It nearly bisects Mull and is familiar as the Lochgyle of Campbell's poem, *Lord Ullin's Daughter*.

> 'Now who be ye, would cross Lochgyle,
>   This dark and stormy water?'
> 'O, I'm the chief of Ulva's isle,
>   And this Lord Ullin's daughter.'

In the mouth of the loch is the islet of Inchkenneth, where Johnson and Boswell were entertained by Sir Allan Maclean and spent 'the most agreeable Sunday he had ever passed.'

Staffa is an uninhabited islet of columnar basalt, formed by volcanic action, and is 1 mile long and about ¼ mile wide. Weather permitting, the steamer passengers are landed in a lifeboat from Gometra so that they may inspect Fingal's Cave, one of the marvels of the world for its dimensions, its fantastic columnar formations, and its beautiful colouring. The arch at the entrance is 66 feet in height, and the cave is 227 feet deep. The first visitor from the outside world was Sir Joseph Banks, who heard of it by chance in 1772. There are other caves on Staffa, but no time is allowed for their inspection.

> The pillared vestibule,
> Expanding yet precise, the roof embowed,
> Might seem designed to humble Man, when proud
> Of his best workmanship by plan and tool
>
>   WORDSWORTH.

Iona, where passengers land again for a stay of an hour and a half, is a barren, treeless island, 3 miles long, 1½ wide, and situated about 1 mile from the south-west extremity of Mull. Formerly called I or Hy, Ioua Insula (whence, by a copyist's error, Iona), and Icolmkill, it is famous as the cradle of Scottish Christianity, for in the year 563 St Columba landed here from Ireland with twelve companions, established a monastery, and used the island as a base for his evangelistic journeys. Though repeatedly burnt by the Norsemen, the monastery was refounded again and again until its destruction in 1561. It has once again been rebuilt. There is a hotel on the island, which has a population of about 230 and belongs to the Duke of Argyll. A night or two might well be spent here. Articles made of green Iona marble find a ready sale as souvenirs.

The guide conducts visitors first to the remains of an Austin nunnery, founded in 1203. Then, passing Maclean's Cross, a beautiful work of the fifteenth century, you are led to the Cemetery and St Oran's Chapel, the oldest building on the island, possibly built by Queen Margaret in 1074. Down to the eleventh century the cemetery was the usual burial-place of the Scottish kings and chieftains—including Duncan and Macbeth—and a large number of early sculptured tombstones have survived. The Cathedral, of red granite and recently restored, was rebuilt by Reginald, Lord of the Isles, in 1203, as the church of the Benedictine monastery. The north transept and adjoining choir-wall are assigned to the late eleventh or early twelfth century, the north choir-chapel and most of the cloister buildings to some uncertain middle period, the rest of the church to the late fifteenth or early sixteenth century. Partly built into the west walk of the cloister are the remains of a small chamber which some maintain to be the original cell of St Columba. In front of the Cathedral stands the celebrated Iona Cross, dedicated to St Martin of Tours and decorated with Runic carvings and figures of the Holy Family, David, and Daniel. It dates possibly from the ninth or tenth century. The tracery of the tower windows of the Cathedral and, inside, the carved capitals, the choir-arches, and the abbots' tombs are noteworthy. The old stone protected by a cage beneath the east window is 'St Columba's Pillow.' As one leaves the island the inevitable quotation from Dr Johnson rises to one's lips: 'That man is little to be envied . . . whose piety would not grow warmer among the ruins of Iona.'

On leaving Iona the steamer threads its way through an archipelago of islets and rocks. It was on one of the Torran Rocks, farther on to the right, that David Balfour, in *Kidnapped*, was wrecked. On the left is the island of

Erraid or Earraid—'a jumble of rocks with heather in
among'—on which he was cast ashore and where he lived
on shellfish for a hundred hours before he discovered that
at low tide he could wade across to the Ross of Mull.
'This island,' wrote Stevenson, 'has done me yeoman's
service.   First it was the backbone of *The Merry Men*'
[under the name of Eilean Aros], 'then it made a tolerable
figure in *Kidnapped*.'

On the way back to Oban by the Firth of Lorne you
have a fine series of views of the south coast of Mull,
some of the cliffs of which rise to the height of a thousand
feet.   On the right are the 'Isles of the Sea,' or Garvelloch
Isles, and behind them:

> Scarba's isle, whose tortured shore
> Still rings to Corrievreken's roar.

Scarba rises to 1,470 feet and is noted for its herd of red
deer.   Then Luing, Seil, and finally Kerrera.

An opportunity of seeing something of the Hebrides
(page 168) is afforded by the MacBrayne mail-steamer
that sails thrice weekly from Oban—calling at Tobermory
—for Coll, Tiree, Castlebay in Barra, and Lochboisdale in
South Uist, returning to Oban on the following day.   Coll
and Tiree are flat, wind-swept islands, with an inn apiece.

TOUR IX: OBAN TO FORT WILLIAM VIA
LOCH TAY

Total distance by road: about 280 miles.

INVERARAY — CRIANLARICH — LOCH TAY — KENMORE —ABER-
FELDY — SCHIEHALLION — LOCH RANNOCH — STRUAN —
LOCH LAGGAN — TULLOCH — GLEN ROY.

THIS tour is a roundabout route designed to complete
your hitherto somewhat superficial survey of the Southern
Highlands. The first stage is from Oban, by the way
you came, to Dalmally (26 miles). The railway and the
Glasgow motor-coach go on direct from Dalmally to
Crianlarich (16½ miles), by Glen Lochy and Tyndrum.

Motorists at least—there is a mail-coach service also—
should turn south at Dalmally, and reach Crianlarich
via Inveraray and Arrochar, a long detour that means
an extra 40 miles. This road, which has loose stretches
here and there, with short, sharp hills, passes, 1½ miles out
from Dalmally, a monument to Duncan Ban Macintyre,
the 'Burns of the Highlands.' The view of Loch Awe
and Ben Cruachan from this point is superb. The road
descends to Loch Awe, but at Cladich you bear left and by
a series of steep ascents attain the top of the pass (673 feet),
whence you obtain another splendid view.

Then down the wooded Glen Aray to *Inveraray* (pronounced and often spelt 'Inverary'), the attractively
planned little county town of Argyllshire, long famous as
the centre of the Campbell power. The town was moved
to its present site in 1745 to make way for the Castle,
seat of the Duke of Argyll (Mac Cailean Mhor, Chief of
Clan Campbell). It is beautifully situated on Loch Fyne
(a sea loch) and is surrounded by some of the finest woods
in Scotland. The Town Cross, which came from Iona,
and the beech avenue leading to the Episcopalian Church
should be seen. The Castle and its grounds are open to
visitors from May to October, except on Tuesdays and
Wednesdays.

Neil Munro was born and buried in the town, and 'Inneraora,' Glen Shira, and the surrounding district play a considerable part in his novels and poems. 'Shira Glen, Shira Glen! . . . There, at the foot of my father's house, where the winding river, and north and south the brown hills, split asunder by God's goodness, to give a sample of His bounty. Maam, Elrigmore and Elrigbeg, Kilblaan, and Ben Bhuidhe—their steep sides hung with cattle, and below crowded the reeking homes of tacksman and cottar; the burns poured hurriedly to the flat beneath their borders of hazels and ashes; to the south, the fresh water we call Dubh Loch, flapping with ducks and fringed with shelisters or water-flags and bulrush, and farther off the Cowal hills; to the north, the wood of Drimlee and the wild pass the red Macgregors sometimes took for a back-road to our cattle-folds in cloud of night and darkness.'—*John Splendid.*

The road from Inveraray to Arrochar (22 miles), served by the Glasgow motor-coach, hugs the shore of Loch Fyne, passing the foot of Glen Shira and the ruined tower of Dundarave, which is dated 1598 and is the original of Neil Munro's *Doom Castle.* The road then rounds the head of the loch, but at Cairndow you turn left to tackle the Rest and be Thankful Hill. This is one of the stiffest climbs in Scotland, for the road rises from sea-level to 860 feet, and sinks again to sea-level—and all within a space of 9 miles, with the steepest parts (1 in 7) compressed within $2\frac{1}{2}$ miles, and a hairpin bend at the top. From the top of the pass, where there is a stone seat inscribed 'Rest and be Thankful,' you have a fine view down the wild Glen Croe, over the whole length of the road you have yet to traverse. As you descend the glen the Cobbler is on the left. On reaching the shore of Loch Long you turn left and soon arrive at Arrochar, at the head of the sea loch, where Dunbartonshire is entered. Cf. page 84.

For the next stage, one of the finest on the whole tour —to Crianlarich, 18 miles, with railway and bus available —you cross the isthmus to Tarbet on Loch Lomond, and turn left along the west bank of the lake—with Ben Vorlich (3,092 feet) towering on the left—to Ardlui, at the head of the lake. As you ascend Glen Falloch, side by

side with the tumbling river, you enter Perthshire and
pass the Falls of Falloch. Ben More is conspicuous on
the right, and the view behind you is glorious.

Crianlarich consists of little more than two railway
stations (change here for Killin), a hotel, and a church.
On the east rises the huge mass of Ben More (3,845 feet),
one of the best viewpoints in Scotland; the mountain
behind it is Stobinian (3,821 feet). For Killin, 13½ miles,
you turn right by the switchback road down Glen Dochart,
in company with the railway, passing Loch Dochart, with
its ruined castle, and Loch Tubhair. Luib (pronounced
'Loo-ib'), a tiny hamlet, is an angling resort. Farther on
the Callander road diverges on the right.

Killin (accent on second syllable), situated near the
head of Loch Tay, at the influx of the Dochart and the
Lochay, is a pretty village with many thatched cottages
and an Alpine air. It derives its name from Cil Fhinn,
the cell of Fingal, who is supposed to be buried beneath
an upright stone in a neighbouring field. Finlarig Castle,
between the village and the loch, was once a seat of the
Earls of Breadalbane (pronounced 'Breddáwlbăn'). The
river-island of Inch Bhuidh was the burial-place of the
MacNabs. The Breadalbane Vine, at Kinnell, is one of
the largest in Europe. The scenery of the district is very
striking, and excursions can be made to Glen Lochay,
Glen Lyon, etc.

Loch Tay, a grand lake, 15 miles long and about
¾ mile wide, is famous for its salmon. The salmon-
fishing is preserved, but the trout are free. Steamers
ply normally from Killin Pier to Kenmore at the other
end. There is no railway, but roads with bus services
skirt either bank. The main road—16½ miles to Kenmore
—on the north side of the lake, passes Lawers, at the
foot of Ben Lawers (3,984 feet), the ascent of which is
quite a simple matter, but takes five hours there and back.
There is a superb view from the top, and the slopes are
noted for gentians, saxifrages, moss campion, and other
mountain flora. Ben Lawers, with 8,000 acres, was
acquired by the National Trust in 1950.

Kenmore is a model village situated at the point where
the River Tay flows out of the loch. On an island in the
loch are the ruins of a priory founded by Alexander I in

1122. Taymouth Castle was built in the nineteenth century for the Earl of Breadalbane, and has a splendid park. Motorists who fancy themselves at hill-climbing may try the Amulree road, which rises from 360 feet to 1,672 feet in 3½ miles and has a rough surface, bad turns, and gradients up to 1 in 4⅓. The best excursion, however, is to Glen Lyon, which is said to be the longest glen in Scotland (30 miles) and has grand scenery in its lower part. At its mouth is Fortingal, with a churchyard yew that is claimed to be the oldest tree in Europe. Beyond Bridge of Balgie, 18 miles from Kenmore—a mail-bus runs thus far from Aberfeldy—the road degenerates into a cart track, petering out at Loch Lyon. The only exit from the glen is by a rough road leading south from Bridge of Balgie to Loch Tay (10 miles) and attaining a height of 1,805 feet—1 in 10 up, 1 in 7 down.

Buses run from Kenmore along the south bank of the Tay to the railhead at *Aberfeldy* (6 miles), a nice little town, thronged in summer. The quaint bridge over the Tay was built by General Wade in 1733, and by it is a cairn commemorating the mustering of the Black Watch in 1740. To the south is a rocky gorge with old firs and the pretty Falls of Moness (little water in summer), sung by Burns.

> The braes ascend, like lofty wa's,
> The foaming stream deep-roaring fa's,
> O'erhung wi' fragrant spreading shaws,
> The birks of Aberfeldy.

The direct road from Aberfeldy to Kinloch Rannoch (18 miles) is by the Strath of Appin, but travellers dependent on public conveyances will have to make a detour by rail or bus via Ballinluig and Pitlochry, whence a bus runs to Kinloch Rannoch. Motorists cross the River Tay at Aberfeldy, turn left at Weem—the Rock of Weem (800 feet) is a good viewpoint—and pass Castle Menzies (pronounced 'Mingies'), which is dated 1561 and has a lovely park. You leave Dull, a village with an old market cross, to the right, and a bridge over the River Lyon to the left. On the farther side of the latter are the ivy-clad ruins of Comrie Castle. Then up the valley of the Keltney Burn—fairly steep, 1 in 13—with Garth Castle, built by the 'Wolf of Badenoch,' on the other bank. The graceful cone of Schiehallion comes into view on the left.

The main road ascends to a point 1,262 feet above sea-level, where it commands a panorama hard to beat from any motoring road, and then sinks down to join the road from Pitlochry to Kinloch Rannoch at Tummel Bridge, 8 miles from Loch Tummel.

It is better, however, to take the delightful side-road on the left. This leads over the Braes of Foss, or north shoulder of Schiehallion, affording a glorious prospect and ending in a steep descent into Kinloch Rannoch, 1 in 12, with bad turns.

In recent years the scenery of the Tummel valley has been transformed by the schemes of the North of Scotland Hydro-Electric Board. Lochs Eigheach, Rannoch, Tummel, Ericht, Garry, and Seilich have been dammed, and six power stations have been built in the Tummel valley: Gaur, Rannoch, Tummel, Errochty, Clunie, and Pitlochry. Of these Rannoch, on the north bank of Loch Rannoch, is fed by a tunnel from Lochs Ericht, Garry, and Seilich; and Errochty, on the north bank of Loch Tummel, by a tunnel from a new reservoir created by damming Glen Errochty. The total annual output of the power stations is estimated at 600 million units of electricity.

Kinloch Rannoch means 'the place at the head of Loch Rannoch,' but as a matter of fact is situated at its foot or east end. *Schiehallion* (3,547 feet), perhaps meaning the 'Maiden's Pap,' is the most symmetrical of Scottish mountains, and its quartz peak may be climbed in two to three hours. *Loch Rannoch* is a fine sheet of water, 10 miles long by 1½ miles wide. There are roads on both of its wooded banks, that on the south bank traversing the Black Wood of Rannoch, with its grand old firs. The main road, with bus service, follows the north bank and ends at Rannoch Station, 16½ miles, near Loch Laidon or Lydoch, where it ends in a cul-de-sac in the middle of the Moor of Rannoch—Rannoch means fern. This, the largest and most desolate moor in all Scotland, has a charm of its own and brilliant colouring in summer.

On the eastward journey from Kinloch Rannoch motorists should take the first turning on the left, a short cut to Struan. There is a rare bus by this route, otherwise bus travellers must proceed past Loch Tummel

F

to the Bridge of Garry, where they join the main bus
and railway route via the Pass of Killiecrankie and Blair
Atholl.   The direct road from Kinloch Rannoch to Struan
(13 miles) ascends to 1,089 feet, with a gradient of 1 in
12 and a fine view of Schiehallion, and then drops down
with a similar gradient to Trinafour in Glen Errochty.

At *Struan*, which lies at the foot of the glen, you turn
left and follow the main road and railway to Newtonmore
(30½ miles), as described on pages 126 and 127.   Inverness-
shire is entered at the Pass of Drumochter.   Motorists save
10 miles by turning left at Dalwhinnie and taking a fair
highland road that ascends to 1,294 feet and joins the
main road at Laggan Bridge.

At Newtonmore you can pick up the bus that runs
from Kingussie to Tulloch (there is no railway).   The
road—from Newtonmore to Fort William, 46 miles—first
ascends the upper valley of the Spey, a very pretty section
of the route.   Cluny Castle, on the right, was the seat of
Cluny Macpherson, Chief of Clan Chattan.   The Spey
is crossed at Laggan Bridge.   [A road, now derelict and
quite impracticable for vehicles, continues up the Spey
valley and crosses the Pass of Corrieyairack (2,507 feet)
to Glen Tarff and Fort Augustus—a classic 24-mile walk.
General Wade constructed it in 1735—it is Neil Munro's
New Road—and no other road in these islands rises to over
2,500 feet.   Prince Charlie marched south this way on
28th August 1745.]   The main road mounts Strath Mashie,
overlooking the junction of which with Glen Spey is one
of the best-preserved hill-forts in Scotland—Dundalair,
with thick walls of slate.

Then down again to the hotel at the head of *Loch
Laggan*, a wooded lake 7 miles long and ½ mile wide, with
free trout-fishing   Great alterations, however, have been
made hereabouts in connection with the Lochaber Power
Scheme and the aluminium works at Fort William.   The
waters of the upper Spey are diverted into the River
Pattack and thence into Loch Laggan, which has been
lengthened by 4 miles through the construction of a dam
(700 feet long, 160 feet high) across Glen Spean.   A tunnel,
2¾ miles long, connects Loch Laggan with Loch Treig
(pronounced 'Treeg'), the level of which has been raised
38 feet by the erection of a dam near Tulloch at its north

end. Finally a 15-mile pressure tunnel conveys the water under the slopes of Ben Nevis to the head of the pipe-line above the power house at Fort William.

The road joins the railway at *Tulloch* in Glen Spean— the station lies off the road, to the left—whence you can proceed to Fort William by bus or train. Below Tulloch road and railway pass through the impressive Gorge of Achluachrach. At Roy Bridge all geologists will digress northwards by a rough road to a point 4 miles up *Glen Roy* in order to see its famous Parallel Roads—three distinct terraces extending along both flanks of the valley at corresponding elevations. To quote Sir Archibald Geikie's *The Scenery of Scotland*: 'Each of them is a shelf or terrace cut by the shore-waters of a lake that once filled Glen Roy. The highest is of course the oldest, and those beneath it were formed in succession as the waters of the lake sank. . . . Until Agassiz suggested the idea of a dam of glacier-ice the great difficulty in the way of understanding how a lake could ever have filled those valleys, was the entire absence of any relic of the barrier that must have kept back the water.' There are similar formations in some of the neighbouring valleys.

The River Spean is very pretty below Spean Bridge, and a magnificent mountain-view, with Ben Nevis towering on the left, is disclosed. As you approach Fort William you pass the works of the British Aluminium Co. Operations for the manufacture of aluminium in the electric furnace were started here in 1930. The turbines in the power house develop 120,000 h.p. Supplies of the necessary oxide of aluminium are received in tank wagons from the Burntisland factory. Dispatch of the ingot metal can be made either by railway or from a pier in Loch Linnhe, connected with the factory by a private railway. The employees are housed in the model village of Inverlochy. Permission can be given to inspect the power stations at Fort William, Foyers, and Kinlochleven, but in no case can the aluminium-producing side be visited.

TOUR X: FORT WILLIAM TO SKYE AND THE HEBRIDES, AND BACK TO INVERNESS

Total distance by road (excluding the Hebrides): about 500 miles.

GLENFINNAN—MALLAIG—KYLE OF LOCHALSH—SKYE—LOCH CORUISK—THE COOLINS—PORTREE—THE STORR—THE QUIRAING — DUNVEGAN — THE OUTER HEBRIDES — LEWIS — STORNAWAY — CALLERNISH — HARRIS — NORTH UIST — ST KILDA—BENBECULA—SOUTH UIST—BARRA—LOCH CARRON — GARVE — STRATHPEFFER — DINGWALL — FORTROSE —BEAULY—GLEN AFFRIC.

BOTH for motorists and non-motorists the usual gateway to Skye is Kyle of Lochalsh. There is no regular bus service to Kyle—although there are frequent motor-coach trips to Skye from Inverness and even from Edinburgh—but there is a railway thither from Inverness (via Dingwall) and there is also a line from Fort William to Mallaig, whence there is a daily steamer connection to Skye.

The road from Fort William to Mallaig (47 miles) closely followed all the way by the railway, is almost unmatched for its combination of mountain, moor, loch, glen, and coast scenery. For this reason, and for the Prince Charlie associations, motorists should certainly undertake the trip to Mallaig and back, although the road is a cul-de-sac. From a motoring point of view it is fair as far as Glenfinnan (bus service), then narrow and tortuous, with short, sharp hills (up to 1 in 6) and long stony stretches. You cross the River Lochy outside Fort William and then, at Banavie, the Caledonian Canal. To the right, between the road and Kilmallie Church, beyond Corpach, is an obelisk to Colonel John Cameron of Fassiefern, who fell at Quatre Bras:

> And wild and high the 'Camerons' gathering' rose!
> The war-note of Lochiel . . .

The view of Ben Nevis, behind you, is superb. For 8 miles the road then hugs the north bank of Loch Eil (pronounced 'Eel'), a salt-water arm of Loch Linnhe.

[From the head of Loch Eil a road diverging on the left through a gate returns along the south bank and then skirts the west shore of Loch Linnhe to Inverscaddle Bay and Ardgour, 35 miles from Fort William. Unless you prefer the Corran–Ardgour ferry (motor-car 5s.–7s. 6d.), this is the only vehicular approach—and a very rough, winding, hilly one, with numerous gates—to the remote and lovely Argyllshire districts of Ardgour, Sunart, Ardnamurchan, and Morven. Seven miles beyond Ardgour, at Inversanda, the road forks: left for Lochaline and Drimnin, on the Sound of Mull, 32 and 42 miles from Ardgour; right, up Glen Tarbert, to Strontian (pronounced 'Strontećan'), at the head of Loch Sunart ('Soónărt'), a grand sea-loch. A bus runs daily from Ardgour to Strontian, Salen, and Acharacle. The element strontium was first detected by Cruikshank in 1767 in strontianite, a mineral found in the lead-mines here. The road goes on along the shore of the loch to Salen (pronounced 'Saalen'), 25 miles from Ardgour. Thence a road leads west to Kilchoan (19 miles) in Ardnamurchan, and another north to Acharacle (accent on second syllable), and Loch Moidart (8½ miles). In connection with the Loch Shiel steamer a mail-car runs from Acharacle to Salen and Kilchoan.]

After leaving Loch Eil you have a magnificent view as you descend to *Glenfinnan* at the head of Loch Shiel, past the monument (now vested in the National Trust) erected in 1815 where Prince Charlie raised his father's, James VIII's, standard on 19th August 1745, at a rally of the Cameron and Macdonald clans under Lochiel and Tullibardine. The railway viaduct, with its twenty-one arches, was erected in 1898 and is stated to be the earliest concrete structure of its kind. A steamer plies daily on Loch Shiel, a lonely, roadless, freshwater lake, 18 miles long and 1 mile wide, with romantic scenery. It divides Argyllshire from Inverness-shire, and at its south-west end is Acharacle. At the narrows you pass Eilean Fhionain, the 'Isle of the Dead,' with a ruined chapel and a burial ground.

Beyond Glenfinnan the road rises to 400 feet and thereafter is one of the trickiest roads in Scotland. Loch Eilt, with pretty islets at its farther end, is next passed, the road hugging its north bank for 4 miles and the railway its south bank. The sea is reached at the head of Loch Ailort (pronounced 'Éye-lort'), on the south side of which rises Roshven, otherwise known as Fros-Bheinn (2,876 feet). The seascapes are amazingly beautiful from this point onwards: silvery sands, grey rocks, saffron tangle-weed, and broad panoramas of island-studded sea.

The next sea-loch is Loch nan Uamh or 'Loch of the Caves.' On 25th July 1745 Prince Charlie landed at Borradale, on the north shore of the loch, from a French frigate, *La Doutelle*. He was taken off at the same spot by *L'Heureux* fourteen months later, on 20th September 1746, having spent the five months since Culloden as a fugitive in the Highlands and the Hebrides, with a price of £30,000 on his head. In the course of his wanderings he passed through Borradale twice, sailing thence for Benbecula on 26th April and landing there from Skye on 10th July.

Arisaig overlooks Loch nan Cilltean, the entrance to which is guarded by seal-haunted islands. Eigg, with its Scuir, is conspicuous out at sea. The road then runs between the sea and a flat and fertile countryside. Rum, with its four pyramidal peaks, and the Coolins in Skye come into view. In Mr L. A. G. Strong's own words: 'The setting for *The Brothers* and *The Jealous Ghost* is the country between Arisaig and Morar. Aeneas's house in *The Brothers* is actually Camus Darach ("The Bay of the Oaks"), 4 miles from Arisaig and 2½ miles from Morar. The house at which the Macraes are supposed to live is at Cross, on the headland of Ru' Achaid Mhor above the burn. The other places will be easily recognised on a map of the district. The same for *The Jealous Ghost*.'

The short River Morar, which is next crossed, is the outlet of the freshwater Loch Morar, which, with a depth of over 1,000 feet, is the deepest hole in Europe. Twelve miles long, it is almost entirely surrounded by mountains and is studded with islets at its west end. There is a small hydro-electric scheme here, which has raised the level of the loch by 8 feet. There are short but stiff 1 in 6 gradients on the road near Morar Station.

Mallaig, with a good hotel, is the terminus of the road and the railway. It is a small fishing port at the south

entrance to Loch Nevis (pronounced 'Névvis') and, though
not attractive in itself, is a headquarters for the exploration—by boat, for there are practically no other roads in
this area—of two of the grandest and remotest sea-lochs
in the Highlands: Loch Nevis ('Loch of Heaven') and
Loch Hourn ('Loch of Hell').   Between the two lies the
mountainous district of Knoydart ('k' silent), which
culminates in Ladhar Beinn (3,343 feet).   There is an
inn at Inverie, on the north shore of Loch Nevis.

A MacBrayne steamer sails daily all the year round
from Mallaig through the Sound of Sleat to Kyle of
Lochalsh, and thence to Raasay and to Portree in Skye.
Thrice a week it calls *en route* at Armadale, in Skye, and
at Glenelg, on the mainland, which is connected with
Kylerhea in Skye by a mail motor-boat.

Once weekly in summer there is an all-day steamer
excursion from Mallaig to Loch Scavaig (page 163), giving
an opportunity to view the grandest scenery in Skye.
Passengers are landed in boats to see Loch Coruisk.

The steamer sailing weekly all the year round from
Mallaig to the Outer Hebrides calls on the way at the
'Small Isles' of Eigg, Rum, and Canna, the voyage back
from which can, in summer, be made on the same day.
The remarkable feature of Eigg (pronounced 'Egg') is its
Scuir (1,289 feet), a 'giant's causeway' of black columnar
pitchstone placed on a ridge 900 feet above the sea.
Eigg was the scene of a terrible deed in the sixteenth
century, when the whole of the Macdonald population,
200 men, women, and children, took refuge in the Cave of
Francis from the raiding Macleods of Skye, who suffocated
them by kindling a huge fire at the mouth of the cave.
Muck—'Isle of Swine,' i.e. porpoises—is not touched at.
Rum is almost entirely composed of splendid mountains,
the highest of which are Askival (2,659 feet), Ashval, and
Allival, and is preserved as a deer forest.   Canna, a sanctuary for sea birds, is noted for its Compass Hill, which,
owing to the large proportion of iron in its basaltic rock,
has the property of affecting ships' compasses.

Motorists bound from Fort William to Skye follow the
Inverness road along the Caledonian Canal as far as
Invermoriston on Loch Ness, 39 miles (cf. page 136).

[On the way to Invermoriston the opportunity may be taken to visit Glen Garry, the narrow but well-made road through which diverges westwards at Invergarry, on Loch Oich. Loch Garry, the Tomdoun Hotel, and Loch Quoich (pronounced 'Koych') are passed, and the road ends at the head of Loch Hourn (26 miles), a sublime spot, but a breakneck 1 in 6 descent. On the way back you can turn left at the Tomdoun Hotel and take a short cut by a rough road that climbs (1 in 17) to 1,424 feet before descending (1 in 13) to Clunie Bridge on the road to Kyle of Lochalsh.]

The 'Road to the Isles,' from Invermoriston to Kyle of Lochalsh (56 miles—no bus), was originally constructed by General Wade, and was the route followed by Johnson and Boswell in 1773. It ascends Glen Moriston, which is wooded as far as Torgyle. Prince Charlie spent four days, 24th to 28th July 1746, in the Cave of Corriegoe on the north side of the glen, under the care of the 'Eight Men of Glen Moriston' and 'as comfortably lodged as if he had been in a royal palace.' The road then skirts the north bank of the wild Loch Clunie (Cluanie) for 5 miles, passing from Inverness-shire to Ross-shire half-way along the loch. Beyond the inn at Clunie Bridge, where the road from Glen Garry comes in, you ascend to 889 feet, and then descend Glen Shiel, a superb defile enclosed by bare and savage mountains.

The head of Loch Duich is reached at Invershiel, just past Shiel Bridge. The hills enclosing this grand sea-loch are the 'Five Sisters of Kintail.' They form part of the Kintail Estate, a National Trust property of 15,000 acres, including Ben Attow (page 178). Kintail Lodge is now a hotel (nearest village, Dornie). The best viewpoint, and a superb one, is Scour Ouran (3,505 feet), a simple 2½-hour climb. Near Shiel Bridge was fought, on 11th June 1719, the Battle of Glenshiel, in which General Wightman's government troops defeated 2,000 Highlanders—mostly Macraes and Mackenzies. The Highlanders were led by the Earl of Seaforth, but the Marquis of Tullibardine and George Keith, Earl Marischal, were also present. They were assisted by 300 Spaniards, who had landed in Loch Alsh from two frigates, all that a tempest had left of a fleet of thirty vessels dispatched from Cadiz by Cardinal Alberoni to help the cause of the Old Pretender. The Spaniards surrendered, and the Scots took to the hills. From Invershiel a rough road runs west over the pass of Mam Rattachan (1,116 feet), with gradients up to 1 in 6 and bad turns, to Glenelg (9 miles). For Kyle, however, you keep along the right-hand side of Loch Duich via Croe Bridge, Kintail Church, and Inverinate, beyond which the Keppoch Hill, 1 in 8 up and down, has to be negotiated. From Croe Bridge an expedition can be made to the Falls of Glomach, 7 miles north-east by the pass west of Glasven; this is the highest (370 feet) and after rain the most impressive waterfall in Scotland. It is vested in the National Trust.

At Dornie you cross the new bridge over the mouth of Loch Long to Ardelve. Eilean Donan, which is connected with the mainland by a bridge, bears an old romantic-looking castle of the Earls of Seaforth, which was bombarded into surrender after the Battle of Glenshiel and has recently been restored by the MacRaes. The road then runs near the north shore of Loch Alsh, and at the village of Lochalsh is joined on the right by the road from Strome Ferry. Then Balmacara, with a youth hostel, and over the hill to Kyle. The Balmacara estate of 8,000 acres is National Trust property.

The village of *Kyle of Lochalsh* lies at the extremity of the peninsula between Loch Alsh and Loch Carron, and is the terminus of a railway from Dingwall on the other side of Scotland. A strait (kyle) only half a mile wide separates it from Skye, with which it is connected by a ferry—not available at certain states of the tide, or on Sundays. Kyle, though it has a good railway hotel and other accommodation, is isolated by ferries, and is thus far from being a good motoring centre. But it is an excellent headquarters for boating excursions among the neighbouring sea-lochs—there are motor-boats, etc., for hire—and it is the starting point of steamer services to Skye and the Outer Hebrides. There is a one-day steamer excursion once a week in summer, via Mallaig, to Loch Scavaig (cf. page 159).

Motorists crossing to Skye (impossible on Sundays) use the ferry over the Kyle to Kyleakin (pronounced 'Kyle-áckin' and meaning 'Straits of Haakon'). Return

* F

fares: car 16s. 11d., if over 12 h.p. 25s., motor-cycle 5s.
Non-motorists either take the steamer to Broadford or
Portree (the finest approach to the island), or cross to
Kyleakin and go on by bus. The steamer calls also at the
large island of Raasay, between Broadford and Portree.
Raasay House, where Dr Johnson and Boswell were
entertained by Macleod, is now a hotel.

> Speed, bonnie boat, like bird on the wing.
>   Onward! the sailors cry.
> Carry the lad that's born to be King
>   Over the sea to Skye.

Skye—in Gaelic Eilean a' Cheo, isle of mist—is a
fascinating and romantically beautiful island, about 50
miles long and 640 square miles in area, forming part of
Inverness-shire. Divided into peninsulas by numerous
sea-lochs, it contains a large variety of lovely but treeless
scenery, including vast stretches of moorland and the most
rugged range of mountains in Great Britain. Early
antiquities abound: brochs, duns, cairns, etc. The climate
is notoriously rainy; the best weather is usually encountered in spring, May and June being perhaps the finest
months. Skye, like Islay, Mull, Harris, etc., enjoys
extraordinarily mild winters, the mean January tempera-
ture (41–42°) being the same as that of Devonshire. The
islanders are mostly crofters engaged in cattle-rearing and
sheep-farming, and many still live in primitive low cabins,
the rough thatch of which is weighted with stones.

Hotel accommodation is good, but apt to be over-
crowded in July, August, and September. The main
roads are in better condition than those on the adjoining
mainland, and are nearly all served by buses, but roads
are rare and buses infrequent. The best of Skye is only
to be seen by the walker, but distances are so great that
some use of the buses or of a car—brought from the
mainland or hired—is almost essential for getting about.
Non-motorists should stay at Sligachan and devote most
of their time to the Coolins, but they should see Dunvegan
and the Quiraing also, possibly by coach from Portree.

Strangely enough, few authors seem to have chosen
Skye as a locale for their novels. Mrs Virginia Woolf's
To the Lighthouse is set in Skye, but the lighthouse itself
is based on the Cornish lighthouses—St Ives, Eddystone,

etc. Some of the most exciting adventures of John Buchan's *Mr Steadfast* occur among the Coolins.

Castle Moil, a gaunt ruin half a mile east of Kyleakin, was the seat of the Mackinnons and dates from the fifteenth century. The tale goes that it was built by a Danish Princess, 'Saucy Mary,' who stretched a chain across the strait, and took toll from every ship that passed. The fine moorland road from Kyleakin to Portree—motor-bus thrice daily in summer and once in winter—has been reconditioned and even provided with entirely new sections. It affords splendid views of the island-studded sea and the mountains of Skye and Ross-shire. Broadford, 8 miles from Kyleakin, is a prosperous-looking place, with a hotel. The limestone isle of Pabay, opposite, is noted for its rich store of fossils. Broadford is a good centre for excursions in Eastern Skye. A beautiful coast road, with a bus, leads thence south-ward through the peninsula of Sleat (pronounced 'Slate') —with views of the mainland and Lochs Nevis and Hourn—to Isle Ornsay, Armadale Castle, the modern Gothic seat of Lord Macdonald, and Ardvasar, 22 miles.

The great excursion from Broadford, however, and one which nobody should leave Skye without 'doing,' is to Loch Scavaig and Loch Coruisk (pronounced 'Corroósk'), the finest approach to which is by sea, e.g. by excursion steamer from Fort William, Kyle of Lochalsh, and Mallaig. It can be accomplished in various ways, the laziest being the conducted trip by motor-coach or hired car from Portree to Elgol, and thence by motor-boat. The classic route is by the road—third-rate, but with grand scenery— leading south-west from Broadford, via Torran (view of Blaven, 'heaving its huge bulk on high'), the head of Loch Slapin, and Strathaird House, to Elgol on the shore of Loch Scavaig, 14½ miles. Either at Torran or at Elgol—the height above which commands one of the loveliest views in Scotland—a motor-boat should be hired for the visit to Loch Coruisk; in the former case the Spar Cave may be seen *en route*, if the tide is low and the sea calm. Prince Charlie embarked at Elgol on 4th July 1746, on the way from Raasay to Mallaig. Sturdy walkers leave the road at Strathaird House, 10 miles from Broadford, and cut across the peninsula to Camasunary, a lonely farmhouse.

Thence they cross a stream by stepping stones, and go round the foot of Trodhu, negotiating on the way the 'Bad Step,' a narrow ledge above the sea. This is sensational rather than dangerous, provided you take the proper route at a height of about 15 feet above highwater level. *Loch Coruisk*, connected by a short stream with Loch Scavaig, is a green freshwater lake at the foot of the black and jagged Coolins. No other spot in the British Isles presents such a desolate, savage, awe-inspiring scene. If previously ordered, a guide and pony will be in waiting on the ridge of Drumhain, east of the loch, to convoy the traveller down Glen Sligachan (pronounced 'Sleégǎchǎn') to the Sligachan Hotel, 8 miles. The walk all the way from Broadford to Loch Coruisk and the Sligachan Hotel is a good 25 miles, over a terrain of the roughest and most tiring description.

The road from Broadford to the Sligachan Hotel (18 miles) follows the north coast for most of the way, leaving the granitic Red Hills or Red Coolins (2,403 feet) on the left, and the large island of Scalpay on the right, opposite the quaintly named hamlet of Strollamus. It then rounds the head of Loch Ainort and cuts across a peninsula, with Lord Macdonald's Forest—Glamaig (2,537 feet)—on the left, to the mouth of Loch Sligachan, opposite the south end of Raasay. Above the other bank of the loch rises Ben Lee (1,456 feet).

The Sligachan Hotel, at the head of the loch, is a summer headquarters for the *Coolins*, a region of unrivalled fascination for climbers, geologists, artists, anglers, and nature-lovers. The Coolin (or Cuillin) range, savagely impressive with its shattered sky-line, never dropping below 2,500 feet, and its blue-black gabbro rocks, provides the best mountaineering in the British Isles. A guide is essential for novices. The compass is unreliable owing to the amount of iron in the rock. At least seven of the twenty odd peaks exceed 3,000 feet: the nearest to the hotel and the one most frequently climbed, is Sgurr-nan-Gillean (3,167 feet), which was first conquered by Professor James D. Forbes in 1836 and takes at least five hours there and back. The easiest route, and difficult enough at that, is by the south-east shoulder, from the head of Glen Sligachan, and is marked by small cairns and nail-marks on the rocks. All except experts descend the same way. The 'Pinnacle' or north-east route is only for the highly skilled. Bruach-na-Frithe, the 'Brae of the Forest' (3,143 feet), a neighbouring height on the west, is quite a simple climb in fair weather, four hours up and three hours down, and the view from the top is finer; the route thither is by the track beside the Red Burn to the pass called Beallach a' Mhaim. The highest of the Coolins is Sgurr Alasdair (3,251 feet), ascended from Glen Brittle by the Coire Lagan, a superb corrie, and the uncomfortable 'Stone Shoot.' Sgurr Alasdair is named in honour of Sheriff Alexander Nicolson, who made its first ascent in 1873. Glen Brittle and Loch Brittle are reached by a rough road (14½ miles) diverging left from the Dunvegan road at the head of Loch Harport. Glen Brittle, the chief base for climbers in the Coolins, has a hotel (Glenbrittle House) and a youth hostel.

Loch Coruisk, if not already visited, must on no account be omitted. The simplest route—three hours, and ponies available—is up the waterlogged Glen Sligachan, with Marsco (2,414 feet) on the left and the grand Harta Corrie on the right; then, bearing right-handed, over the ridge of Drumhain, opposite Clach Glas (2,590 feet), a haunt of the golden eagle, and the scarred face of Blaven (3,042 feet). A much more exciting and strenuous route is by the north bank of the stream called Allt Dearg Mor, then left, up the Coire na Creiche (the grand corrie to the right of Bruach-na-Frithe) and over the main ridge of the Coolins, keeping to the right of Bidein.

From Sligachan the main road ascends north and descends Glen Varragill to *Portree* (9½ miles), the 'King's Port,' capital and only town of Skye. It has a fishing fleet, a woollen factory, and three hotels, and is the best headquarters in the island for non-motoring tourists, owing to its central position and its bus services: to Kyleakin, to Staffin and Flodigarry, and to Uig, Kilmuir, Duntulm, and Kilmaluag. Motor-coaches start daily in summer for various tours: Quiraing, Dunvegan–Bracadale–Sligachan, Loch Coruisk, Armadale, etc. The room in which, according to tradition, Prince Charlie said good-bye to Flora Macdonald, on 30th June 1746, is shown at the Royal Hotel. 'Prince Charlie's Cave,' 5 miles north, is probably not genuine, but provides a good excuse for a boating trip along the interesting coast.

North of Portree extends the peninsula of Trotternish. Motorists should take the road to Staffin—16½ miles, fair but stony in parts—along the east coast of the peninsula, which passes Lochs Fada and Leathan and commands grand views of mountain and sea. Those who are energetic hill-climbers should leave the car at Loch Leathan and climb the *Storr* (2,360 feet), with its bizarre rock-pinnacles. The lovely lawn on top commands what some authorities consider to be the finest sea-and-mountain view in Scotland. The Old Man of Storr is a conspicuous obelisk of black trap-rock, 160 feet in height.

Staffin has a youth hostel, a bathing beach, and cliff scenery, including the Kilt Rock. The coast road goes on to Uig (17 miles) round the north end of the peninsula, via the Flodigarry Hotel, Kilmaluag, and the fragmentary ruins of Duntulm Castle, once the seat of the Macdonalds of Sleat; thence south, passing Kilmuir graveyard, where Flora Macdonald is buried, and near Monkstadt or Mougstot House, below which, at Port Kilbride, she landed from Benbecula, with Prince Charlie disguised as her maid, 'Betty Burke,' on 29th June 1746. The direct road over the hills from Staffin to Uig—9 miles, with gradients of 1 in 11 and hairpin bends—rises to 852 feet, and from the top of the pass a rough track leads to the right along the foot of the cliffs to the *Quiraing*, which must on no account be omitted. It is a fantastic chaos of towers and pinnacles, composed of amygdaloidal trap, and including the 'Prison,' the 'Needle' (120 feet high), and the 'Table.' Clamber up to the top of the last to get a most impressive sea-view.

Uig (pronounced 'Oóig' and meaning 'corner') is a pleasant scattered village with an inn and a youth hostel, situated on a bay of Loch Snizort, a wide sea-loch. Then southwards, passing near Kingsburgh, the successor of Flora Macdonald's married home, where she and her husband entertained Johnson and Boswell on 12th September 1773, the former occupying the very bed in which Prince Charlie had slept. If you do not need to return to Portree, which is 15 miles from Uig, you can turn right for Dunvegan at a point 2½ miles beyond Snizort Church.

The rather dreary road from Portree to Dunvegan—
22 miles, hilly but in good condition and with no excessive
gradients—is traversed daily by a bus. It leaves the
Uig road to the right, and skirts the heads of Loch Snizort
Beag and Loch Greshornish (two arms of Loch Snizort).
At the Fairy Bridge a road goes off on the right to serve
the peninsula of Vaternish, which is pronounced and sometimes spelt Waternish. Farther on you get a splendid
view over Loch Bracadale, and then turn right for *Dunvegan* (pronounced 'Dunvéggan'), which lies at the head
of an island-dotted sea-loch and has a small hotel and
several boarding houses. Dunvegan Castle, the ancestral
home of MacLeod of MacLeod (pronounced 'MacLoúd'),
is claimed to be the oldest inhabited castle in Scotland.
It is a venerable building of various periods, looking, in
the words of Dr Johnson, who spent a week here, 'as if it
had been let down from heaven by the four corners, to be
the residence of a Chief.' The north-east tower is
fourteenth century, the 'new house' with the Fairy
Tower sixteenth, and the west wing seventeenth. The
present approach is by a bridge, but formerly the only
entrance was by the sea gate. Visitors are admitted on
Tuesday and Thursday afternoons from 1st May to
mid October, and at other times by arrangement. The
celebrated Fairy Flag, religiously preserved here, is supposed to have the power, on being waved, of saving the
clan from three great dangers. It has already been
waved twice—at the battles of Glendale and the Stony
Dyke.

West of Dunvegan lies the peninsula of Quirinish,
dominated by two hills called MacLeod's Tables (1,538
and 1,601 feet). A rough road leading along the west
shore of Loch Dunvegan passes Boreraig, with a memorial
cairn to the famous school of piping maintained here in
the sixteenth, seventeenth, and eighteenth centuries by
the MacCrimmons, who held their land of MacLeod by the
tenure of piping. The course lasted seven years, and the
student had to learn by heart nearly three hundred tunes.

The picturesque road from Dunvegan to Sligachan, a
bus route of 24½ miles, completing the circuit of Skye,
commands grand views of Loch Bracadale, with its islands
and its various arms, and of the Coolins. At the Point

of Idrigil are 'MacLeod's Maidens,' three stack-rocks of basalt. The road, though with fair surface, is winding, with several bad turns, and hilly, with a dangerous ascent (1 in 11) at Coillore, beyond the village of Bracadale. From Sligachan you leave the island by the way you came, via Broadford and the ferry to Kyle of Lochalsh.

> Jerusalem, Athens, or Rome,
> I would see them before I die;
> But I'd rather not see any one of the three
> Than be banished for ever from Skye.
>
> ALEXANDER NICOLSON.

Back again at Kyle of Lochalsh, it will occur to many people that now or never is the time to see the *Outer Hebrides*. There are two steamer services from Kyle: daily all the year round (with connection from Mallaig), to Stornoway in 4½ hours, calling at Applecross on the mainland, and thrice a week to Harris and North and South Uist (once a week via Mallaig). Car from 40s.

There are air services from Glasgow four times weekly to Barra, Benbecula, and Stornoway, and thrice weekly from Inverness to Stornoway.

The Outer Hebrides, Pliny's Hebudes, and now known collectively as the 'Long Island,' consist of a chain of islands divided from each other by narrow sounds. Their aggregate length, from the Butt of Lewis on the north to Barra Head on the south, is 130 miles. Geologically the islands are composed of grey-pink archaean gneiss, the oldest known rock, found nowhere else except in Sutherland and the St Lawrence district of Canada, and they have existed 'since before the Himalayas were beneath the seas.' Except for Harris, which is mountainous, their surface is a waterlogged moorland, barren, peaty, treeless, and flecked with innumerable small lochs. The white shell-sands, however, provide marvellous sea-bathing, and with the flowery machair and the isolated hills often form the most fascinating landscapes. Hotel accommodation is scanty, and most of the few tourists who come to the islands are anglers, artists, yachtsmen, or just lovers of wild nature. The trout-fishing is free, but the salmon are strictly preserved. The numerous early antiquities include chambered cairns, earth-houses, standing stones, brochs, and especially duns, the last-named often constructed in the middle of a loch. The crofters, Gaelic-speaking though partly of Norse origin— the Hebrides were under Norse domination until 1266— live in primitive stone and turf cabins, sometimes without even a fire-place for their peat fires. The beauty of their Gaelic folk-songs and folk-poems was discovered by Mrs Kennedy-Fraser. Agriculture, the herring and lobster fisheries, and seaweed-burning for iodine are practically their sole occupations, and distress is endemic. Large numbers of the crofters have emigrated to Canada, and the Song of the Exiles, a Canadian boat-song of unknown authorship, expresses their nostalgia.

> From the lone shieling of the misty island
>   Mountains divide us, and the waste of seas—
> Yet still the blood is strong, the heart is Highland,
>   And we in dreams behold the Hebrides.

Many novelists have chosen these romantic islands as a setting, e.g. William Black, in *A Princess of Thule*, his best novel (Lewis), and Neil Munro, in *Children of Tempest* (South Uist). Some of the mystical works of 'Fiona Macleod' (William Sharp) deal with the Hebrides: *Pharais: a Romance of the Isles*, *The Sin Eater* (Celtic tales), etc. Miss Agnes Mure Mackenzie's *The Quiet Lady* is localized in Stornoway and North-east Lewis; the opening part of *Between Sun and Moon* is placed in South Lewis; and the Hebridean island where most of the action of *Single Combat* passes is mainly based on South Lewis. Mr George Blake's *Sea Tangle* moves from Skye to the coast of Ross about Gruinard Bay, thence to an imaginary island in the Minch and, ultimately, St Kilda. Mr J. J. Bell's novel of adventure, *Atlantic Gold*, has much of its setting in the Outer Hebrides. For Barra, read *St Clair of the Isles*, or *The Outlaws of Barra*, by Elizabeth Helme.

Lewis, 'The Lews,' is the northern and largest portion of the largest and northernmost island. It forms part of Ross-shire. *Stornoway*, with five hotels and a youth hostel, is the only town in the Outer Hebrides and the chief fishing port. Its kippers and 'matje' herrings are noted. Lewis Castle, modern, with wooded grounds, was presented to the town by the late Lord Leverhulme, who bought Lewis in 1918 and made vastly expensive, but unavailing, efforts to improve the economic condition of the islanders by the development of the fishing industry. One of his enterprises was the opening of numerous retail fish-shops (MacFisheries Ltd.) to serve as an outlet for the Hebridean fisheries. His efforts met with more appreciation in Harris, which he acquired after his failure in Lewis.

The roads of Lewis, though stony, are fair and free from bad hills. Almost every village in the island is connected with Stornoway by a daily bus service, and there are charabanc excursions in summer. Most of the inns have a car for hire. A road runs west from Stornoway to *Callernish*, or Callanish (16 miles), at the head of Loch Roag and 2 miles beyond the inn of Garynahine. Callernish is famous for its Standing Stones, which are second in importance to Stonehenge alone among the Bronze Age monuments of Britain. The stones are thirty-nine in number, arranged in the form of a cross, with an avenue on the north and a chambered cairn in the centre. The road goes on along the west coast, via Carloway with its conspicuous and well-preserved broch, 30 feet high on one side, to Barvas, and thence (fords) to Port of Ness, 34 miles from Callernish. Port of Ness is a fishing hamlet near the lighthouse and fine cliff scenery of the Butt of Lewis. The natural arch of rock here is supposed to have been made by the Devil so that he could fasten a chain to Lewis and drag it away with him. It is 27 miles back to Stornoway, turning left at Barvas, where there is an inn.

Harris, the southern portion of the main island, is hilly, like the adjoining districts of Lewis. Together with the rest of the Outer Hebrides, it belongs to Invernessshire. Harris tweeds, with their reek of peat-smoke, are much imitated on the mainland, where they are woven by machinery. Nowadays it is very difficult to obtain a genuine Harris tweed, even on the Islands, as, though they are woven by hand, all the other processes—dyeing, scouring, teasing, breaking, carding, spinning, finishing— are in most districts performed by machinery. The road from Stornoway to Tarbert—35½ miles, with very poor surface after it leaves Lewis—is served by a daily bus, connecting at Tarbert on certain days with a service to Rodil. You pass the oddly shaped Loch Seaforth and skirt the slopes (with gradients of 1 in 9) of Clisham, in North Harris, which, with 2,622 feet, is the highest mountain in the Long Island. Tarbert, where the steamers call, is situated on the narrow isthmus, barely half a mile wide, between North and South Harris. It has a hotel.

Scalpay, an island at the mouth of East Loch Tarbert, was a frequent refuge of Prince Charlie's during his wanderings as a hunted fugitive in the Hebrides, between 27th April 1746, when he arrived at Benbecula from Borradale, and 28th June, when he left with Flora Macdonald for Skye. The 'Island that Likes to be Visited' of Sir J. M. Barrie's *Mary Rose* is believed to be in West Loch Tarbert; if you go searching for it, remember that it is six acres in area, uninhabited, a hundred yards from a greater island, quite close to the inn, near the whaling station, and that it has firs, a few rowan-trees, and a tiny pool out of which a stream flows.

The road goes on via Borve Lodge, a former residence of Lord Leverhulme's, and Scarista (accent on first syllable), on the west coast, with a splendid bathing beach, to Leverburgh (20½ miles), as Obbe was renamed in honour of Lord Leverhulme, who built a harbour and established a fishery there. All his schemes collapsed, however, on his death in 1925. It has an inn and lies on the Sound of Harris, beautiful with its archipelago of islands. The prominent bare hill to the east is Roneval (1,506 feet). The road ends at Rodil, 4 miles farther, where the ancient church of St Clement should be seen. It dates from the early sixteenth century and is the only church of any architectural importance in the isles. The curious sculptured panels on the west tower belong to the class termed in Ireland 'shiela na gigs.' Inside there are three tombs of the Macleods of Dunvegan, one of which (1528) ranks among the finest in all Scotland.

The next island, going south, is *North Uist* (pronounced 'Yoóist'), an amazing network of fresh- and salt-water lochs, diversified by half a dozen isolated hills, the highest of which is Eaval (1,138 feet). The view from the summit of any one of these is eerie in the extreme—the land all lochs, the sea all islands. The principal settlement and the steamer port of call is Lochmaddy, with a hotel and a golf-course. A road (35 miles) encircles the island. An interesting expedition might be made to the Monach

Isles, 5 miles west, which are inhabited by a score of Macdonalds.

[*St Kilda*, or Hirta, is the largest of a lonely group of about sixteen islets in the Atlantic, 40 miles west of North Uist but forming part of Harris. Cruising steamers call there at rare intervals. The islands have belonged from time immemorial to the Macleod of Macleod, but in 1930 the last of the permanent population, thirty-six souls, were evacuated at their own request. The superb cliffs of the main island, rising to 1,200 feet on the north-east side, are the home of numberless sea-birds: fulmar petrels, puffins, guillemots, etc., and the gannets breed on the neighbouring islet of Boreray. The St Kilda wren (*Troglodytes troglodytes hirtensis*), mouse (*Mus muralis*), and field-mouse (*Apodemus hirtensis*) are unique species.]

Benbecula lies between North and South Uist, and at low water is connected with both by fords, which vehicles can cross—strangers should take a guide or ask local advice. A road, 5 miles long, with an inn at either end, traverses the island from Gramisdale Ford on the north to Creagorry Ford on the south.

South Uist is more hilly, with Ben More (2,034 feet) and Hecla (1,988 feet) as its principal peaks. Like Benbecula, it is crossed from north to south by a road with an inn at either end: from Carnan, opposite Creagorry, to Pollachar, 28½ miles. Lochboisdale, on the east coast, near the south end, is the steamer port and chief settlement, with a hotel. There is a golf-course at Askernish, on the west coast, 5 miles from Lochboisdale, and at Milton, 2 miles north of Askernish, are the ruins of Flora Macdonald's birthplace. It was in a hut near Ormaclett, 3 miles farther north, that she first met Prince Charlie and agreed to take him over to Skye. The prince spent twenty-two days (15th May to 5th June) in comparative comfort at a forester's cottage in Glen Corodale, at the east foot of Ben More.

Beyond the small island of Eriskay (pronounced 'Érriskay')—where, on 23rd July 1745, Prince Charlie first set foot on Scottish soil, spending the night in a cottage—lies *Barra*, whose population (about 2,000), like that of most of the Southern Hebrides, is Roman Catholic. It derives its name from St Barr or Finbarr of Cork. The port is Castlebay, with two hotels and the majestic ruins of Kiessimul Castle, once the home of the MacNeils, on a rock in the bay. Though very archaic in appearance, it is not older than 1427. Heaval, the hill above the village, is the highest in the island (1,260 feet). The road that encircles the island is 12 miles in length. The vast white sands of Traigh Mhòr are noted for their cockle-beds.

The 'Long Island' ends in a string of small islands: Vatersay, Sandray, Pabbay ('priest's isle'), and the now uninhabited Mingulay, with the weirdest and most startling cliff scenery, and Berneray, with a lighthouse and Barra Head, the southernmost point of the Outer Hebrides and one of the wildest and grandest spots in Scotland, with cliffs nearly 600 feet high.

The last section of this tour—Kyle of Lochalsh to Inverness—crosses Ross-shire from west to east and can be accomplished by railway. The road, 84 miles, is good on the whole, but loose in parts. In settled weather robust walkers should, without fail, choose either Glen Affric or the Glen Cannich route (page 177). Motorists leave Kyle by the way they came, passing Balmacara, turn left at Lochalsh, and cross a roughish col (683 feet), 1 in 10, to Strome Ferry, 14 miles. The direct road, though 3 miles shorter, has a very poor surface and bad hills, but if you should go that way do not fail to see the wholly delightful village of Plockton, which lies at the mouth of Loch Carron. At Strome Ferry you cross *Loch Carron* (car 10s., motor-cycle 2s.). No Sunday services. An inn (closed), a youth hostel, and the scanty ruins of Strome Castle, which once belonged to the Macdonalds of Glen Garry, and are now National Trust property, await you on the far side of the ferry. The road then follows the north bank of this beautiful sea-loch, via the attractive village of Jeantown, alias Lochcarron, 4 miles.

[A magnificent digression, with a bad 1 in 9 hill, may be made west from Jeantown to Kishorn or Courthill (youth hostel), 4½ miles, at the head of Loch Kishorn and at the foot of Ben Bhan (2,936 feet), a mountain of Torridon sandstone. Thence either to Shieldaig (10 miles farther), a pretty village on Loch Torridon, with an inn; or by the stony, zigzag road to Applecross (13½ miles), which rises from sea-level to 2,054 feet in 6 miles, with 1 in 7 gradients, and is probably the most difficult and sensational hill in Scotland. Applecross is a fishing village with a temperance inn, facing Skye. The Stornoway steamers call here.]

Beyond Jeantown the road and the railway ascend Glen Carron, with impressive views of the grand mountains on either side, notably Fuar Tholl (2,968 feet) on the left and Moruisg (3,026 feet) on the right. Loch Doule, in a countryside of young forests, is passed; then Loch Scaven and, beyond the divide, Loch Gowan. The scenery becomes bare and desolate. At Achnasheen, 25 miles from Strome Ferry, the Gairloch road comes in on the left. On the left rises Fionn Ben (3,060 feet), on the right Scuir Vuillin (2,845 feet). The landscapes become more wooded as you descend Strath Bran, passing Loch Achanalt and Loch Culen. On the right you get a glimpse of Loch Luichart, the source for a new electric power scheme.

At *Garve*, 16 miles from Achnasheen, with a hotel, opens Strath Garve, through which runs the road to Ullapool. The scenery around Loch Garve is very fine. The sprawling massif to the north is Ben Wyvis (pronounced 'Wivvis' or 'Weevis'), which rises to 3,426 feet and is rarely free from snow. The road then passes near the Falls of Rogie, on the left, in a delightful setting of rock, heather, and birches, and at the Achilty Hotel a road diverges for the pretty Loch Achilty and the Falls of Conon, in the beautiful Strath Conon. At Contin the road to the right affords a short cut, by Moy Bridge and Urray, to Muir of Ord.

The main road goes on to *Strathpeffer* (9½ miles from Garve), the most fashionable spa in Scotland, a peaceful modern township with excellent hotels and attractive villas. The railway station is the terminus of a branch line from Dingwall. Strathpeffer's strong sulphur and iron waters are of proved efficacy for rheumatism and skin diseases. The season is from May to September. The surrounding countryside is pleasant in a tame, well-tended way. Archaeologists should inspect the vitrified fort (cf. page 134) of Knockfarrel, 3 miles east, on the ridge known as the Cat's Back from its strip of woodland.

At *Dingwall*, which lies at the head of Cromarty Firth, $4\frac{1}{2}$ miles from Strathpeffer, you reach the east coast, having thus crossed Scotland from sea to sea. Its name is of Norse origin: Thingvollr, Field of the Thing or Parliament. Though the county town of Ross and Cromarty, it consists almost entirely of a single long street. The Town House is eighteenth century. An obelisk on Green Hill commemorates General Sir Hector Macdonald ('Fighting Mac'), a native of the town, who joined the Gordon Highlanders as a private, became one of the most successful generals in the Boer War, but shot himself in Paris as the result of an opprobrious accusation.

From Dingwall the main road (a bus route) and the railway run south, via Conon Bridge (pronounced 'Connon') and Muir of Ord, to Beauly, $8\frac{1}{2}$ miles, crossing the neck of the Black Isle, i.e. the peninsula between the Firths of Cromarty and Beauly. The Black Isle is neither an isle nor black, but very green and fertile, and altogether rather attractive. It is said to be so called because snow rarely lies there in winter. Besides the railway from Muir of Ord to Fortrose there are buses from Dingwall to Cromarty, from Cromarty to Rosemarkie, and from Rosemarkie to Fortrose and Muir of Ord. For motorists—turn left at Conon Bridge—this means a 50-mile detour. Cromarty (pronounced 'Crómmarty') is a decayed little town near the mouth of Cromarty Firth, the bottleneck entrance to which is guarded by two headlands known as the Sutors (i.e. shoemakers). A thatched cottage near the east end of the main street was the birthplace in 1802 of Hugh Miller, the journeyman stone-mason who became a famous geologist and man of letters; it dates from 1650 and is vested in the National Trust. Fortrose, with its neighbour Rosemarkie, is a growing seaside resort. A stone shaft at Rosemarkie marks the site of the last burning for sorcery in Scotland. Fortrose Cathedral, mostly a ruin, is a fragment of a very beautiful example of Decorated Gothic, built between 1330 and 1485. The Chapter House and the south side of the choir and nave survive. Between Muir of Ord and Beauly you pass from Ross-shire to Inverness-shire.

Beauly, meaning 'beau lieu' and pronounced 'Bewly,' is indeed beautifully situated on the river of the same name, not far from its mouth. It has a large market square and the sandstone ruins of a priory church that was built in a severe Gothic style, being founded for Cistercians in 1230 by Sir John Bisset of Lovat.

The main road from Beauly to Inverness (12½ miles) crosses the River Beauly at Lovat Bridge and then hugs the shore of Beauly Firth. But at all costs do not fail to visit the Beauly Valley and Glen Affric, the scenery of which—a lovely combination of river, woods, lochs, and mountains—is unsurpassed of its kind in these isles. A bus runs twice a day from Beauly to Tomich near the head of Strath Glass, 20 miles, but walk it if you possibly can—to Affric Lodge, 28 miles.

The road is narrow but in quite fair condition. It branches off to the right on this side of Lovat Bridge and leads direct to Kilmorack, while the River Beauly curves south past Beaufort Castle, the modern seat of Lord Lovat, chief of the Frasers. Near Kilmorack Bridge are the Falls of Kilmorack, where the river dashes over rapids in a setting of forest and porphyry cliffs. The gorge farther upstream is more impressive. Between Kilmorack and the beginning of Glen Affric there is an alternative road on the other bank of the river. The road on the north bank passes through the Druim Pass (pronounced 'Dream'), a ravishing spot with its birchwoods and its red sandstone rocks rising from the middle of the stream. The scenery then becomes less exciting. You pass Erchless Castle, former seat of the Chisholm family, which owned the valley for centuries. From Struy Bridge, over the River Farrar, a primitive by-road ascends through the birch-woods of Glen Strathfarrar, wildest of valleys, to Loch Bunacharan, Loch Mhuilinn or Muillie, a scenic jewel, and Loch Monar, 15 miles. Out of the shooting season, accommodation is occasionally to be found at the keepers' lodges.

Our road now ascends the pastoral and comparatively tame Strath Glass (glass=grey-green)—the River Beauly changes its name to Glass at Struy Bridge—and near its farther end we reach Cannich or Invercannich, with the Glen Affric Hotel, near the point where the Glass is joined by the tributary Cannich. This is the last hotel, going westwards, for many a long mile, and it makes an excellent headquarters for walkers. Apart from the Glen Affric Youth Hostel at Allt Beithe, which does not provide food, the only accommodation beyond the hotel—and that by no means to be depended on—is at a rare keeper's lodge or shepherd's hut. A side-road helps one to explore the wonderful scenery of Glen Cannich (cannich = cotton-grass), with its rocks and heather, its birch- and pine-woods, its waterfalls, and its lochs. The glen, which was the farthermost point reached by Prince Charlie in his wanderings (5th–6th August 1746), ends at the farther end of Loch Mullardoch (13 miles), whence a track goes on past Loch Lungard to Loch na Leitreach (9 miles), near the Falls of Glomach. Here you join the rough road down Glen Elchaig to Ardelve and the Loch Duich Hotel, 12 miles. Cf. page 161.

At Cannich a model village has been built for the staff employed on the Glen Affric scheme, an undertaking (1946–51) of the North of Scotland Hydro-Electric Board that produces 230 million units annually. The principal works consist of a dam 2,385 feet long and 116 feet high at Loch Mullardoch in Glen Cannich; a 3¼-mile tunnel from Loch Mullardoch to Loch Beneveian in Glen Affric; a dam 516 feet long and 86 feet high at Loch Beneveian; and another 3¼-mile tunnel from Loch Beneveian to the main power station at Fasnakyle in Strath Glass. The levels of the two lochs have been raised, but the beauty of the scenery has otherwise hardly been affected.

A mile or so above Cannich the road begins to ascend *Glen Affric*. The power station at Fasnakyle is a building of beautiful design. The road then passes through a long defile known as Chisholm's Pass, which is a superb conjunction of forest and mountain scenery. Pine-woods give way to open moorland, and the new road runs high above the north bank of Loch Beneveian. The road ends near Affric Lodge (12 miles from Invercannich), a keeper's lodge close to the east end of the lovely Loch Affric, with its old Scots firs. Affric means 'grey water.' On the right rises Sgurr na Lapaich (3,401 feet), and behind it are the twin peaks of Mam Soul (3,862 feet) and Carn Eige

(3,877 feet). Strong walkers may go up on Glen Affric, past the youth hostel at Allt Beithe, 9 miles from Affric Lodge, and then via Glen Grivie, keeping to the right of Ben Attow (3,385 feet), to the Loch a' Beallach. Leaving this to the right, you cross the Beallach or Pass of Kintail (1,700 feet), beyond which you have a steep descent to Croe Bridge and Loch Duich, 16 miles from Affric Lodge. The nearest accommodation is at Ardelve, 8 miles farther on. Cf. page 161.

On the way back from Glen Affric motorists may return by the other bank of the Glass and Beauly, or from Cannich take the road east, which climbs a 1 in 9 hill and descends Glen Urquhart (bus service to Inverness), with its beautiful woods and Loch Meiklie, to Drumnadrochit on Loch Ness, 12½ miles. Glen Urquhart is the only glen running up from Loch Ness that is cultivated. As John Bright wrote in the visitors' book of the Drumnadrochit Hotel:

> In Highland glens 'tis far too oft observed
> That man is chased away, and game preserved.
> Glen Urquhart is to me a lovelier glen—
> Where deer and grouse have *not* supplanted men.

From Drumnadrochit you regain Inverness as described on page 136.

TOUR XI: INVERNESS TO INVERNESS VIA CAPE WRATH AND JOHN O' GROATS

Total distance by road: about 550 miles.

LOCH MAREE — GAIRLOCH — ULLAPOOL — LOCH ASSYNT — LOCHINVER — SCOURIE — DURNESS — CAPE WRATH — TONGUE — BETTYHILL — THURSO — JOHN O' GROATS — WICK — HELMSDALE — DUNROBIN CASTLE — DORNOCH — TAIN—FEARN—BLACK ROCK.

THE first half of this tour—by the north-west coast to Thurso—is one of the finest motor drives in the whole country. The landscapes are of the wildest: fantastically shaped and tinted mountains, rock-strewn moors, salt- and fresh-water lochs, beaches of white sand, and island-studded sea. The colours are brilliant after rain. There are no towns, and the villages mostly consist of scattered crofts with a church and a post office. Inns are few and far between, but there are a number of youth hostels; the former, frequently booked up by anglers, are clean and comfortable, with plain, largely home-grown fare. Railways are absent from this north-west corner of Scotland, which is given over to deer forest. Bus services are rare along the coast road, and where they exist function only once daily or even less frequently. The mail-cars take passengers and are often useful—inquire locally. Some of the Scottish Motor Transport and Strathpeffer coaches penetrate as far as Gairloch, Ullapool, and Tongue. The chief points on the coast are connected by motor-bus with Garve, Invershin, Lairg, or Inverness, and there are occasional connections by sea-going steamers, so that those who are dependent on public transport can work out a circular tour, filling up gaps by means of hired cars or Shanks's pony.

The roads are narrow, winding, and hilly, though breakneck gradients are rare. Tar is unknown, and the road surface is loose and shingly, or rutted, or grass-grown. There are very few garages where repairs can be carried out, and motorists should take plenty of petrol, provisions, and rugs.

The road and railway from Inverness to Achnasheen, 44 miles, are described in the preceding tour. Ross-shire is entered a short distance beyond Beauly. Motorists who have already seen Dingwall, Strathpeffer, etc., should take the short cut from Muir of Ord to Contin. Non-motorists go by train to Achnasheen and mount the Gairloch and Aultbea bus, which awaits the arrival of the morning train from Inverness.

From Achnasheen, where 'Parallel Roads' (cf. page 155) are discernible, the road to Gairloch (28 miles) diverges right from the Strome Ferry road and runs for 3 miles along the north bank of the desolate Loch Rosque. It then mounts to 815 feet and descends Glen Docharty— 1 in 12, with bad curves. Suddenly you obtain a marvellous view of Loch Maree, with the precipices of Slioch on its north bank. Kinlochewe, near the head of the lake, has a good hotel with fishing. There is rock-climbing too on Ben Eay or Eighe (3,309 feet), a white quartzite massif rising to the west. If you stop off here, take the roughish road, served by a daily bus, to Torridon (10½ miles), which is situated amid incredibly lovely scenery at the head of the saltwater Loch Torridon. All round rise lofty mountains, notably Liathach (3,456 feet), a terraced mass of Torridonian sandstone topped with white quartzite.

Beyond Kinlochewe the Gairloch road runs along the west bank of *Loch Maree*, a Highland gem of surpassing beauty. It is a good trouting lake; it is said that the salmon, though plentiful, are never caught. On your left are hanging woods; on the other side of the lake towers Slioch (3,217 feet), succeeded farther on by the less precipitous Ben Lair (2,817 feet). The road crosses the Bridge of Grudie, a pretty spot, leaves the lakeside for a while, and rejoins it at Talladale and the Loch Maree Hotel. Boats can be hired here for the exploration of the score of romantic, fir-clad islands in the lake, where sea-gulls and grey lag geese breed. Eilean Suth-ainn (Suinn) is over a mile long, and has three little lakes on it. Garbh Eilean and Eilean Ruairidh (Rory Isle) are reputed the most beautiful. The little Isle Maree is

named after St Maelrubha or Mulrube, who came from
Bangor, Co. Down, A.D. 671, to found a monastery at
Applecross. It has a ruined chapel and an old burial-
ground.

At Slatadale the road quits the loch, rises to 427 feet
with a 1 in 14 gradient—remember to look back at the
view—and then descends, 1 in 19, with bad turns, through
the wooded Kerrysdale, past Loch Batnaskalloch and the
Falls of Kerry. *Gairloch*, on the sea-loch of that name
(=short loch), with its bright, clean sands, is a pretty
hamlet with a large and somewhat incongruous hotel.
Bathing, boating, and fishing (both sorts) are the chief
amusements. There is a splendid view of the mountains
to the south, topped by Ben Alligin (3,232 feet). A
favourite walk from the hotel is up the pretty glen called
Flowerdale.

The road from Gairloch to Ullapool, 56½ miles, ascends
(1 in 9, with bad turns) to 456 feet and passes Loch
Tollie, commanding a grand view of Loch Maree. It
then drops down (1 in 9) to run alongside the River Ewe,
a short stream connecting Loch Maree, which was probably a sea-loch itself once, with Loch Ewe and the sea.
Poolewe, with an inn, lies at the head of Loch Ewe. The
grounds of Inverewe, National Trust property, with rare
and sub-tropical plants, are open on Wednesdays and
Saturdays, and on Sunday mornings. Then along the
east side of Loch Ewe, the shores of which are dotted with
crofts. From Aultbea (pronounced 'Awltbáy'), which
has a good hotel and a youth hostel, you cross the neck of
a peninsula to Gruinard Bay (pronounced 'Grínniard').
The sea views, with the magic islands at the mouth of
Loch Broom, are enchanting. The clachans of Laide—
which has boats for hire—Sand, with its great sandhills,
and the curiously named First Coast and Second Coast
are passed. Then, after a climb, comes the notorious
Little Gruinard Hill, 1 in 8, with hairpin bends, by which
you descend to Little Gruinard Bay, an idyllic spot with
its sub-tropical glade and its deserted golden sands.
Beyond Mungasdale you go up again (1 in 12), over a
ridge, and down (1 in 16) to Badcaul, on the south shore
of Little Loch Broom. From the Dundonnell Hotel, a
snug little hostelry at the head of this sea-loch, walkers

and cyclists can save 20 miles by taking the cart-road
to the left, which ascends in a mile to 700 feet, crosses a
col between the hills, and then descends (1 in 5) to Aultnaharrie, 6 miles, whence there is a ferry to Ullapool.

The motoring route—'Destitution Road,' made during
the famine of 1851—ascends Strath Beg, deep, narrow,
and wooded, to Dundonnell Forest. Views to the right
of the grand red Challich Hills—An Teallach, the Forge,
3,483 feet. After reaching a height of 1,110 feet the road
descends to the fertile and sheltered Strath More, where
it joins the Garve–Ullapool route—a bus route, 32 miles—
at the estate of Braemore. Here, in a romantic wooded
gorge (National Trust property), are the fine Falls of
Measach. The uppermost fall has been described as
resembling 'the graceful drapery of a Shetland shawl.'
The road then descends Strath More (1 in 10 and bumpy),
reaches the head of the saltwater Loch Broom ('Loch of
Showers'), and follows its east bank.

Ullapool, a strange sort of place, not far from the mouth
of the loch, is a crofting township and a not very flourishing fishing port, founded by the British Fishery Society
in 1788. The climate is extraordinarily mild. There
are half a dozen hotels, besides a youth hostel, and bathing, boating, fishing, and golf are available. The 'Summer Isles' at the mouth of the loch are a great place for
picnics.

The scenery of the district between Loch Broom and
Loch Assynt is the strangest in all Scotland. From a
broken surface of archaean gneiss, pitted with small lochs,
rise isolated, fantastically shaped peaks of Torridonian
sandstone. The road from Ullapool to Lochinver is 37½
miles via Ledmore, as far as which it is distinctly an
adventurous road, with 1 in 10 hills, sharp turns, and
rough surface. At Ardmair you have a wonderful view
of the isle-strewn mouth of Loch Broom and of Ben More
Coigach (2,438 feet). The road turns inland and crosses
Strath Kanaird obliquely.

[At the Drumrunie signpost an alternative road to
Lochinver diverges on the left, saving 6½ miles and
winding through a deserted countryside with very beautiful landscapes; it is very stony, however, and so narrow
that there is no room for two cars to pass each other. It

passes between Cul Beg (2,525 feet), weirdest-looking of mountains, and Stack Polly or An Stac (2,009 feet), on one side, and Loch Lurgain and Loch Baddagyle (Bad a Ghaill) on the other. Stack Polly, with its pinnacles of shattered sandstone, has been compared with 'a porcupine in a state of extreme irascibility.' The Lochinver road turns right at the end of Loch Baddagyle—straight on for Achiltibuie and the Summer Isles Hotel, at the mouth of Loch Broom—and then approaches the sea from time to time. Stack Polly remains constantly in sight. At Inverkirkaig, which some consider the gem of the north-west coast, you cross the River Kirkaig into Sutherland.]

The main road—if you can so call it—ascends from Drumrunie to 771 feet, enters Sutherland, and descends to Elphin (gates), which is complete with church, post office, and school. Sutherland, i.e. 'southern land,' so called by the Norsemen of Orkney and Shetland, is the most thinly populated county in Great Britain—only seven persons to every ten square miles. This is partly the result of the much-abused 'Sutherland Clearances' of 1810–20, when the tenants in the interior were removed to the coast, and their arable holdings converted into sheep-farms. But this was only a part of the general Highland Clearances of 1750–1850, whereby thousands of peasant cultivators were driven from their homes and compelled to emigrate to Canada and the United States. The growth of deer-forests is a comparatively recent phenomenon.

Leaving Loch Veyatie and the Cam Loch to the left, you reach the Ledmore road junction, where you join the road from Invershin to Lochinver—50 miles, traversed daily by buses from Invershin and Lairg. About 1½ miles along this road, to the right, is the Altnacealgach Hotel, an angling resort on the bank of Loch Borralan. The Lochinver road, with a much-improved surface, runs north, passes the little Loch Awe, with its wooded islets, and drops down to the Inchnadamph Hotel at the head of *Loch Assynt*. The cottages hereabouts are built of locally quarried white marble. This grand loch is surrounded by mountains on all sides except the west: on the south side, at a distance, Canisp (2,779 feet) and Suilven (2,399 feet); on the east, Ben More Assynt (3,273 feet) and other lower hills; on the north, Glasven (2,541 feet) and the jagged Quinag (2,653 feet). Suilven, one of the most remarkable mountains in Great Britain, is known also as the Sugarloaf from its shape when seen edgewise, i.e. east and west. Owing to the variety of rock—Lewisian gneiss or 'Old Boy,' Cambrian quartzite, Torridon sandstone—this is classic ground for geologists and botanists. The road skirts the north bank of the loch for seven of the loveliest miles in Scotland. Ardvreck Castle, a ruin on the edge of the lake, was built by the Macleods of Assynt in the late sixteenth century. It served as a prison for the Marquis of Montrose, who, after his defeat at Invercarron, fled into the mountains but was seized and betrayed by his old friend Neil Macleod—Aytoun's 'deed of deathless shame.' The road to Kylesku Ferry branches off to the right at Skaig Bridge. Towards the end of Loch Assynt you pass the charming little Loch Letteressie, on the right. Then down the bank of the rushing River Inver.

Lochinver, with the Culag Hotel, is an ideal little holiday resort at the head of a small sea-loch, with a view westward to Lewis. The bathing and fishing are excellent. It is said that there are two hundred and forty freshwater lochs in the parish. The fantastically shaped mountains in its hinterland afford excellent climbing; Suilven especially, 'a series of rocky cliffs piled in terraced succession upon each other,' affords a marvellous view, and its ascent, though rough and wearisome, is not difficult, provided the tourist route (i.e. the stone shoots) is adhered to. Inverkirkaig and the Falls of Kirkaig should be visited also.

The ordinary route from Lochinver to Scourie, 31 miles, is to return by the way you came as far as Skaig Bridge, turn left, scale the col (813 feet) between Quinag and Glasven—a 1 in 12 gradient, with bad surface, but with magnificent views in either direction from the top—and descend steeply to the Kylesku Ferry, which crosses a sea-loch from Unapool to Kyle Strome, at the point where Loch Glencoul and Loch Glendhu unite to form Loch Cairnbawn.

[An interesting alternative route from Lochinver to Scourie is by the coast road, narrow and winding, with many bad hills, to Drumbeg, 15 miles. A conveyance of sorts can be obtained thus far, and a boat can be hired at Drumbeg to take you across Eddrachillis Bay to Badcall. Or adventurous spirits can push on to Kylesku.]

The free car-ferry at Kylesku functions daily, including Sunday, all the year round, from 9 a.m. till 7 p.m. or dusk. There is a delay of 1½ hours at low tide. Modest inn on the south side. The ferry saves a sixty-mile detour via Lairg. The feature of the district on the other side of the loch is the vast number of lochs, small but deep, interspersed with outcrops of gneiss. The road improves, but there are 1 in 10 hills. As you approach the coast again near Badcall (youth hostel), superb views of Eddrachillis Bay and its islets are revealed. East rises the symmetrical peak of Ben Stack (2,364 feet). *Scourie* (rhymes with 'floury') is a township of white houses on a small bay, with a good hotel, a tiny church, and silvery sands. The bathing and fishing are first rate, and the great thing to do is to hire a motor-boat and explore the deserted island of Handa, the grand red sandstone cliffs of which, 400 feet high, are the breeding place—in May, June, and July—of countless guillemots, razorbills, puffins, cormorants, terns, and gulls. The view of the mountain from the island is superb.

The next stage, Scourie to Durness (26 miles), is served daily by a bus, with a change at Laxford Bridge. There is a bad 1 in 7 hill out of Scourie, and the road is narrow and tortuous. [At Laxford Bridge the road to Lairg (37 miles—buses from Scourie and Durness) goes off on the right, passing Lochs Stack, More, Merkland, Ghriam, and Shin (with the Overscaig Hotel). Loch Shin has been described as 'a huge ditch without bays, without promontories, without rocks, without trees, without houses, without cultivation.']

Laxford is Norse for salmon loch. To the right are Arkle (2,580 feet) and Foinaven (2,980 feet), with its bleached walls, and Reay Forest (pronounced 'Ray'), the Duke of Sutherland's vast deer preserve. The Durness road proceeds through a chaos of rocks and lochs. From Rhiconich, with the Brae Hotel, near the head of the saltwater Loch Inchard, a steep, stony road

diverges left for Kinlochbervie, 4 miles, a crofting township with the Garbet Hotel. Our road, constructed by
the Duke in 1831, crosses the desolate Gualan moor and
attains a height of 596 feet. Then down to Strath Dionard, with Grann Stacach or Cranstackie (2,650 feet) and
Ben Spionnaidh (2,537 feet) rising on the right. The road
descends the strath, crossing the river, to the Kyle of
Durness, a shallow sea-loch, and follows its east bank
for a while, past two or three brochs and the Cape Wrath
Hotel.

Durness (accent on last syllable), where you at last
attain the north coast of Scotland, is a scattered village
on a promontory. At Balnakill, on the Kyle, there is a
ruined church that dates from 1619 and was once a cell
of Dornoch Abbey; it contains the quaint tomb of Donald
Makmurchou, and Robert Donn, the 'Burns of the
North,' who could neither read nor write, is buried in the
graveyard. A walk should be taken to Far-Out Head,
at the end of the promontory, but *the* thing to see at
Durness—preferably by boat—is the Cave of Smoo, which
is reached from a point a mile along the Tongue road
(landmark, a square white house). Sir Walter Scott
describes it in his diary. The outer cavern can be entered
on foot at low tide; the inner chamber contains a waterfall
and is always under water.

Another interesting expedition from Durness is to
Cape Wrath, 14 miles to the west. The Kyle of Durness
has to be crossed, but the Keoldale ferry will only take a
motor-cycle (6s.). The Cape Wrath Hotel keeps a car on
the west side to take parties to the lighthouse; or in fine
weather you can go by motor-boat from Durness. The
road across the Parph moors of the Cape Wrath peninsula
has a sequence of 1 in 10 hills, but, being so little used,
it has an excellent surface. It rises to 535 feet and
commands fine views. On the right is the red granite
face of Scrishven. Two shepherds' cottages are the only
dwellings passed. Cape Wrath, the north-west extremity
of Scotland, has grand cliff scenery and a lighthouse, but
no other habitation. Visitors are shown over the lighthouse, which affords a fine view of the north coast of
Scotland, and westward to Lewis. The word Wrath is
really the Norse *Hvarf*, a turning point. Here, much more

than at John o' Groats, you feel you are at the end of all things.

At Durness we turn our faces in an eastward direction. The road to Tongue (37 miles), a series of long loops, runs close to the coast at first, with an excellent surface and 1 in 13 hills, but is soon faced with a forbidding obstacle in the shape of Loch Eriboll, a 10-mile sea-loch, which it is forced to encircle, leaving Ben Spionnaidh and Grann Stacach on the right. The road round the peaty head of the loch is poor and stony. Heilem Ferry takes passengers only; walkers save 9 miles by using it. After passing Eriboll, on the east bank of the loch, the road, a series of switchbacks, turns east again and crosses the outflow of the freshwater Loch Hope at Hope Lodge. [From this point a poor by-road, with soft surface, runs south to Altnaharra, 21½ miles, skirting Loch Hope and the foot of Ben Hope (3,040 feet), which is noted for its rare alpines. In Strath More, a beautiful green valley once well populated but a victim of the Sutherland Clearances, you pass the waterfall of Alltnacaillich and the broch of Dun Dornaigil or Dornadilla, a portion of which is 22 feet high. In the background towers Ben Hee (2,864 feet), the highest point of Reay Forest.]

The Tongue road, made by the Duke of Sutherland in 1830, crosses a dreary peat-moss called the Mhoine, rising to 741 feet, with splendid views, and then descending to the shore of the Kyle of Tongue (youth hostel). The ferry takes passengers and motor-bikes, saving 8½ miles. The road once more has to round the head of the loch and is narrow, tortuous, and rough. Then an ascent and descent of 1 in 9.

Tongue, on the east side of the loch, is a delightful little place with more foliage than is usual in these parts. It has the Bungalow Hotel, with fishing and shooting, and the ruined Castle Varrich. The House of Tongue, a seat of the Duke of Sutherland, first erected in 1678, was once the seat of Lord Reay, head of Clan Mackay. Excellent bathing, boating, and sea-angling are to be had among the islands at the mouth of the Kyle, and the cliff scenery of Kennageall or Whiten Head, west of the Kyle, is very fine.

[East of Tongue the scenery rapidly decreases in grandeur as one gradually returns to civilization and tarred

G 2

roads. Caithness is really rather a dull county, not Highland at all but rather Norse, at least near the coast—as the place-names show. Consequently the traveller will not be ill advised if he decide to cut short this tour by making for Lairg direct. If he does so, he will miss the kudos of having reached John o' Groats, but not very much else. The road from Tongue to Lairg (37 miles), traversed by a daily bus, crosses a barren moorland. It runs south between Loch Laoghal (Loyal), which is 7 miles long and of interest to ornithologists, and Ben Laoghal (2,504 feet), an isolated and precipitous mass with an impressive group of four granite peaks; it then passes the Altnaharra Hotel, near a cross-roads at the west end of Loch Naver, and crosses the Crask, a pass (828 feet) on the west side of Ben Klibreck (3,154 feet).]

If you decide on John o' Groats after all, you take the road for Thurso, 44½ miles from Tongue. It runs at some distance from the sea. At Borgie Bridge (6½ miles) you join the bus route from Skerray to Thurso (once or twice daily). The next valley is Strath Naver, where you turn left and cross the river near its mouth. *Bettyhill*, with a good hotel (fishing and shooting), is situated on Torrisdale Bay and overlooks a waste of sands which offer a sanctuary for sea birds. Farr Bay is a delightful cove. The Naver is a famous salmon stream, and Strath Naver is worth exploring. It once maintained a population of 1,200, but its river meadows have long since been converted into sheep-farms. The rough road through the valley leads to Loch Naver and Altnaharra, 25 miles.

The Thurso road runs parallel with the coast, a mile or two from it. The third bridge east of Bettyhill crosses the Kirtomy Burn, and a couple of miles north of it is the Aird of Kirtomy, with a curious natural tunnel under Kirtomy Point. The road continues to wind up and down through a region dotted with crofts. Strathy is a fishing and quarrying village. There is a hotel at Melvich, near which are the Bighouse Rocks, well worth stopping for. The Halladale River is crossed, and you soon enter Caithness. The roads at once improve. Reay, on Sandside Bay, has a golf-course.

Thurso, the most northerly town and railway station on the Scottish mainland, is old but not very sightly. It is situated on Thurso Bay, at the mouth of the Thurso River. The name is Norse and means Thor's river. After fishing the chief industry (now rapidly declining) is the quarrying and export of Caithness flags, slabs of old red sandstone, which are much used locally for roofing and fencing. Near the harbour are the ruins of St Peter's Church, sixteenth or seventeenth century. Thurso Castle, east of the river, is the seat of Viscount Sinclair, and a statue opposite the church commemorates Sir John Sinclair, the first baronet, who did so much to improve agriculture in the north of Scotland. In the Town Hall are preserved the collections of Robert Dick, a local baker and self-taught geologist and botanist.

Walk west along the cliff, past the ruined palace of the Bishops of Caithness, to Scrabster, whence steamers sail daily to Orkney, etc. Beyond it rises Holburn Head, with wild cliffs of flagstone and a detached bird-rock called the Clett. You can return from Scrabster by bus. If you intend to visit Orkney and/or Shetland, Thurso is the usual starting point (but cf. page 196).

The road east from Thurso to John o' Groats (20 miles) passes through a dull, well-cultivated countryside, via Castletown, Dunnet (with the Northern Sands Hotel), Mey, Canisbay, and Huna. There is a sketchy bus service, with a change or two *en route*. The churches of Dunnet and Canisbay are pre-Reformation, with quaint saddleback towers. Dunnet is 3½ miles from Dunnet Head, the most northerly point of the mainland, with a tall lighthouse. There is a glorious view from here of the north coast and, across the Pentland Firth, of the Orkneys. Barrogill Castle, or the Castle of Mey, half-way between Dunnet and John o' Groats, is the new residence of the Queen Mother. *John o' Groats*, consisting chiefly of a hotel, is commonly looked upon as the northernmost point in Scotland—for the purpose of motor reliability trials, etc. As a matter of fact it is only the north-easternmost point on a main road, nearly 900 miles by road from Land's End, the south-western extremity of England. The flagstaff by the hotel marks the site of John o' Groat's House, which, according to the story usually told—there are variants, however—was built in memory of Jan de Groot, a Dutchman who migrated to

Scotland in the time of James IV. To prevent quarrels over precedence among his descendants, the house was octagonal, with eight doors and an eight-sided table, enabling each member of the family to take the head. The beach hereabouts is composed of powdered sea-shells, and cowries (buckies) may be found. There is a fine view of Pentland Firth, the isle of Stroma, and the Orkneys. A two-mile walk should be taken to see the scenery at Duncansby Head, the north-eastern extremity in Scotland, with its sandstone chasms, stack rocks, and reefs.

At long last you turn southwards again. There is a through bus service all the way to Inverness. The road from John o' Groats to Wick (17 miles) crosses Warth Hill (412 feet), whence a fine view of the Orkneys is obtained, and passes Keiss, a fishing village with a ruined castle (end of sixteenth century) by the sea. *Wick*, which derives from the Norse *vik*, a bay, is the 'dry' county town of Caithness, a railway terminus, and a celebrated fishing port, with a harbour built by Telford in 1800 for the British Fishery Society. Its busy season is in July and August, when the herring fleet is in. An amazing and gruesome sight it is to watch the fisher-girls gutting and packing the herrings at full speed. The coast scenery in both directions is worth exploring, especially near the 'Old Man of Wick,' a fourteenth-century keep, 1½ miles south.

There is a good bus service all the way from Wick to Inverness by the coast road. The railway describes a wide loop inland, regaining the coast at Helmsdale. The road to Helmsdale (37 miles) leaves Wick by the suburb of Pulteneytown, which was founded about 1808 by the British Fishery Society. The country traversed is somewhat featureless, but well cultivated, with many crofts. The sea is some distance to the left, and the coastline is fringed with ruined castles. Loch Hempriggs is passed on the right. Lybster (pronounce 'y' as in 'lie') is a fishing village, now almost derelict. Beyond Latheron, which has a detached bell-tower, conspicuous on the shoulder of the hill, the road becomes hillier and hillier. There is a 1 in 17 hill into Dunbeath, and a 1 in 14 out of it. Dunbeath Castle, by the sea, built in 1633, is an admirable example of Scottish domestic architecture, showing French influence.

This is the country of Mr Neil M. Gunn. When a traveller going north by the main road crosses the Ord of Caithness, he sees before him that immense stretch of rock-bound coast, the northern shore of the Moray Firth, which Mr Gunn has called the Grey Coast. In the dead months of the year, when the grass has withered, that bleak coast is grey enough; and this greyness may be emphasized in the mind by the knowledge of the ebb of a virile fishing life and of prosperity. Upon this northern iron-bound coast, then, you can fairly safely find the scenes in *Morning Tide*, *The Grey Coast*, and *Sun Circle*, which goes back to early Viking times. A fourth novel, *The Lost Glen*, belongs to the Pentland Firth—westward into Sutherland.

Berriedale, a charming spot, is approached from either side by a steep hill: 1 in 12 down and 1 in 9 up. These hills are very tricky, and careful driving is necessary round the hairpin bends. Note the sidings provided for runaway vehicles to be steered into—an early example of 'Safety First.' Berriedale Castle, a ruin by the sea, belonged to the Earls of Caithness. Langwell House, on the hill between the two glens, is the shooting-lodge of the Duke of Portland, who owns the vast Langwell Forest. A permit from the factor is required to go through it in order to climb the mountains of Scaraben (2,054 feet), Maiden Pap (1,587 feet), and Morven (2,313 feet), the last-named a triangular peak conspicuous from most parts of Caithness.

The next section of the road is superb, running high up on the mountain side above the sea and winding round the heads of several ravines. The black posts serve to guide travellers when the road is covered with snow. A height of 747 feet is attained on the plateau known as the Ord of Caithness, the boundary between Caithness and Sutherland. It is courting fate for a Sinclair to cross the Ord on a Monday, for the Earl of Caithness and three hundred men crossed it on a Monday in 1513, to leave their bones at Flodden. *Helmsdale* is a decayed fishing village, at the mouth of the River Helmsdale or Ullie, with a decrepit harbour and lighthouse. It too has its ruined castle, once a seat of the Earls of Sutherland, and reconstructed in 1616. This was the scene of a grim tragedy in 1567, when the Earl and Countess were poisoned at supper by Isobel Sinclair in order that her son, the Earl of Caithness, might inherit. Caithness, however, accidentally drank of the poison and perished along with the Sutherlands.

The road from Helmsdale to Dornoch (28 miles) runs between the sea and the mountains of Sutherland, the railway keeping it company. The beach is marvellous hereabouts, with miles of clean sand. A stone by the wayside at Loth commemorates the slaying of the last wolf in Scotland, in or about the year 1700. Between the road and the railway, 1½ miles farther on, is the large broch of Kintradwell or Cinn Trolla. Brora has brown coal or lignite mines, nevertheless it is a golfing, fishing, and bathing resort. It lies at the mouth of the River Brora, the strath of which, with a loch dominated by the Carrol Rock (684 feet), repays exploration.

Just before the road reaches Golspie it passes to the right of *Dunrobin Castle*, the princely seat of the Duke of Sutherland, with a splendid park and a private railway station. The Castle dates in its oldest part from the end of the thirteenth century, but is mostly a creation of the nineteenth. The public is admitted to the Castle grounds and to the ducal museum of northern antiquities. Golspie is a nice little seaside resort. On the hill above it is Chantrey's huge statue of the first duke.

The road now crosses the head of Loch Fleet, or estuary of the River Fleet, by way of the 'Mound,' an embankment constructed by Telford in 1815, by means of which a large area of land was reclaimed from the sea. Between the Mound and Bonar Bridge the railway describes a wide loop inland, via Lairg and Invershin, the starting points of the buses to the north-west coast (Tongue, Durness, Kinlochbervie, Scourie, Lochinver, etc.). Great sheep sales are held at Lairg in August.

Dornoch, near the sea, is the terminus of a branch line from the Mound and is a couple of miles off the main road, but should on no account be skipped. Though but a tiny place (pop. 800), it is the county town—in fact the only town—of Sutherland, and most attractive. The ruins of the Cathedral of the Bishops of Caithness were ruthlessly transformed into a parish church in 1835. It was built by Bishop Gilbert of Moray (d. 1245), the last Scotsman to be canonized. The Earls and Dukes of Sutherland are buried here. The rich arcaded work in the choir and transepts and the five-light west window are noteworthy. Of the Bishop's Castle only a tall tower, now incorporated in the County Court, survives. Between the town and the sea are the celebrated golf links, on which the Grass of Parnassus flourishes. There are good hotels, and the bathing is unexceptionable.

From Dornoch to Tain it is only 5 miles in a bee-line, but 44 miles by railway and 29½ by road, which has to make a wide detour round the head of Dornoch Firth. Meikle Ferry, crossing the firth, takes nothing bigger than a motor-cycle (2s.). The road leads along the north side of the firth, through woodlands, and passes Skibo Castle, which was built by Andrew Carnegie on an estate of 40,000 acres acquired in 1898, and remained his favourite residence until the First World War. At Bonar Bridge (pronounced 'Bónnar'), the boundary between Sutherland and Ross-shire, the road crosses the neck of the Kyle of Sutherland and is rejoined by the railway. Then east again, along the south shore of the firth, to *Tain*, a quaint old place with excellent golf. See the picturesque old tower, once the jail, and the Church of St Duthus (or St Duthac, an eleventh-century Bishop of Ross), built in 1471 and a good specimen of Decorated Gothic.

Easter Ross, the flat, fertile, and highly farmed district between the firths of Dornoch and Cromarty, is the 'Garden of the North.' The main road from Tain to Dingwall (25 miles), accompanied by the railway, runs direct to Alness, but you should make the digression to see *Fearn* (pronounced 'Fern'), which possesses an old Abbey Church, founded for Augustinians in 1338 and roughly restored. Archaeologists should see the Cross at Shandwick and the sculptured stone attached to the village church of Nigg, both in the vicinity of Fearn. The main road to Dingwall leaves Invergordon a couple of miles to the left, but most people will be curious to see that famous naval base on the north bank of Cromarty Firth.

Rejoining the main road at Alness (pronounce 'al' as in 'pal,' with accent on first syllable), a delightful spot, you perceive, on a hill to the right—Knock Fyrish, 1,483 feet—a bizarre structure erected by General Sir Hector Munro, who served with distinction in India and captured Negapatam in 1781. The monument is a copy of the gate of that town. You must digress again, to the right just before reaching Evanton, to see the amazing gorge eroded in the old red conglomerate and known as the Black Rock of Novar. It is 110 feet in depth and at its narrowest only 17 feet across the top. The River Glass rushes through it with a deafening roar. Between Evanton and Dingwall the road hugs the shore of Cromarty Firth.

Dingwall, Beauly, and the rest of the road to Inverness (21 miles) have already been described on pages 175 and 176.

TOUR XII: ORKNEY AND SHETLAND

KIRKWALL — MAESHOWE — STENNESS — STROMNESS — SKARA
BRAE — HOY — LERWICK — SCALLOWAY — MOUSA —
HILLSWICK—UNST.

THE *Orkneys*—the name is probably a Celtic-Norse amalgam, meaning 'whale islands'—are divided from the mainland of Scotland by Pentland Firth, which at its narrowest
point, Duncansby Head to South Ronaldsay, is 6½ miles
wide. It has an evil reputation for its swift tide-race
and its storms. The Orkneys are composed of Old Red
Sandstone and number about seventy islands (of which
twenty-nine are inhabited), apart from countless rocky
islets and skerries, i.e. rocks awash at high tide. The
largest island is Mainland, erroneously called Pomona.
The coastline of the Orkneys is remarkably indented,
except for the west coast of Hoy and Mainland, with their
rugged cliffs. The islands are somewhat bare and treeless,
and, apart from Hoy, of low elevation. The climate is
mild, however, owing to the influence of the Gulf Stream,
and the soil is fertile. The Orcadians, largely Norse in
origin, are practically all farmers, with a reputation for go-
ahead enterprise. Some of the land is still held on the
Norse 'udal' tenure, i.e. an absolute freehold based on
uninterrupted possession, without written title. The
Orkneys and Shetlands were conquered in the year 875 by
Harold Haarfager ('Fair Hair') and remained Norse until
1468, when Christian I pledged them to his son-in-law
James III of Scotland as surety for the payment of his
daughter Margaret's dowry. For tourists the principal
attractions of the islands are their primitive, unspoilt
character, the marine scenery, the abundance of prehistoric remains—'Shetland for scenery, Orkney for
antiquities'—and the trout-fishing. There is golf at
Kirkwall, Stromness, and St Mary's Hope. The mid-
summer nights grow progressively shorter the farther
north one goes, and in the Shetlands there is hardly any
darkness.

Scott's *The Pirate* deals picturesquely, but with less than his usual veracity, with Shetland. Modern Orkney novelists are Mr Eric Linklater, with *White Maa's Saga, The Men of Ness*, and *Magnus Merriman*, and Mr J. Storer Clouston, with *Garmiscath, The Spy in Black, The Man from the Clouds*, and *The Two Strange Men*. *White Maa's Saga* deals with Orkney (Kirkwall, Scapa Flow, etc.) and 'Irondoon,' i.e. Aberdeen. In *The Men of Ness*, which treats of Orkney in Viking times, 'Ragnarshall' and 'Ness,' the two principal houses, are situated respectively on the present estates of Binscarth and Westness, and 'Orkahowe' is Maeshowe. *Magnus Merriman* is concerned with Edinburgh and Orkney (Kirkwall, Stromness, Dounby, the Loch of Harray, and West Mainland). 'Taffrail's' thriller, *The Man from Scapa Flow*, centres round the salvage operations. Mr Clouston has also written *A History of Orkney* (1932).

The mail route to Orkney is by steamer, daily except Sundays, from Scrabster (near Thurso) to Stromness in $2\frac{1}{2}$ hours (motor-car £4–6 return), but there are also services from Leith and Aberdeen, including round trips and cruises to Orkney and Shetland. For details apply to the North of Scotland & Orkney & Shetland Steam Navigation Co., Matthews Quay, Aberdeen. There are daily air services from Glasgow and Inverness (or from Aberdeen), via Wick, to Orkney, and thence to Shetland.

The steamer from Thurso crosses the Pentland Firth, passing Dunnet Head and leaving the islands of Stroma and Swona well to starboard. To port are Hoy and the pasture-holm of Switha. The steamer then enters Scapa Flow by way of the Sound of Hoxa, between Flotta, to port, and Hoxa Head on South Ronaldsay, to starboard. Scapa Flow, which was the anchorage of the Grand Fleet during both World Wars (particularly Long Hope and Gutter Sound), is an inland sea surrounded by islands and entered by four (formerly six) sounds. The German Fleet surrendered at the Armistice in 1918 was interned here, around the island of Cava (off Hoy), but on 21st June 1919 nearly all the ships were scuttled by their crews. Of the 70 vessels, which included 10 battleships and 14 cruisers, 39 vessels (8 battleships, 5 battle cruisers, 1 cruiser, and 25 destroyers) were raised between 1924 and 1947. In 1939, as a result of the torpedoing of the *Royal Oak*, causeways were constructed from Mainland to Burray, and from Burray to South Ronaldsay, and these were opened as a public road in 1944.

At the narrowest part of Mainland, which is here only two miles wide, lies *Kirkwall*, on a landlocked bay—the name means Church Bay—the chief town of the county of Orkney. It is a quaint little place, with three or four hotels and with narrow streets and old gabled houses reminiscent of Norway. The Highland Park Distillery was founded in 1789, but the district is now 'dry.'

The chief thing to see at Kirkwall is the Cathedral of St Magnus, an impressive red-sandstone building in a plain Romanesque style, with Early Pointed additions. Now used as the parish church, it was founded in 1137 by Rognvald, or Ronald, Jarl (Earl) of Orkney, in honour of his uncle and predecessor St Magnus, treacherously slain on Egilsay. Their bodies were found inside two pillars during a recent restoration. The Cathedral was not completed until the fifteenth or sixteenth century, from which period dates the fine east window. As R. W. Billings wrote in *The Baronial and Ecclesiastical Antiquities of Scotland*: 'Among all the architectural glories of the middle ages, there is scarcely any other that presents so startling a type of the capacity of the Church of Rome to carry the symbols of its power, its wealth, and its high culture into distant regions, as this Cathedral edifice, built in the twelfth century, in one of the most remote dependencies of a small and secluded European power.' A feature of the church is the 'mort brods,' funerary boards or hatchments suspended from the walls. There are monuments to John Rae and William Baikie, the explorers. The vestry contains some old brass alms-dishes. The tower, which may be ascended, commands an interesting view.

The ruin on the south side of the Cathedral is that of the Bishop's Palace, which has a massive round tower. Haakon IV, King of Norway, died here of a broken heart after the Battle of Largs, and his remains rested in the Cathedral until their removal to Trondhjem. Adjacent on the east are the remains of the Earl's Palace, which was built by Patrick Stewart, the tyrannical Earl of

Orkney, who was executed at Edinburgh in 1614. Wideford Hill (741 feet), 3 miles west of Kirkwall, is a good object for a walk, as it affords an excellent and instructive view of all Orkney.

The main roads on Mainland are exceptionally good, with no bad hills. The bus from Kirkwall to Stromness (16 miles) passes Finstown and, 3 miles farther on, *Maeshowe*, a great conical mound containing stone chambers with runic inscriptions and intriguing graffiti. A guide will be found at the neighbouring farm of Tormiston. The second road on the right, farther on, leads to the famous Standing Stones of *Stenness*. It first passes the remains of a small stone circle, on the right, and then crosses the Bridge of Brogar, a natural causeway between the Loch of Stenness and the Loch of Harray. The Ring of Brogar, a little farther on, consists of unwrought monoliths of the local sandstone, of which thirty-six—twenty-one upright—survive out of the original sixty or so. The stone with a circular hole through which lovers used to take the 'Promise of Odin,' as related in *The Pirate*, has disappeared. The Loch of Stenness is famous for its trout, and the largest ever recorded in the British Isles was taken here. A short way along the main road is the Standing Stones Hotel.

Stromness, the only other town in Orkney, is a queer, rambling little fishing port with the Stromness Hotel. There is an unforgettable view of Scapa Flow and Hoy from the graveyard on the cliff to the west, and the Ness at the mouth of the harbour is also a good viewpoint.

The west coast of Mainland, north of Stromness, has some very attractive cliff scenery, and those who possibly can should tackle the fifteen-mile walk to Birsay, returning by bus. The Bay of Skaill is about half-way, and on its south side are the Hole o' Rowe, a natural arch, and *Skara Brae*, a well-preserved Stone Age or 'Pictish' village, recently excavated. It dates (according to some authorities) from about 1500 B.C., and consists of huts, equipped with stone beds, dressers, and other fixtures, and opening on narrow covered alleys. Farther on is Marwick Head, with a memorial tower to Lord Kitchener, who was drowned close by on 5th June 1916, together with his staff and seven hundred officers and men of H.M.S.

Hampshire, when the cruiser struck a mine on the way to Archangel. Birsay, with the Barony Hotel, visited for shooting and fishing, has a ruinous sixteenth-century palace of the Earls of Orkney.

The Southern Orkneys can be visited by local steamer from Stromness. They include—from east to west—Burray, with a broch, South Ronaldsay, Flotta, and Hoy. South Ronaldsay can be approached by the causeway connecting it with Burray and Mainland (bus service). St Margaret's Hope, a bay at the north end of South Ronaldsay, with the Murray Arms, is named after Margaret, the little Maid of Norway, betrothed to the future Edward II, who died on board ship in the Orkneys in 1290 on the way from Bergen to succeed her grandfather Alexander III on the throne of Scotland. *Hoy* is the second largest of the Orkney Islands and has the finest scenery. Its chief 'remarkables' are at the north end and include the stupendous twelve-mile wall of dark cliffs on its northwest coast, in the neighbourhood of St John's Head, and the Old Man of Hoy, an isolated column 450 feet high and pierced with arches. The domical Ward Hill is the highest point in the Orkneys (1,565 feet) and commands a magnificent view. In the valley south-east of it is the Dwarfie Stone, a great rock hollowed out into chambers. There is accommodation at Longhope, on the north shore of Walls, the southern peninsula.

The Northern Orkneys are served by steamers from Kirkwall. On Shapinsay is Quholm, the home of the parents of Washington Irving, who was born in an emigrant ship on the way to the States. Rousay (pronounced 'Rówzy') has fine cliffs and, at Rinyo, a complete Stone Age village of the same type as Skara Brae. Adjacent, to the west, is Egilsay ('Church Isle'), where St Magnus was murdered. Its ruined church has a round tower resembling those of Brechin and Abernethy. Between Rousay and Mainland is the uninhabited island of Eynhallow, with the remains of a Cistercian abbey. The scenery of Calf Sound, between Eday and its 'Calf,' is among the best in Orkney. Near Pierowall (hotel), on Westray, are the ruins of Noltland Castle, which is assigned to the sixteenth century; Noup Head, farther west, is a grand promontory and a haunt of sea-fowl. Papa Westray,

an island north-east of Westray, derives its curious name
from the hermits that once inhabited it. The other
islands—Stronsay, Sanday (Kettletoft Hotel), and North
Ronaldsay—are of less interest.

The *Shetland Islands*, known officially as Zetland and
deriving their name from the old Norse Hjaltland (perhaps
meaning 'high land'), number a hundred or more, of
which twenty-four are inhabited. They lie about 50
miles north of the Orkneys and resemble them in general
characteristics. The cliff scenery is grander, and Mainland, by far the largest island, has a coast-line so much
indented by long fjord-like 'voes' that, although it is
480 miles in length, there is no spot on the island more
than 3 miles from the sea. The climate is wetter and
more stormy than that of Orkney, but the range of tem-
perature is only fourteen degrees, no other place in the
world, except the Falkland Isles, having such a slight
variation. Shetland is noted for its tiny, shaggy ponies
and for its sheep, which produce a fine wool that is
knitted into exquisite shawls. Fish, mutton, and por-
ridge are staple foods of the islanders. The trout-fishing
and sea-angling attract many visitors. Notable traits
of the Shetlanders are their hospitality and the industry
of their women, who manage the farms while their menfolk
are away at sea, and spend their spare time in knitting.
There are steamer services from Kirkwall to Lerwick
in 8 hours, and from Aberdeen direct in 14 hours (motor-
car £7 12s. return). Also daily air services from Glasgow
and Aberdeen (or from Inverness), all via Wick and
Orkney: from Orkney to Shetland in ¾ hour, from Aberdeen to Shetland in 2½ hours.
Half-way between Orkney and Shetland is Fair Isle—
which means the same as Farö, i.e. sheep island—a
lonely island with a population of about a hundred. It
is famous for its jumpers and other hosiery. The whole
island, which lies in the path of bird migration, has been
purchased since the war by an ornithologist who has
established a bird sanctuary and hostel there. The
southernmost point of the Mainland of Shetland is Sumburgh Head, west of which rise the imposing cliffs of
Fitful Head.

Lerwick—meaning Clay Bay and pronounced 'Lerwick'—is the capital of Shetland, with two hotels, and is situated on the east coast of Mainland. Its fine harbour is sheltered by Bressay. Lerwick is a quaint, irregularly built old town, mainly dependent on its fisheries. In summer the harbour is crowded with herring-boats from all parts. The six-oared 'sixern,' a Scandinavian type of fishing-boat, is still occasionally to be seen. Fort Charlotte, at the north end of the town, was originally built by Cromwell's soldiers. The broch of Clickimin, a mile west of Lerwick, is considered to be the best extant specimen after Mousa.

The chief excursion from Lerwick is by ferries to the islands of Bressay (inn) and Noss. Permission to land on the latter, on which Shetland ponies are bred, must be obtained from the factor at Maryfield, Bressay. The Ward of Bressay, a hill 742 feet high, is an excellent viewpoint. At Bard Head, the southern extremity of Bressay, is the Orkneyman's Cave, with stalactites and an echo. You should visit it by boat, armed with torches. The features of Noss are the Noup, a fine headland (592 feet) on the west coast, and, south of it, the Holm of Noss, a bird-rock.

Buses run from Lerwick to *Scalloway*, 7 miles, a fishing village with inns, at the head of Clift Sound. Scalloway Castle, a ruin, was built in 1600 by the hated Patrick Stewart. There is a fine view from the Witch's Hill, to the west. Splendid boating excursions may be made among the islands. To the north of Scalloway is Tingwall Loch, with an island on which the Shetland 'thing' or Parliament used to assemble.

The road to Dunrossness (20 miles, with bus service), southernmost parish of Mainland, leaves the Lerwick–Scalloway road half-way between the two places. It runs near the east coast, passing Quarff, Cunningsburgh, and Sandwick. You should obtain permission at Sand Lodge, Sandwick, to ferry across to the uninhabited island of *Mousa* (pronounced 'Mooza'), which is famous for its possession of the only approximately perfect broch in Scotland, 158 feet in circumference and 45 feet high. It is constructed of dry stone, without cement, and bulges out below and again towards the top to prevent its being scaled. The doorway, low and narrow, gives on a passage leading to the open area inside. The tower consists of two concentric walls, each 5 feet thick, the space between which was occupied by small living-rooms and a winding staircase leading to the upper galleries, while the open centre may have been used for cattle. It is related in the *Orkneyinga Saga* that, about 1155, Erlend carried off the widow of the Earl of Atholl to 'Moseyarborg' and held it successfully against her son Harald, Earl of Orkney. Scott described it as Norna's tower in *The Pirate*, but transferred its location to Fitful Head. Farther south the road leaves the Loch of Spiggie to the right, and forks: right for Fitful Head (928 feet) and its magnificent cliffs; left for Sumburgh Head, with a lighthouse, the airport, and the ruins of Jarlshof, the Earl's Farm, a Norse farmhouse where Iron Age remains have been excavated. The story of *The Pirate* opens here.

A fair road runs north from Lerwick or Scalloway, throughout the length of Mainland, and there are bus services, Lerwick–Walls–Sandness and Lerwick–Brae–Hillswick, which afford the visitor some idea of the beauty of the west coast. From Walls, on Vaila Sound, a mail-boat sails every fortnight to the small and solitary island of Foula (pronounced 'Foola'), which is 16 miles west of the nearest land and has become known through the film entitled *The Edge of the World*. Its cliffs are the loftiest (1,220 feet) and grandest in the British Isles. Landing is impossible in stormy weather. The inhabitants number about 150. The island is a great breeding place of sea-birds, including the bonxie or great skua.

Near Brae (inn), on Busta Voe, Mainland contracts to an isthmus 35 yards wide—the Mavis Grind or Gull's Bridge. *Hillswick*, in the parish of Northmaven, 34 miles from Lerwick, has the comfortable St Magnus Hotel, belonging to the steamer company, and is the centre for the exploration of northern Shetland. Beyond Ronas Voe rises Ronas Hill, the highest in the islands (1,475 feet); it is composed of red granite and commands a superb view. To the west is the peninsula of Esha Ness, a most interesting district, with the quaint fishing village of Stenness, fantastic stack-rocks and blow-holes, the natural archway of Dore Holm, the Grind of the Navir or

Gate of the Giants, a vast staircase chiselled by the waves in the face of the porphyry cliffs, the Hole of Scraada, a cauldron communicating with the sea by an underground passage, and the chasm of Calders Geo.

The North Isles of Shetland, served thrice a week by a steamer from Lerwick, are Whalsey, Yell, Fetlar, and Unst. *Unst* most deserves a visit, for it has good fishing and shooting, wild coast scenery, and numerous antiquities. Its sheep produce the best wool in the Shetlands. The steamer calls at Uyeasound (pronounced 'Yoóasound') and at Baltasound (pronounced 'Báwlta-sound'), where there is a boarding-house. On the north coast of Unst are Burra Firth and Herma Ness, the Ultima Thule of Shetland. The lighthouse on Muckle Flugga, a rock off the Ness, is the northernmost habitation in the British Isles (60° 51′ 2″ N. lat.).

> Farewell to Northmaven,
>   Grey Hillswicke, farewell!
> To the calms of thy haven,
>   The storms on thy fell . . .
> Farewell the wild ferry,
>   Which Hacon could brave,
> When the peaks of the Skerry
>   Were white in the wave.

INDEX

The figures in square brackets are map references

ABBOTSFORD, 59, [2]
Aberbrothock, 112
Aberchirder, 129, [15]
Aberdeen, 115, [15]
Aberdour, 98, [2, 9]
Aberfeldy, 152, [8, 11]
Aberfoyle, 90, [7, 11]
Abergeldie Castle, 119
Aberlady, 43, [2, 9]
Aberlour, 129, [14]
Abernethy, 113, [8, 9]
—— Forest, 128
Aboyne, 119, [15]
Acharacle, 157
Achiltibuie, 183
Achilty, 174
Achintee, 138
Achluachrach, 155
Achnacarry, 137
Achnacloich, 141
Achnasheen, 174, 180, [16, 21]
Adam, Robert, 45, 51
Affric Lodge, 177
Agricola, 65, 93, 106
Ailsa Craig, 75, [4]
Aird of Kirtomy, 188
Airlie Castle, 110
Air Services, 29, 87, 168, 196
Alexander, William, 130
—— I, 98, 151
—— II, 60, 132
—— III, 78, 199
Allival, 159
Alloa, 96, [7, 8, 11]
Alloway, 76, [4]
Allt a Mhuillin, 138
Allt Beithe, 177, 178
Alltnacaillich, 187
Almond, River, 54, [2, 8]
Almondbank, 108
Alness, 193, [17, 19]
Altnacealgach, 183, [18]
Altnaharra, 187, 188, [18]
Alva, 104, [7, 8, 11]
Alvah, Bridge of, 130
Alyth, 110, [9]
Amulree, 108, 152, [8, 11]
Andrew, St, 33, 101
Angus, 110, 112, [9]
Annan, 67, [3, 5]
——, River, 64, 65, [3, 5]
'Annie Laurie,' 69
Anstruther, 99, [9]
Antonine Wall, 93
Aonach Dubh, 142
—— Eagach, 142
Appin, 140

Applecross, 174, 168, [16, 22]
Arbigland, 70
Arbroath, 112, 97, [9]
Ardchonell, 144
Ardelve, 161, 177
Ardgoil, 83
Ardgour, 157, [10]
Ardlamont Point, 86, [6]
Ardlui, 150, 89, 91, [11]
Ardmair, 182, [18, 21]
Ardmore Point, 145
Ardnamurchan, 145, 157, [12, 22]
Ardoch, 106
Ardrishaig, 86, 85, [6, 13]
Ardrossan, 77, [6]
Ardtornish Castle, 145
Ardvasar, 163, [22]
Ardvreck Castle, 184
Argyll, Dukes of, 84, 104, 143, 147, 149
——, Marquis of, 46, 106, 138
Argyllshire, 84, 85, 86, 88, 145, 149, 157, [10]
Arisaig, 158, [10, 16, 22]
Arkaig, River, 137
Arkle, 185
Arklet Water, 89
Armadale, 163, 159
Aros Castle, 145
Arran, 84, [4, 6]
Arrochar, 84, 150, [6–7, 11]
Arthur's Seat, 44, 54
Ashestiel, 59
Ashval, 159
Askernish, 172
Askival, 159
Atholl, Dukes of, 125, 123
—— Sow, 126
Auchencairn, 71, [5]
Auchmithie, 112
Auchrannie, Slug of, 110
Auchterarder, 106, [8]
Auchtermuchty, 102, [9]
Auldearn, 133, [14, 17]
Aultbea, 181, [21]
Aultnaharrie, 182
Aviemore, 127, [14, 17]
Avon, River, 129, [14]
Awe, River, 143
Ayr, 76, [4, 6–7]
——, River, 76, [4, 5, 7]
Ayton, 41, [2]

Badcall, 185, [18, 21]
Badcaul, 181
Badenoch, 127, [11, 17]

205

Badenoch, Boar of, 126
'Badenoch, Wolf of,' 123, 128, 131, 152
Baird, J. L., 83
Balavil, 127
Balfron, 93, [7, 8]
Balgownie, Brig o', 116
Baliol, John de, 70
Ballachulish, 140, [10]
Ballantrae, 75, [4]
Ballater, 119, [14]
Ballindalloch Castle, 128
Ballinluig, 124, [8]
Balloch, 88, [7]
Ballochbuie Forest, 120
Balmacara, 161, [16]
Balmaha, 89, [7, 11]
Balmoral Castle, 119, [14]
Balnakill, 186
Balquidder, 107, [8, 11]
Baltasound, 203, [24]
Balvenie Castle, 129
Banavie, 138, 156
Banchory, 118, [15]
Banff, 129, 32, [15]
Bankend, 68, [3, 5]
Bannockburn, 94, [7, 8]
Barcaldine Castle, 140, [10]
Bard Head, 201
Barholm Castle, 71
Barness, 41
Barra, 172, 148, [13]
—— Head, 173, 168
Barrie, Sir James, 111, 171
Barrogill Castle, 189
Barvas, 170, [20]
Bass Rock, 42, [9]
Bealach nam Bo, 90
Beallach, the 178
Beaton, Cardinal, 100, 101
Beaufort Castle, 176, [17]
Beauly, 176, [17]
——, River, 176, [17]
—— Firth, 175, 176, [17]
Bell, Henry, 83
——, J. J., 81, 169
Bellochantuy, 86, [6]
Bell Rock, 112, [9]
Bemersyde, 61
Ben A'an, 90
—— Alder, 126
—— Alligin, 181
—— an Tuirc, 85
—— Arthur, 84
—— Attow, 160, 178, [16]
Benbecula, 172, 171, [13]
Ben Bhan, 114
—— Chonzie, 108
—— Cleuch, 104
—— Cruachan, 143, [10]
—— Dearg, 125, [8, 11, 14]
—— Douran, 142
—— Eay, 180, [16, 21]
—— Eighe, 180
—— Fhada, 142
—— Hee, 187
—— Hope, 187
—— Klibreck, 188, [18]

Ben Lair, 180
—— Laoghal, 188
—— Lawers, 151, [8, 11]
—— Ledi, 90, 106
—— Lomond, 89, [7, 11]
—— Loyal, 188, [18]
—— Lui, 142
—— MacDhui, 122, [14]
—— More (Cowal), 83
—— —— (Mull), 145, [12]
—— —— (Perthshire), 151
—— —— (South Uist), 172, [13]
—— —— Assynt, 184, [18]
—— —— Coigach, 182
—— Muich-Dhui, 122
Bennan Head, 85
Ben Nevis, 138, [10, 16]
—— Nuis, 84
—— Rinnes, 129
—— Spionnaidh, 186
—— Stack, 185, [18]
—— Tarsuinn, 84
—— Tee, 137
—— Vair, 140
—— Venue, 90, [7, 11]
—— Vorlich (Dunbartonshire), 150
—— —— (Perthshire), 107, [8, 11]
—— Vrackie, 125, [8]
—— Wyvis, 174, [17]
Ben-y-Gloe, 122, 125, [8, 14]
Beregonium, 140
Berneray, 173
Berriedale, 191, [19]
Bervie, 114, [9, 15]
Berwick-upon-Tweed, 39, [2]
Bettyhill, 188, [18]
Bibliography, 36
Bieldside, 118, [15]
Bighouse Rocks, 188
Birkhall, 119
Birnam, 124, [8]
Birrenswark, the, 65
Birsay, 199, [23]
Bishop's Seat, 83
Black, William, 145, 169
—— Cavern, 85
—— Isle, 175, [17]
Blackford, 106, [7, 8, 11]
Black Mount, 142
Blackness, 94, [2, 8]
Black Rock of Novar, 194
Blackwater Loch, 85, [6]
Blackwater Reservoir, 149, [10–11]
Black Wood of Rannoch, 153
Blair Atholl, 125, [8, 11]
Blair Castle, 125, [8, 11]
Blairgowrie, 123, [8]
Blairs College, 118
Blake, George, 78, 169
Blantyre, 91
Blaven, 165, 163, [22]
Boat of Garten, 128, [14]
Boddam, 117, [1, 5]
Bogie, River, 129, [15]
Bonar Bridge, 193, [18]
Bonnington Linn, 92

Boreraig, 167
Boreray, 172
Borgie Bridge, 188, [18]
Borgue, 75, [5]
Borradale, 158
Borve Lodge, 171
Bothwell, 91, [7]
——, Earl of, 51, 62
Bowhill, 63
Bowling, 82, [7]
Bowmore, 88, [13]
Boyne Castle, 130
Bracadale, 168, [22]
Bracklinn Falls, 106, [7, 8, 11]
Brae, 202
Braehead, 54
Braemar, 120, 32, [14]
Braemore, 182
Braeriach, 122, [14]
Bran, River, 124
Brander, Pass of, 143, [10]
Breadalbane Vine, 151
Brechin, 112, [9]
Bressay, 201, [24]
Bridgeness, 93
Bridge of Allan, 105, 32, [7, 8, 11]
—— of Balgie, 152, [8, 11]
—— of Orchy, 142, [11]
—— of Weir, 78, [7]
Brig o' Turk, 90, [7, 8, 11]
British Aluminium Co., 55, 98, 136, 140, 155
Broadford, 163, [16, 22]
Broadshaw, 132
Brodick, 84, [4, 6]
Brodie Castle, 132, [14]
Brogar, 198
Brora, 192, [19]
Broster, D. K., 137
Brown, Bridge of, 128
——, George Douglas, 77
Broxburn, the, 41
Bruach-na-Frithe, 165
Bruar Water, 126, [8, 11]
Bruce, Robert, 60, 65, 69, 72, 74, 79, 94, 97
——, Sir William, 50, 103
Brunanburh, 65
Buccleuch, Dukes of, 48, 54, 57, 63, 98
Buchaille Etive, 142
Buchan, 116
——, Anna, 59
——, John, 70, 108, 163
Buchanan Castle, 91
Buchan Ness, 117, [15]
Buckhaven, 98
Buckie, 130, [14]
Bullers of Buchan, 117, [15]
Burghead, 31, [14, 19]
Burnmouth, 40
Burns, Robert, 31, 54, 68, 75, 76, 77, 83, 126, 152
Burnswork, the, 65
Burntisland, 98, [2, 9]
Burnt Islands, 86
Burra Firth, 204, [24]

Burray, 199, [23]
Burrow Head, 73, [4]
Busta Voe, 202
Bute, 83, 84, 86, [6]
——, Marquises of, 83, 103, 132
Butt of Lewis, 170, 168, [20]
Bynack Lodge, 122

Cadzow, 92
Caerlaverock Castle, 68, 72, [3, 5]
Cairndow, 150, [6, 10–11]
Cairn Gorm, 122, [14]
Cairngorm Mountains, 121, 127, [14]
Cairnsmore of Fleet, 72, [4, 5]
Cairn Toul, 122, [14]
Cairnwell Pass, 123, [8, 14]
Caithness, 188–90, [19, 23]
Calders Geo, 203
Caledonian Canal, 135
Calendar, A Scottish, 31
Calf Sound, 199, [23]
Callander, 106, 90, [7, 8, 11]
Callernish, 170, [20]
Cally, Bridge of, 123
Calton Hill, 52
Camasunary, 163
Cambuskenneth Abbey, 95
Cambuslang, 92
Cam Loch, 183
Campbell Castle, 104
Campbeltown, 85, [6]
Campsie Fells, 93, [7, 8]
—— Glen, 93
Canisbay, 189, [23]
Canisp, 183, [18, 21]
Canna, 159, [22]
Cannich, 176
——, River, 177, [16–17]
Caravanning, 25
Carberry Hill, 44, 103
Cardoness Castle, 71
Cardross, 82, [6–7]
Carfin, 92
Carlaverock Castle, 68, 72, [3, 5]
Carlingwark Loch, 70
Carlisle, 66, [3]
Carlops, 58, [2]
Carloway, 170, [20]
Carluke, 92, [7]
Carlyle, Thomas, 65, 43
Carnach, 142
Carnan, 172, [13]
Carnassary Castle, 87
Carn Dearg, 139
Carnegie, Andrew, 97, 193
Carn Eige, 177
Carnoustie, 112, [9]
Carradale, 85, 86
Carrbridge, 128, [14]
Carrick, 74, [4]
—— Castle, 83
Carrol Rock, 192
Carronbridge, 69, [5]
Carr Rocks, 99
Carskey, 86
Carsluith Castle, 71

Carsphairn, 71, [5]
Carswell, Catherine, 81
Castlebay, 173, 148, 32, [13]
Castlecary, 93
Castle Campbell, 104
—— Douglas, 70, [5]
—— Grant, 128
—— Kennedy, 74, [4]
—— Menzies, 152
—— Moil, 163
—— Roy, 128
Castles, the, 84
Castletown, 189, [19, 23]
Castle Urquhart, 136
—— Varrich, 187
Caterthuns, the, 113
Cat's Back, 175
Cauldron of the Dungeon, 72
Cava, 196
Cawdor Castle, 133, [14, 17]
Cellardyke, 99
Challich, 182
Charles I, 97
—— II, 50-2, 101
—— Edward, Prince, 44, 46, 50, 55, 62, 69, 94, 126, 133, 137, 154, 157, 158, 160, 163, 165, 167, 171, 172, 177
Chisholm's Pass, 177
Cinn Trolla, 192
Cir Mhor, 84
Clachan, 85, [6, 13]
Clach Glas, 165
Clachmannan, 96, [7, 8]
Cladich, 149, [10]
Clava, Stones of, 133
Clett, the, 189
Clickimin, 201
Clift Sound, 201
Clisham, 170
Cloch Lighthouse, 78, [6]
Clouston, J. Storer, 196
Clunie, River, 120, 121
—— Bridge, 160, [16]
Cluny Castle, 154
Clyde, Falls of the, 92, [7]
——, Firth of, 76-8, 82, 83, [4, 6]
——, River, 64, 78-80, 82, 92, [2, 5, 7]
Clydebank, 82
Clyde Law, 64
Clynder, 83
Cobbler, the, 84, 89, [6, 10-11]
Cockburnspath, 41, [2, 9]
Cocklaw, 41
Cock of Arran, 85
Collenogle Ford, 90
Collace, 168, [22]
Coldingham, 40, [2]
Colintraive, 83, 86, [6]
Coll, 148, [12]
Collieston, 116, [15]
Colonsay, 88, [13]
——, Little, 146
Columba, St, 146
Comlongon Castle, 67
Common Ridings, 31, 32
Comrie, 107, [8, 11]

Comrie Castle, 152
Connel Ferry, 143, 140, [10]
Conon, Falls of, 174
—— Bridge, 175, [17]
Contin, 174, [17]
Coolins, the, 164
Corpach, 156, [10, 16]
Corra Linn, 92
Corran, 139, 157
Corrie, 84, 85, [6]
Corriegoe, 160
Corriemulzie, Linn of, 120
Corrieyairack, Pass of 154, [11, 17]
Corstorphine, 53, [2, 8-9]
Cortachy Castle, 111
Coulport, 83
Coupar Angus, 110, [9]
Courthill, 173
Cove, 83, [6]
Cowal, 83, 86, [6]
Craigandarrach, 119
Craig Beg, 127
—— Cluny, 120
—— Dhu, 127
Craigellachie (Banffshire), 129, [14]
—— (Inverness-shire), 127
Craigendoran, 82
Craighouse, 87, 88, [13]
Craigmillar Castle, 57
Craignethan Castle, 92
Craigour, 125
Craig Phadrig, 134
Crail, 99, [9]
Cramond Bridge, 54
Cranstackie, 186
Crask, the, 188, [18]
Crathes Castle, 118, [15]
Crathie Church, 119, [14]
Creagorry, 172, [13]
Cree, River, 72, [4]
Creetown, 72, [4]
Crianlarich, 151, [11]
Crieff, 107, 32, [8, 11]
Criffel, 70, [5]
Crinan Canal, 86, [6, 13]
Crockett, S. R., 70
Croe Bridge, 161, 178
Croidh-la, 127
Cromarty, 175, [17]
—— Firth, 175, 193, 194, [17]
Cromwell, Oliver, 41, 46, 50
Crossaig, 92, [7]
Crossraguel Abbey, 75
Cruachan, Falls of, 143
Cruden Bay, 117, [15]
Cuillins, the, 164, [22]
Cul Beg, 183
Culbin Sands, 131
Culblean, 119
Cullen, 130, [14-15]
Cullochy, 137
Culloden, 133, 31, [17]
Culross, 96, [2, 8]
Cults, 118, [15]
Culzean Castle, 75
Cumberland, Duke of, 55, 133, 137

Cumbernauld, 93, [7, 8]
Cumbrae, Great, 78, 84, [6]
——, Little, 78, 84, [6]
Cunningsburgh, 201
Cupar, 102, [9]
Cycling, 27

Dairsie Castle, 102, [9]
Dalbeattie, 70, [5]
Dalkeith, 57, [2]
Dalmally, 142, [10–11]
Dalmellington, 71, [4–5, 7]
Dalmeny, 54
Dalmuir, 82
Dalnaspidal, 126, [8, 11, 17]
Dalriada, 143
Dalry, 71, [5]
Dalveen Pass, 69, [5, 7]
Dalwhinnie, 126, 154, [11, 17]
Dark Mile, 138
Darnaway Castle, 132
Darnick Tower, 60
Darnley, Earl of, 51
David I, 51, 60, 62, 95, 97, 105, 113, 131
—— II, 47, 99
Davidson, John, 78
Dee, River (Aberdeen), 114, 118–22, [15]
——, —— (Kirkcudbright), 70, [5]
——, Linn of, 121, [14]
——, Pools of, 122
Denny, 93, [7, 8]
Derry Lodge, 122
Destitution Road, 182
Deveron, River, 129, 130, [14, 15]
Devil's Beef Tub, 64, [3, 5]
—— Elbow, 123, [8, 14]
Devon, River, 104, [7, 8]
Dick, Robert, 189
Dingwall, 175, [17]
Dinnet, 119, [14]
Dippen, 86, [6, 13]
Dirleton, 43, [2, 9]
Divach Falls, 136
Dochart, River, 151, [11]
Dollar, 104, [7, 8]
Don, River, 116, [15]
Donn, Robert, 186
Doon, River, 76, [4, 7]
Dore Holm, 202
Dornie, 161, [16]
Dornoch, 192, [19]
—— Firth, 193, [18–19]
Douglas, Sir Archibald, 40
——, Catherine, 109
——, George, 77
——, 3rd Earl of, 42, 70
——, 4th Earl of, 69
——, 6th Earl of, 47
——, 8th Earl of, 95
Doune, 106, [7, 8, 11]
Drem, 42
Drimnin, 157
Druim Pass, 176

Drumbeg, 185, [21]
Drum Castle, 118, [15]
Drumhain, 164, 165
Drummond Castle, 108
Drummore, 74, [4]
Drumnadrochit, 178, 136, [17]
Drumochter, Pass of, 126, [8, 11, 17]
Drumrunie, 182
Dryburgh Abbey, 61, [2]
Dryhope Tower, 64
Drymen, 91, [7]
Duart Castle, 145
Dufftown, 129, [14]
Dull, 152
Dulnain Bridge, 128, [14]
Dumbarton, 82, 94, [7]
Dumfries, 68, 32, [3, 5]
Dunaverty Bay, 86
Dunbar, 41, [2, 9]
Dunbartonshire, 84, 89, 93, 150, [6, 7]
Dunbeath, 190, [19]
Dunblane, 105, [7, 8, 11]
Dun Buy, 117
Duncan, 111, 133, 147
Duncansby Head, 190, 195, [19, 23]
Dundalair, 154
Dundarave, 150
Dundee, 109, 102, [9]
——, Viscount, 125
Dundonnell, 181, [21]
Dun Dornadilla, 187
—— Dornaigil, 187
Dundrennan Abbey, 71, [5]
Dunedin, 46
Dunfermline, 96, [2, 8]
Dunglass House, 41
Dunkeld, 123, [8]
Dunmore Hill, 107
Dunnet, 189, [19, 23]
—— Head, 189, 196, [19, 23]
Dunnottar Castle, 114, [15]
Dunollie Castle, 144
Dunoon, 83, 32, [6]
Dunrobin Castle, 192, [19]
Dunrossness, 201
Dunsinane, 124
Dunstaffnage Castle, 143, 110
Duntocher, 82
Duntulm Castle, 166
Dunure, 76, [4, 6]
Dunvegan, 167, [22]
Durness, 186, [18]
Dwarfie Stone, 199
Dysart, 98, [9]

Earlsferry, 99
Earn, River, 107
Earraid, 148
Easter Ross, 193
East Linton, 41, [2, 9]
—— Loch Tarbert, 171, [20]
—— Wemyss, 98, [9]
Eaval, 171
Ecclefechan, 65, [3, 5]

Eday, 199, [23]
Eddrachillis Bay, 185, [21]
Edinburgh, 44, 31, 32, 94, [2, 9]
—— Festival, 53
Edward I, 46, 55, 94, 110, 136
—— II, 94, 199
—— III, 40, 43, 46, 109
Edzell, 113, [9, 15]
Egilsay, 199, 113, 197, [23]
Eglinton Castle, 77
Eigg, 159, [22]
Eildon Hills, 60, 62
Eilean Donan, 161
—— Fhionain, 157
—— Ruairidh, 180
—— Suinn, 180
—— Suthainn, 180
Elderslie, 78
Electric Brae, 75
Elgin, 131, [14]
Elgol, 163, [22]
Elie, 99, [9]
Ellen's Isle, 90
Ellisland, 69
Elphin, 183, [18, 21]
Elvanfoot, 69, [5, 7]
Erchless Castle, 176, [17]
Eriboll, 187, [18]
Ericht, River (near Blairgowrie), 123
——, —— (Loch Ericht), 126, [11]
Eriskay, 172
Erraid, 148
Erskine, 79
Esha Ness, 202
Esk, River (Dumfries-shire), 66, [3]
——, —— (Midlothian), 44
Ettrick, 63
——, River, 63, [3]
—— Forest, 63, [2]
Evanton, 194, [17]
Ewe, River, 181
Eyemouth, 40, [2]
Eynhallow, 199, [23]

Fair Isle, 200, [24]
Fairlie, 77, 84, [6]
Fairy Bridge, 167, [22]
Falkirk, 55, [8]
Falkland, 103, [9]
Falloch, Falls of, 151
Far-Out Head, 186
Farrar, River, 176, [16 17]
Farr Bay, 188
Fasnakyle, 177
Fast Castle, 40, [2]
Fearn, 193, [17, 19]
Feolin, 87, [13]
Fergusson, Robert, 50
Fetlar, 203, [24]
Fettercairn, 113, [9, 15]
Fettes College, 54
Feugh, Bridge of, 119
Fiddich, River, 129
Fife, 96, 55, 99, 102, [9]
—— Ness, 99, [9]

Fincharn Castle, 144
Findhorn Bay, 131, [14]
—— Glen, 132, [14, 17]
Findochty, 130, [14]
Findon, 114, [15]
Fingal, 144, 146, 151
Fingal's Cave, 146
Finlarig Castle, 151
Finstown, 198, [23]
Fintry, 93
Fionn Ben, 174
First Coast, 181
Fitful Head, 200, 202, [24]
Fleet, River, 192, [18]
Flodigarry, 166, [22]
Floors Castle, 62
Flotta, 196
Flowerdale, 181
Fochabers, 130, 32, 129, [14]
Foinaven, 185, [18]
Folda, 110
Ford, 144, [10, 13]
Forest Lodge, 122
Forfar, 112, [9]
Forres, 132, [14]
Forrest, Henry, 100
Fort Augustus, 136, [16–17]
Forth, River, 90, 95, 96, [7]
——, Firth of, 53, 55, 94, 96, 97, [9]
—— and Clyde Canal, 93
—— Bridge, 55, [2, 8]
Fortingal, 152, [8, 11]
Fortrose, 175, [17]
Fort William, 138, 32, 155, [10, 16]
Foss, Braes of, 153
Foula, 202, [24]
Fowlis Wester, 108
Foyers, 136, 155, [17]
Fraserburgh, 130, [15]
Fros-Bheinn, 158
Fuar Tholl, 174
Furnace, 85, [6, 10]

Gairloch, 181, [16, 21]
Gairlochy, 138, [10, 16]
Galashiels, 59, 31, [2]
Galloway, 69, 74
——, New, 71, [4, 5]
Galt, John, 77
Callavan, 144
Garbh Eilean, 180
Gardenstown, 130
Gareloch, 83, [6]
Garelochhead, 83, [6–7]
Garleton Hill, 43
Garliestown, 73, [4]
Garnock, River, 77
Garry, River, 125, 126, [8, 11]
Garth Castle, 152
Garve, 174, 182, [17]
Garvelloch Isles, 148
Garynahine, 170, [20]
Gatehouse of Fleet, 71, [4, 5]
Gearr Aonach, 142
Gibbon, Lewis Grassic, 113

Gibbs, James, 115
Gigha, 86, 87, [6, 13]
Girvan, 75, [4]
Glamis Castle, 110, [9]
Glasgow, 80, 32, [7]
Glas Maol, 123, [8–9, 14]
Glass, River (Inverness-shire), 176, [17]
——, —— (Ross), 194
Glasven (Ross), 161
—— (Sutherland), 184, [18]
Glen Affric, 177, [16]
—— Alva, 104
—— Aray, 149, [10]
—— Ashdale, 84
—— Avon, 122, [14]
Glenbarry, 129, [14–15]
Glen Brittle, 164
—— Callater, 121
—— Cannich, 177, [16]
Glencaple, 68, [3, 5]
Glen Carron, 174, [16]
—— Clova, 111, [9, 14]
—— Clunie, 121, 123, 120, [14]
Glencoe, 141, [10]
Glen Corodale, 172
—— Croe, 150
—— Dee, 122
—— Derry, 122
—— Dochart, 151
—— Docharty, 180
—— Doe, 136
Gleneagles, 106, [8]
Glen Elchaig, 177
Glenelg, 159, 161, [16]
Glen Errochty, 153, 154
—— Esk, 113, [9, 14–15]
—— Etive, 141, [10]
—— Falloch, 150, [11]
—— Feshie, 127
Glenfinnan, 157, [10, 16]
Glen Fruin, 83
—— Garry, 160, 137, [10, 16]
—— Grivie, 178
Gleniffer, 79
Glen Iorsa, 84
—— Isla, 110, [9]
Glenlivet, 129
Glen Lochay, 151, [11]
—— Lochy, 142
—— Loy, 138
Glenluce, 73, [4]
Glen Lui, 122
—— —— Beg, 122
—— Lyon, 152, [8, 11]
—— Morag, 83
—— More, 135, [16, 17]
Glenmore Lodge, 122, 128
Glen Moriston, 160, [16–17]
—— Muick, 119, [14]
—— Nevis, 139
—— Ogle, 107, [8, 11]
—— Orchy, 142, [10–11]
—— Prosen, 111, [9]
—— Quharity, 111
—— Rosa, 84
—— Roy, 155, [11, 17]
—— Sannox, 84

Glen Shee, 123, [8]
—— Shiel, 160, [16]
—— Shira, 150
—— Sligachan, 164, 165
—— Spean, 154, [11, 17]
—— Spey, 127, 154
—— Strathfarrar, 176
—— Tarbert, 157
—— Tarff, 154, [17]
—— Tilt, 122, [8, 14, 17]
—— Truim, 126
—— Turret, 107
—— Urquhart, 178, 136, [17]
—— Varragill, 165
—— Vorlich, 107
Glomach, Falls of, 161, 177
Glossary, 33
Goat Fell, 84, [6]
Golspie, 192, [19]
Gometra, 146, [12]
Gordon, Dukes of, 127, 129, 130
—— Castle, 131
Gourdon, 114
Gourock, 78, [6]
Gowrie, 1st Earl of, 108
——, 3rd Earl of, 109
Graham's Dyke, 93
Gramisdale, 172
Grampian Mountains, 95, 108, 109, [10–11]
Grange, 129
Grann Stacach, 186
Grant, Castle, 128
Granton, 54, [2, 9]
Grantown, 128, [14]
Great Glen, 135, 138
Greenloaning, 106, [7, 8, 11]
Green Loch, 128
Greenock, 78, [6–7]
Gretna Green, 65, [3]
Grey Mare's Tail, 64, [3, 5]
Grim's Dyke, 93
Grind of the Navir, 202
Grogport, 86
Grudie, Bridge of, 180
Gruinard Bay, 181, [21]
Gualan, the, 186
Guard Bridge, 102, [9]
Gullane, 43, [2, 9]
Gull's Bridge, 202
Gunn, Neil M., 196
Gutter Sound, 196

Haakon IV, 78, 19
Habbie's How, 58
Haco IV, 78, 197
Haddington, 43, [3, 9]
Haig, Earl, 60
Halidon Hill, 40
Halladale River, 188, [19]
Hamilton, 91, [7]
——, Patrick, 100
Handa, 185
Harris, 170, [20]
Hawick, 63, 31, [3]
'Heart of Midlothian,' 48
Heaval, 173

Hebrides, 168, 148, 159, [12, 13, 20]
Hecla, 172
Heilem Ferry, 187
Helensburgh, 82, 32, [6–7]
Helmsdale, 191, [19]
Herma Ness, 203, [24]
Hermitage Castle, 62
Highland Games, 32
Hillswick, 202, [24]
Hirta, 172
Hoddam Castle, 65
Hogg, James, 63, 64
Holburn Head, 189
Hole o' Rowe, 198
Holm Sound, 199
Holy Isle, 85, [4, 6]
Holyrood Palace, 50
Hope Lodge, 187, [18]
Hotels, 29
Hoxa, Sound of, 196
Hoy, 199, [23]
Huna, 189, [19]
Huntingtower Castle, 108
Huntly, 129, [14]

Idrigil, Point of, 168
Inchcape Rock, 112
Inchcolm, 98, [2, 9]
Inchkeith, 98, [2, 9]
Inchkenneth, 146
Inchmahome, 91
Inchmurrin, 89
Inchnadamph, 183, [18]
Innellan, 86, [6]
Innerleithen, 59, [2]
Inver (near Balmoral), 120
—— (near Birnam), 124
——, River, 184
Inveraray, 149, [6, 10]
Invercannich, 176
Invercarron, 184
Invercauld, 120
Inverewe, 181
Inverey, 120, [14]
Inverfarigaig, 136
Invergarry Castle, 137, 160
Invergordon, 193, [17, 18]
Inverie, 159, [10, 16]
Inverinate, 161, [16]
Inverkeithing, 97, [2, 8–9]
Inverkirkaig, 183
Inverliver, 144
Inverlochy, 155
—— Castle, 130
Invermoriston, 136, 159, [17]
Inverness, 133, 32 [17]
Inversanda, 157, [10, 12]
Inverscaddle Bay, 157
Invershiel, 160
Invershin, 193, 179, 183, [18]
Inversnaid, 89, 91, [6–7, 11]
Inverugie Castle, 117
Iona, 146, [12]
Irongray, 69
Irvine, 77, 32, [4, 7]
Irving, Edward, 67

Isla, River, 110, [9]
Islay, 87, [13]
Isle Ornsay, 163, [16, 22]
—— of Whithorn, 73, [4–5]
Isles of the Sea, 148

Jacob, Violet, 113
James I (of Scotland), 109
—— II, 47, 62, 63, 95
—— III, 54, 94, 95, 100, 195
—— IV, 50, 55, 95
—— V, 49, 54, 66, 94, 103
—— VI (I of England), 47, 50, 94–6, 108, 109, 117
—— VIII (Old Pretender), 112, 157, 161
Jarlshof, 202
Jeantown, 173
Jedburgh, 62, [3]
John o' Groats, 189, [19, 23]
Johnson, Samuel, 117, 144, 146, 147, 160, 162, 165
Johnstone, 78, [7]
Jones, Paul, 70, 71
Jura, 87, [13]

Keiss, 190, [19, 23]
Keith, 129, [14]
——, George, 5th Earl Marischal, 115, 114
——, ——, 10th Earl Marischal, 117, 114, 160
——, Marshal, 117
Kelso, 61, [2]
Kemp, G. M., 45
Kenmore, 151, [8, 11]
Kennageall, 187
Kenneth Macalpine, 110
Kentallen, 139
Keoldale, 186
Keppoch, 161
Kerrera, 144, 139, 145, [10, 12]
Kerry, Falls of, 181
Kerrysdale, 181
Kidd, Captain, 78
Kiessimul Castle, 173
Kilbirnie, 78, [6–7]
Kilbrennan Sound, 86, [6]
Kilchattan Bay, 83, [6]
Kilchoan, 145, 157, [12]
Kilchurn Castle, 142
Kilconquhar, 59
Kilcreggan, 83, [6]
Kildonan Castle, 85, [4, 6]
Killearn, 93, [7, 8]
Killiecrankie, Pass of, 125, [8]
Killin, 151, [8, 11]
Kilmacolm, 78, [7]
Kilmallie, 156
Kilmaluag, 166, [22]
Kilmarnock, 77, [4, 7]
Kilmartin, 87, [6, 10, 13]
Kilmelfort, 87, [6, 10, 12]
Kilmorack, 176, [17]
Kilmuir, 166
Kilnaughton Bay, 88

Kilninver, 87, [10, 13]
Kilpatrick, Old, 82, 79, 93, [7]
Kilravock Castle, 133
Kilt Rock, 166
Kilwinning, 77, [6]
Kincardine (Fife), 96, [7, 8]
—— Castle, 113
—— O'Neil, 119, [15]
Kincraig, 127, [17]
Kinghorn, 97, [2, 9]
Kingsburgh, 166
King's Caves, 85
King's House (near Balquhidder), 107
Kingshouse (Moor of Rannoch), 142, [10]
Kingussie, 127, 32, [11, 17]
Kinlochbervie, 186, [18, 21]
Kinlochewe, 180, [16, 21]
Kinlochleven, 140, 155, [10–11]
Kinloch Rannoch, 153, [8, 11]
Kinloss Abbey, 131, [14]
Kinnaird Castle, 113
Kinnoull Hill, 109
Kinross, 103, [8]
Kintail, 160
——, Pass of, 178
Kintradwell, 192
Kintraw, 87
Kintyre, 85, [6]
Kinveachy, 128
Kippen, 93, [7, 8, 11]
Kirkaig, River, 183
Kirkbean, 70, [5]
Kirkcaldy, 98, [9]
Kirkcudbright, 71, [5]
Kirkmadrine, 74
Kirkmaiden, 74
Kirk o' Field, 51
Kirkoswald, 75, [4, 6–7]
Kirkwall, 197, [23]
Kirriemuir, 111, [9]
Kirtomy Point, 188
Kishorn, 173, [16]
Kitchener, Earl, 199
Knockfarrel, 175
Knock Fyrish, 194
—— of Crieff, 107
Knox, John, 43, 49, 50, 95, 100, 108
Knoydart, 159
Kyleakin, 161, 32, [16, 22]
Kyle of Durness, 186, [18]
—— of Lochalsh, 161, [16]
—— of Sutherland, 193
—— of Tongue, 187, [18]
Kylerhea, 159
Kylesku, 184, [18, 21]
Kyles of Bute, 86, [6]
Kyle Strome, 184

Ladhar Beinn, 159
Ladybank, 102, [9]
Lagg (Arran), 85, [4, 6]
—— (Jura), 88, [13]
Laggan, River, 90
—— Bay, 87, [13]

Laggan Bridge, 154, [11, 17]
—— Locks, 137
Laide, 181
Lairg, 192, 183, 185, 188, [18]
Lamberton, 40
Lamlash, 85, [4, 6]
Lammermuirs, the, 41
Lanark, 92, 31, [7]
Lang, Andrew, 101
Langholm, 32, [3]
Langside, 104
Langwell House, 191
Largo, 99, [9]
Largs, 78, [6]
Larig Ghru, 122
Larne, 74
Lasswade, 57
Latheron, 190, [19]
Laurencekirk, 113, [9, 15]
Lawers, 151, [8, 11]
Laxford Bridge, 185, [18]
Leadburn, 58, [2]
Leadhills, 59, [5, 7]
Ledmore, 183, [18]
Leith, 54, 44, [2, 9]
Lennoxlove, 43
Lennoxtown, 93, [7, 8]
Leny, Pass of, 106, [7, 8, 11]
——, River, 106
Lerwick, 201, 31, 32, [24]
Leuchars, 102, [9]
Leven, 99, [9]
——, River, 82, 88
Leverburgh, 171, [20]
Leverhulme, Lord, 170, 171
Lewis, 169, [20]
Lhanbryde, 131, [14]
Liathach, 180
Liberton, 57
Lincluden Abbey, 69
Linklater, Eric, 196
Linlithgow, 55, 31, [2, 8]
Linton, East, 42, [2, 4]
Lismore, 139, [10, 12]
Little Colonsay, 146
—— Gruinard, 181, [21]
Livingstone, David, 91
Loanhead, 57
Loch a' Beallach, 178
Lochaber, 138, 154, [10–11]
Loch Achanalt, 174
—— Achilty, 174
—— Achray, 90, [7, 11]
—— Affric, 177, [16]
—— Ailort, 158, [10, 16]
—— Aline, 145, 157, [10, 12]
—— Alsh, 161, [16]
—— Alvie, 127
—— -an-Eilean, 127
—— Ard, 91, [7, 11]
—— Arkaig, 137, [10, 16]
—— Arklet, 89, [7, 11]
—— Assynt, 183, [18, 21]
—— Avon, 122, [14]
—— Awe (Argyll), 144, 143, 149, [6, 10]
—— —— (Sutherland), 183
Lochay, River, 151, [11]

Loch Bà, 142
—— Bad a Ghaill, 183
—— Baddagyle, 183
—— Batnaskalloch, 181
—— Beinn a'Mheadhoin, 178
—— Beneveian, 177, [16]
Lochboisdale, 148, 172, 32, [13]
Loch Borralan, 183
—— Bracadale, 167, [22]
—— Brittle, 165, [22]
—— Broom, 182, 183, [18, 21]
—— ——, Little, 181, [21]
—— Brora, 192, [19]
—— Bunacharan, 176
—— Cairnbawn, 184
—— Carron, 173, 161, [16]
—— Chon, 91, [7, 11]
—— Clunie, 160, [16]
—— Coruisk, 164, 161, [22]
—— Craignish, 87
—— Creran, 139, [10, 12]
—— Culen, 174
—— Dochart, 151
—— Doule, 174, [16]
—— Drunkie, 90
—— Duich, 160, [16]
—— Dunvegan, 167, [22]
—— Earn, 107, [8, 11]
Lochearnhead, 107, [8, 11]
Loch Eck, 83, [6]
—— Eigeach, 153
—— Eil, 156, [10, 16]
—— Eilt, 157, [10, 16]
—— Enoch, 72
—— Eriboll, 187, [18]
—— Ericht, 126, 153, [8, 11, 17]
—— Etchachan, 122
—— Etive, 141, 139, 140, 143, [10]
—— Ewe, 181, [21]
—— Fada, 166
—— Feochan, 87
—— Fleet, 192, [19]
—— Fyne, 85, 83, 87, 149, 150, [6, 10]
—— Garry   (Inverness-shire), 160, [10–11, 16]
—— —— (Perthshire), 126, 153, [8, 11, 17]
—— Garth, 137
—— Ghriam, 185
Lochgilphead, 85, [6, 13]
Loch Glencoul, 184
—— Glendhu, 184
—— Goil, 84, [6, 10]
Lochgoilhead, 83, [6, 10–11]
Loch Gowan, 174
—— Greshornish, [9]
—— Gruinart, 88, [13]
Lochgyle, 146
Loch Harport, 165, [22]
—— Hempriggs, 190
—— Hope, 187, [18]
—— Hourn, 159, [16]
—— Inchard, 185
Lochinch Castle, 74
Loch Indaal, 88, [13]
—— -in-Dorb, 129, [14]

Loch Insh, 127, [14]
Lochinver, 184, [21]
Loch Katrine, 89, [7, 11]
—— Ken, 71, [5]
—— Kinord, 119
—— Kishorn, 173, [16]
—— Laggan, 154, [11, 17]
—— Laidon, 153, [11]
—— Laoghal, 188
Lochlea, 77
Loch Leathan, 166
—— Lee, 113, [9, 14]
—— Letteressie, 184
—— Leven (Argyll), 139, [10]
—— —— (Kinross), 103, [8]
—— Linnhe, 138–40, 157, [10, 12]
—— Lochy, 137, [10, 16]
—— Lomond, 88, 150, [7, 11]
—— Long (Argyll), 83, 84, 150, [6, 11]
—— —— (Ross), 161
—— Loyal, 188, [18]
—— Lubnaig, 106, [8, 11]
—— Luichart, 174, [17]
—— Lungard, 177
—— Lurgain, 185, [21]
—— Lydoch, 153
—— Lyon, 152, [11]
Lochmaben, 64, [3, 5]
Lochmaddy, 171, 32, [12, 20]
Loch Maree, 180, [16, 21]
—— Marlie, 123
—— Meiklie, 178, [17]
—— Melfort, 87
—— Merkland, 185, [18]
—— Mhuilinn, 176
—— Moidart, 157
—— Monar, 176, [16]
—— Morar, 158, [10, 16]
—— More, 185, [18]
—— Morlich, 122, 128, [14]
—— Muick, 119, [14]
—— Muillie, 176
—— Mullardoch, 177, [16]
Lochnagar, 121, [14]
Loch na Keal, 146, [12]
—— na Leitreach, 177
—— nan Cilltean, 158
—— nan Uamh, 158
—— Naver, 186, [18]
—— Ness, 135, [17]
—— Nevis, 159, [10, 16]
—— of Butterstone, 123
—— of Clunie, 123
—— of Craiglush, 123
—— of Harray, 198
—— of Lows, 123
—— of Spiggie, 202
—— of Stenness, 198, [23]
—— of the Lowes, 64
—— Oich, 137, [11, 17]
—— Quoich, 160, [10, 16]
—— Rannoch, 153, [8, 11]
Lochranza, 83, 84, [6]
Loch Roag, 170, [20]
—— Rosque, 180, [16]
—— Ryan, 73, 75, [4]
—— Scavaig, 163, 161, [22]

Loch Scaven, 174
—— Seaforth, 170, [20]
—— Seilich, 153
—— Shiel, 157, [10, 16]
—— Shin, 185, [18]
—— Skeen, 64, [3, 5]
—— Slapin, 163, [22]
—— Snizort, 166, [22]
—— Stack, 185, [18]
—— Sunart, 157, 145, [12]
—— Tarbert, East, 171, [20]
—— ——, West (Argyll), 86, 87, [6, 13]
—— ——, —— (Harris), 171, [20]
—— Tay, 151, [8, 11]
—— Tollie, 181
—— Torridon, 180, 174, [16, 22]
—— Treig, 154, [11, 17]
—— Triochatan, 142
—— Trool, 72, [4]
—— Tubhair, 151
—— Tulla, 142, [11]
—— Tummel, 125, 153, [8, 11]
—— Turret, 108
—— Vaa, 128
—— Vennachar, 90, [7, 8, 11]
—— Veyatie, 183, [18, 21]
—— Voil, 107, [11]
Lochy, River, 138, 156, [10, 16]
Lockerbie, 65, [3, 5]
Lockhart, J. G., 61
Lodgings, 30
Lomond Hills, 103, 53, [9]
Longhope, 196
Long Island, 168
Lora, Falls of, 143
Lorimer, Sir Robert, 46, 48, 108
Lorne, 143, [10, 12]
——, Firth of, 148, [10, 12]
Lossiemouth, 131, [14, 19]
Loth, 192
Lothian, East, 41, 42, [2]
Lovat Bridge, 176, [17]
Luce Bay, 72, [4]
Luib, 151, [11]
Luing, 148, [10, 12]
Lunan Bay, 112, [9]
Lundin Links, 99
Luss, 89, 32, 83, 91, [7, 11]
Lybster, 190, [19]
Lynwilg, 127, [17]
Lyon, River, 152, [8, 11]

McAdam, J, L., 74
Macbeth, 111, 124, 132–4, 147
Macdonald, Flora, 143, 165, 172
——, George, 129, 130
——, Gen. Sir Hector, 175
MacDonald, Ramsay, 131
Macduff, 130, [15]
Macduff's Castle, 98
Machars, the, 72, [4]
Machir Bay, 88
Machrie (Arran), 85, [6]
—— (Islay), 87
Machrihanish, 85, [6]
Macintyre, Duncan Ban, 149

Mackenzie, Agnes Mure, 114, 118, 169
Mackintosh, C. R., 81
MacLeod's Maidens, 168
—— Tables, 167
Macpherson, Ian, 128
——, James, 127
Maeshowe, 198
Magus Muir, 102
Maidenkirk, 74
Maiden Pap, 191
Mainland (Orkney), 195, [23]
—— (Shetland), 200, [24]
Malcolm Canmore, 96, 124
Mallaig, 158, 32, [10, 16, 22]
Mam Rattachan, 161
—— Soul, 177, [16]
Mar, Earl of, 106, 112
—— Castle, Old, 120
Maree, Isle, 180
Margaret, St, 46, 96, 147
Mar Lodge, 120
Marsco, 165
Marwick Head, 198
Mary of Guise, 103
Mary Queen of Scots, 41, 44, 47, 50, 51, 55, 57, 62, 66, 71, 91, 94–6, 101, 102, 104
Mauchline, 77, [4, 7]
Mavis Grind, 202
Maxwelltown, 69, [3, 5]
Maxwelton House, 69
May, Isle of, 99, [9]
Maybole, 75, [4, 6]
Mealfourvonie, 136
Mearns, the, 113
Measach, Falls of, 182, [18]
Meigle, 110, [9]
Meikle Ferry, 193
Meikleour, 110, [8]
Melfort, Pass of, 87
Melrose, 60, [2]
Melvich, 188, [19]
Mennock Pass, 69, [5, 7]
Menstrie, 104, [7, 8, 11]
Menteith, Lake of, 90, [7, 8, 11]
Menzies Castle, 152
Merchiston Castle, 57
Merrick, 72, [4]
Merse, the, 40, [2]
Methil, 98, [9]
Methven, 108, [8]
Mey, 189, [19, 23]
——, Castle of, 189
Midlothian, 44, 48, 58, [2, 9]
Mhoine, the, 187
Miller, Hugh, 175
Milnathort, 103, [8]
Milngavie, 93, [7]
Milton, 172
Mingary Castle, 145
Mingulay, 173
Moffat, 64, [2, 5]
Moil, Castle, 163
Monach Isles, 171, [12]
Monadhliath Mountains, 127, [17]
Moness, Falls of, 152
Monk, General, 42, 43, 58

Monkstadt House, 166
Monmouth, Duke of, 92
Monreith, 73
Montrose, 112, [9]
——, Dukes of, 84, 91
——, Marquis of, 48, 63, 104, 112, 133, 138, 184
Morar, 158, [10, 16, 22]
——, River, 158
Moray, 128, 130, [14]
—— Firth, 130, 132, 134, 136, 191, [14, 17]
Morrone Hill, 121
Moruisg, 174
Morven (Aberdeenshire), 119, [14]
—— (Argyll), 145, 157, [10, 12]
—— (Caithness), 191
Mossgiel, 57
Mote of Urr, 70
Motherwell, 92, [7]
Motoring, 25
Mougstot House, 166
Moulin, 124, [8]
Mound, the, 192, [19]
Mount Stuart, 83
Mousa, 201, [24]
Moy Bridge, 174, [17]
Muchalls, 115, [15]
Muck, 159, [22]
Muckle Flugga, 203
Muirfield, 43
Muirhead, 93
Muir of Ord, 175, [17]
Mull, 144, [10, 12]
——, Sound of, 145, 157, [10, 12]
—— of Galloway, 74, [4]
—— of Kintyre, 85, [6]
—— of Oa, 88, [13]
Mungasdale, 181
Mungo, St, 80, 81
Munro, Neil, 150, 169
Murray's Monument, 72, [4]
Musselburgh, 44, [2, 9]
Mylne, Walter, 100

Nairn, 132, [14, 17]
——, River, 132, 133, [17]
Napier, John, 57
National Trust for Scotland, vii, 47, 65, 71, 76, 94, 96, 104, 111, 125, 134, 141, 151, 157, 160, 161, 174, 175, 181, 182
Naver, River, 188, [18]
Neidpath Castle, 59
Ness, River, 133, [17]
Nethy Bridge, 128, [14]
New Abbey, 70, [5]
Newark Castle (Fife), 99
—— —— (Renfrewshire), 78
—— —— (Selkirkshire), 63
Newburgh, 116, [15]
New Galloway, 71, 72, [4, 5]
Newhaven, 54
Newtonmore, 127, 154, [11, 17]
Newton Stewart, 72, [4]
Newtown St Boswells, 61, [2]
Nigg, 193, [17]

Ninian, St, 73
Nith, River, 68, 69, [3, 5]
Noltland Castle, 199
North Ballachulish, 139, [10]
—— Berwick, 43, [2, 9]
—— —— Law, 42
—— Esk, River (Angus), 114, [9, 15]
—— ——, —— (Midlothian), 58
Northmaven, 202
North Ronaldsay, 200, [23]
—— Uist, 171, [12]
Noss, 201
Noup Head, 199, [23]

Oa, the, 88, [13]
Oban, 143, 32, 87, [10, 12]
Obbe, 171, [20]
Ochil Hills, 103, 104, 105, [8–9]
Oich, River, 137, [17]
Old Kilpatrick, 82, 79, 93, [7]
—— Man of Hoy, 199, [23]
—— —— of Storr, 166
—— —— of Wick, 190
'Old Mortality,' 68, 114
Onich, 139, [10]
Orchardton, 71
Orchy, River, 142
Ord of Caithness, 191
Orkney Islands 195, [23]
Orkneyman's Cave, 201
Ormaclett, 172
Oronsay, 88, [13]
Ossian's Cave, 142
Outer Hebrides, 168, 148, 159, [12, 13, 20]
Overscaig, 185, [18]
Owen, Robert, 92

Pabay, 163
Pabbay, 173, [13]
Paisley, 78, [7]
Papa Westray, 199, [23]
Pap of Glencoe, 142
Paps of Jura, 88, [13]
Parallel Roads, 155, 180, [11, 17]
Park, Mungo, 63
Parph, the, 186
Partick, 82
Pattack, River, 154
Pease Dean, 41
Peebles, 58, 31, [2]
Penicuik, 59, [2]
Penifuer, 90
Pennan, 130, [15]
Penpont, 69, [5]
Pentland Firth, 189–91, 195, 196, [23]
—— Hills, 53, 58, [2]
Perth, 108, [8]
Peterculter, 118, [15]
Peterhead, 117, 112, [15]
Philiphaugh, 63
Pierowall, 199, [23]
Pinkie, 44, 91
Pirnmill, 85, [6]

Pitcairngreen, 108
Pitlochry, 124, 32, [8]
Pittenweem, 99, [9]
Playfair, W. H., 45
Plockton, 173, [16]
Pluscarden Abbey, 132, [14]
Pollachar, 172
Pomona, 195, [23]
Poolewe, 181
Port Appin, 139, [10, 12]
—— Askaig, 87, [13]
—— Charlotte, 88, [13]
—— Ellen, 88, [13]
—— Glasgow, 78, [6–7]
Portgordon, 130, [14]
Port Kilbride, 166
Portknockie, 130, [14–15]
Port Logan, 74, [4]
—— Mary, 71
—— nan Gallan, 88
Portobello, 44, [2, 9]
Port of Ness, 170
Portpatrick, 74, [4]
Portree, 165, [22]
Portsonachan, 144, [10]
Portsoy, 130, [15]
Port William, 73, [4]
Prestonpans, 44, [2, 9]
Prestwick, 29, 77, [4, 6–7]
Pulteneytown, 190

Quarff, 201
Queensferry, North, 55, [2, 8]
——, South, 54, [2, 8–9]
Queen's View, 125, [8, 11]
Quholm, 199
Quinag, 184, [18, 21]
Quiraing, 166, [22]
Quirinish, 167
Quoich, Linn of, 121, [14]

Raasay, 162, [22]
Raehills Glen, 64
Railways, 28
Ramsay, Allan, 51, 58
Randolph's Leap, 132
Rannoch, Moor of, 153, 139, [11]
—— Station, 153, [11]
Reay, 188, [19]
—— Forest, 185, 187, [18]
Red Hills, 164
Reekie Linn, 110
Renfrew, 29, 87, [7]
Renfrewshire, 78
Rennie, John, 62
'Rest and be Thankful,' 150, [6, 11]
Revoan Pass, 128
Rhiconich, 185, [18]
Rhinns of Galloway, 74, [4]
—— of Islay, 88
Rhu, 83, [6]
Rhymer's Glen, 60
Rinyo, 199
Rizzio, David, 51
Robert III, 83

Rob Roy, 91, 107
Rodil, 171, [20]
Rogie, Falls of, 174
Roman Wall, 93
Ronaldsay, North, 200, [23]
——, South, 199, 195, 196, [23]
Ronas Hill, 202, [24]
—— Voe, 202
Roneval, 171
Rory Isle, 180
Rosemarkie, 175, [17]
Roseneath, 83, [6]
Roshven, 158
Roslin, 58
Rosslyn, 58
Ross-shire, 170, 173, 175, 176, 180, 193, [16–17]
Rosyth, 98, [2, 8]
Rothesay, 83, 32, [6]
Rothiemurchus, Forest of, 127
Rousay, 199, [23]
Rowardennan, 89, [7, 11]
Roxburgh, 62, 32
Roy Bridge, 155, [11, 17]
—— Castle, 128
Rum, 159, [22]
Rumbling Bridge (near Birnam), 124
—— —— (near Dollar), 104, [8]
Rutherglen, 91, [7]
Ruthven, 127
—— Castle, 108
Ruthwell, 67

Saddell, 85, 86, [6]
Saddle, the, 84
St Abbs, 40, [2]
—— —— Head, 40
—— Andrews, 99, 31, 32, [9]
—— Boswells, 61, [2]
—— Bride's Chapel, 107
—— Fillans, 107, [8, 11]
—— John's Head, 199
—— Johnstoun, 108
—— Kilda, 172
—— Margaret's Hope, 199, [23]
—— Mary's Isle, 71
—— —— Loch, 63, [2]
—— Monans, 99, [9]
—— Ninians, 94, [7, 8]
—— Ninian's Cave, 73
Salen (Mull), 145, [10, 12]
—— (Sunart), 157, [10, 12, 22]
Saltcoats, 77, [4, 6]
Sand, 181
Sanday, 200, [23]
Sandhead, 74, [4]
Sandray, 173, [13]
Sandside Bay, 188
Sandwick, 201, [24]
Sanquhar, 69, [5, 7]
Sark, River, 65
Sayers, Dorothy L., 70
Scalloway, 201, [24]
Scalpay, 171, [20]
Scapa, 196, 197, 199
—— Flow, 196, [23]

Scaraben, 191, [19]
Scarba, 148, [10, 13]
Scarista, 171
Schiehallion, 153, [8, 11]
Scone, 110, [8–9]
Scott, Michael, 60, 61
——, Sir Walter, 45, 49, 51, 57, 59–63, 114, 186
Scottish Tourist Board, viii
Scourie, 185, [18, 21]
Scour Ouran, 160
Scraada, Hole of, 203
Scrabster, 189, 196, [19]
Scrishven, 186
Scuir Vuillin, 174
Seamill, 77, [6]
Second Coast, 181
Selkirk, 63, 31, [2]
——, Alexander, 99
Sgurr Alasdair, 164, [22]
—— na Lapaich, 177
—— -nan-Gillean, 164
Shandon, 83, [6]
Shandwick, 193
Shanter, 75
Shapinsay, 199, [23]
Sharp, Archbishop, 101
——, William, 169
Shelter Stone, 122
Shepherds of Etive, 142
Sheriffmuir, 105
Shetland Islands, 200, [24]
Shiel Bridge, 160, [16]
Shieldaig, 174, [16]
Sidlaw Hills, 109, 124, [8–9]
Sinclair, Sir John, 189
Skaig Bridge, 184, [18]
Skaill, Bay of, 198
Skara Brae, 198
Skelmorlie, 78, [6]
Skerray, 188
Skibo Castle, 193
Skye, 162, [16, 22]
Slains, Old Castle of, 117
Slatadale, 181
Sleat, 163
——, Sound of, 159, [16, 22]
Slioch, 180
Slug Road, 114, [15]
Sluie, 132
Sma' Glen, 108, [8, 11]
Small Isles, 159
—— Pier, 87
Smeaton, John, 109, 130
Smith, Adam, 50, 98
Smoo, Cave of, 186, [18]
Solway Firth, 65, 68, [5]
—— Moss, 66, 103
Souter Johnnie, 76
Southend, 86, [6]
South Esk, River, 111, [9]
—— Queensferry, 54, [2, 8–9]
—— Ronaldsay, 199, 195, 196, [23]
—— Uist, 172, 148, [13]
Spar Cave, 163
Spean, River, 155
—— Bridge, 155, 137, [16]

Spey, River, 127–9, 131, 154, [11, 14, 17]
—— Bay, 131, [14]
Spittal of Glenshee, 123, [8, 14]
Spynie Palace, 131
Stac, An, 183
Stack Polly, 183
Staffa, 146, [12]
Staffin, 166, [22]
Stanely Castle, 79
Stanley, 123, [8]
Steamers, 28
Stenness (Orkney), 198
—— (Shetland), 202, [24]
Stevenson, R. L., 48, 54, 58, 75, 120, 124
Stirling, 94, [7, 8, 11]
Stobinian, 151
Stonebyres Linn, 92
Stonefield, 91
Stonehaven, 114, [15]
Stornoway, 169, [20]
Storr, the, 166, [22]
Strachur, 83, [6, 10]
Strae, River, 142
Stranraer, 74, [4]
Strathaird House, 163
Strath Beg, 182
Strathblane, 93, [7]
Strath Bran, 174, [16–17]
—— Brora, 192, [18–19]
—— Conon, 174, [17]
—— Dionard, 186
—— Glass, 176
—— Kanaird, 182, [18, 21]
—— Mashie, 154
Strathmiglo, 102, 103, [8, 9]
Strath More (Ross), 182
—— —— (Sutherland), 187
Strathmore, 109, [8–9]
Strath Naver, 188, [18]
—— of Appin, 152
Strathpeffer, 174, [17]
Strath Spey, 128, 129, [14]
Strathy, 188, [19]
Strathyre, 107, [8, 11]
Stroma, 190, 196, [19, 23]
Strome Castle, 173
—— Ferry, 173, [16]
Stromness, 198, [23]
Stronachlachar, 89, [11]
Strong, L. A. G., 108
Stronsay, 200, [23]
Strontian, 157, [10, 12]
Struan, 126, 154, [8, 11]
Struey Cliffs, 85
Struy Bridge, 176, [17]
Sugarloaf, 184
Suilven, 183, [18, 21]
Sumburgh Head, 200, 202, [24]
Summer Isles, 182
Sutherland, 183, 192, 193, [18–19]
——, Dukes of, 185–7, 192, 193
Sutors, the, 175
Swanston, 57
Sweetheart Abbey, 70
Sweno's Stone, 132

Switha, 196
Swona, 196, [23]

Tain, 193, [18–19]
Talladale, 180
Tam o' Shanter, 75, 76
Tannahill, Robert, 79
Tantallon Castle, 42, [2, 9]
Tarbert (Argyll), 86, 85, [6, 13]
—— (Harris), 171, [20]
Tarbet, 89, 150, [6, 11]
Tay, Firth of, 96, 110, [9]
——, River, 108, 123, 124, 151, 152, [8]
—— Bridge, 110, [9]
Taychreggan, 144
Tayinloan, 85, [6, 13]
Taymouth Castle, 152, [8, 11]
Taynuilt, 143, [10]
Teallach, An, 182, [21]
Teith, River, 90, 106, [7, 8, 11]
Telford, Thomas, 124, 129, 132, 135, 190, 192
Teviot, River, 62, [2, 3]
Thistle, Order of the, 48
Thornhill, 69, [5]
Thornton Junction, 95, [9]
Threave Castle, 70
Thurso, 188, [19, 23]
—— River, 189, [19, 23]
Tibbie Shiel's, 64
Tighnabruaich, 86, [6]
Tillicoultry, 104, [7, 8]
Tillynaught, 129
Tingwall Loch, 201
Tiree, 148, [12]
Tobermory, 145, 32, [12]
Tomachastle, 107
Tomdoun, 160, [16]
Tomintoul, 128, [14]
Tomnahurich, 134
Tongue, 187, [18]
Tor Castle, 138
Torgyle, 160, [16–17]
Tormore, 85
Torran, 163
—— Rocks, 147
Torridon, 180, [16]
Torrisdale Bay (Kintyre), 86
—— —— (Sutherland), 188
Toward Point, 86
Traigh Mhòr, 173
Traprain Law, 42
Traquair House, 59, [2]
Treshnish Isles, 146
Trinafour, 154, [8, 11]
Trodhu, 164
Troon, 77, [4, 6–7]
Trossachs, the, 90, [7, 11]
Trotternish, 166
Troup Head, 130
Truim, River, 126
Tullibardine, Marquis of, 157, 160
Tulloch, 155, [11, 17]
Tummel, Falls of, 125, [8, 11]
——, River, 124, 153, [8, 11]
—— Bridge, 153, [8, 11]

Turnberry, 75, [4, 6]
Tweed, River, 39, 59, 61, 62, 64, [2, 3, 5]
Tyndrum, 142, [11]

Uddingston, 91, [7]
Uig, 166, [22]
Uist, North, 171, [12]
——, South, 172, 148, [13]
Ullapool, 182, [18, 21]
Ullie, River, 191, [19]
Ulva, 146, [12]
Unapool, 184, [18]
Unst, 203, [24]
Urquhart, Castle, 136
Urr, Mote of, 70
Urray, 174
Uyeasound, 203, [24]

Vaila Sound, 202
Varrich, Castle, 187
Vat, Burn of the, 119
Vaternish, 167, [22]
Vatersay, 173, [13]
Victoria, Queen, 95, 119

Wade, General, 106, 123, 152, 154, 160
Walking Tours, 27
Wallace, Sir William, 55, 77, 78, 95, 114, 115
Walls, 202, [24]
Walsh, Maurice, 122, 129, 132
Wanlockhead, 69, [5, 7]
Ward Hill, 199
—— of Bressay, 201
Warth Hill, 190
Waternish, 167, [22]
Water Sound, 199
Watt, James, 78, 135
Weem, 152, [8, 11]
Well of the Heads, 137
Wemyss Bay, 78, [6]
—— Castle, 98, [9]
West Kilbride, 77, [6]
West Loch Tarbert (Argyll), 85, 87, [6, 13]
—— —— —— (Harris), 171, [20]
Westray, 199, [23]
Whalsey, 203, [24]
Whistlefield Hill, 84, [6, 11]
Whitehouse, 85, [6, 13]
Whiteinch, 81, 82
Whitekirk, 42, [2, 9]
Whiten Head, 187
Whithorn, 73, [4]
Whiting Bay, 84, 85, [4, 6]
Whittingehame, 42
Wick, 190, [19, 23]
Wideford Hill, 198
Wigtown, 73, [4]
—— Bay, 71, 72, [4–5]
William the Lion, 112
Winchburgh, 55

Windy Pass, 104
Wishart, George, 100
Wishaw, 92, [7]
Witch's Hill, 201
Wolfe, General, 90
Wordsworth, William, 63, 64, 89, 147
Wrath, Cape, 186, [18]

Yarrow, River, 63, [2]
—— Church, 63, [2]
Yell, 203, [24]
Youth Hostels, 30
Ythan, River, 116, [15]

Zetland, 200